Poetry as Testimon

MW00777435

This book analyzes Holocaust poetry, war poems, working-class poetry, and 9/11 poems as forms of testimony. Rowland argues that testimonial poetry requires a different approach to traditional ways of dealing with poems due to the pressure of the metatext (the original, traumatic events), the poems' demands for the hyper-attentiveness of the reader, and a paradox of identification that often draws the reader towards identifying with the poet's experience, but then reminds them of its sublimity. He engages with the work of a diverse range of twentieth-century authors and across the literature of several countries, uncovering new archival material. The study ends with an analysis of the poetry of 9/11, engaging with the idea that it typifies a new era of testimony where global, secondary witnesses react to a proliferation of media images. This book ranges across the literature of different cultures, and historical events in order to stress the large variety of contexts in which poetry has functioned productively as a form of testimony, and to note the importance of the availability of translations to the formation of literary canons.

Antony Rowland is Chair in Contemporary Literature at the University of Lincoln, UK.

Routledge Studies in Twentieth-Century Literature

Poetry as Testimony

Witnessing and Memory in
Twentieth-century Poems

Antony Rowland

Routledge
Taylor & Francis Group

NEW YORK AND LONDON

First published 2014
by Routledge
605 Third Avenue, New York, NY 10017

and by Routledge
2 Park Square, Milton Park, Abingdon, Oxon OX14 4RN

First issued in paperback 2021

*Routledge is an imprint of the Taylor & Francis Group,
an informa business*

Library of Congress Cataloging-in-Publication Data
Rowland, Antony.
  Poetry as testimony : witnessing and memory in twentieth-century
poems / Antony Rowland.
    pages cm. — (Routledge Studies in Twentieth-Century Literature ; #33)
    Includes bibliographical references and index.
  1. Poetry—20th century—History and criticism. 2. Memory in
literature. 3. Self-disclosure in literature. 4. Psychic trauma in
literature. 5. Witnesses in literature. I. Title.
    PN1083.M4R69 2013
    809.1'9353—dc23
    2013020362

ISBN 13: 978-1-03-224293-4 (pbk)
ISBN 13: 978-0-415-89909-3 (hbk)

DOI: 10.4324/9781315880280

Typeset in Sabon
by IBT Global.

Contents

Acknowledgments

First and foremost, thanks go to Jane Kilby, for discussing much of the material in this book, and for her excellent advice, as well as years of sometimes startling co-teaching. Next, I am extremely grateful to Liz Levine, Emily Ross, and Polly Dodson at Routledge, who were all interested, and trusted, in what I had to write. The British Academy was instrumental to the completion of this book with the award of a Mid-Career Fellowship. Many of the ideas in this book were also formulated during the Arts and Humanities Research Council–funded Research Network entitled 'The Future of Testimony' (2009–11). Without sabbaticals from the University of Salford, and the generous funding support from the Schools of ESPaCH and HuLSS, we would not be here now. Matthew Boswell has also been central to the book's conception: without The Beech in 2005, this book might have been given a completely different title and conceptual thrust.

I would like to thank the following readers, who took precious time out in order to give feedback on the chapters and book/grant proposals: Germaine Loader, Michael Rothberg, Tim Kendall, Emma Liggins, Ben Harker, Lucie Armitt, and Jane (again). The input of Derek Attridge, Shoshana Felman, George Rowe, Sue Powell, Colin McIntyre, James Crowden, Jon Stallworthy, Stef Craps, Robert Eaglestone, Sue Vice, Ursula Tidd, Rick Crownshaw, Rachel Haugh, Robert Sheppard, Peter Boxall, Anthony Rudolf, Debbie Hughes, Emma Hill, Scott Thurston, Anthony Levin, and Sebastian Owen has been appreciated more than this list can convey. I am also grateful to those anonymous readers who provided such positive and helpful feedback on the book proposal, articles, AHRC, and British Academy bids.

Some of the chapters have been reshaped and rewritten on the back of the following articles: 'The Oasis Poets: Perpetrators, Victims and Soldier Testimony', *Comparative Literature*, 63.4 (2011), 366–82 (see www. dukeupress.edu); 'The Lyric as Complicity in Tadeusz Borowski's *Selected Poems*', *Textual Practice*, 26.2 (April 2012), 243–61; '*Voices* Magazine: A Cultural History', *North West Labour History*, 34 (2009–10), 25–31; 'Poetry as Testimony: Primo Levi's *Collected Poems*', *Textual Practice*, 22.3 (September 2008), 487–506 (see www.tandfonline.com). Thanks must go to the journal editors and presses (including Duke University Press) who kindly allowed the republication of some of the material from these articles in book form, and also the generous copyright permissions from Faber and Faber, Chatto and Windus, Nikki Moustaki, and Geoffrey O'Brien. If I have unintentionally neglected any permissions, I shall, of course, correct this in a future edition. I have given papers based on this book's material in New Jersey, Turin, Krakow, London, York, Ormskirk, Liverpool, and Salford (in order of expense), and am thankful for all the thoughtful questions and responses.

Several librarians and archivists have been central to the book's contents and concerns. Steven Walton at the Imperial War Museum (Duxford) introduced me to the Salamander Oasis Trust material and, most importantly, pointed out the overlaps and connections with the London museum's collections (for example, in relation to the recently donated John Jarmain letters and the holdings on Norman T. Morris). Alan and Mike at the Working Class Movement Library in Salford were invaluable to the work on *Voices* magazine. Alan suggested looking at the journal during a visit in 2006; Mike subsequently took his bare feet to many corners of the library on my behalf, chasing up leads and references. It can safely be stated that without their input, that chapter would not have been written. Tadeusz Pioró was an impeccable host during a visit to Warsaw in 2007 and generous with his interview about translating Tadeusz Borowski's poetry. Scott Thurston and I will long remember the luxurious Polish food and Hungarian whites.

Apologies to those whom I will have missed from this list: the project has been a long one, and there have been many helpers and casualties along the way. Oh, and two children too. As is conventional, Emma, Polly, and Clara kept and keep me sane, but, more importantly, deranged, entertained, and confused. I'm still working out how to respond to the request to 'turn off the dark, please, daddy'.

Introduction

Testimony is widely regarded as an unaesthetic form of written or oral attestation to historical suffering, opposed to more self-consciously literary forms such as poetry.[1] In *Testimony*, Shoshana Felman discusses instead Stéphane Mallarmé and Paul Celan poems alongside Albert Camus novels and Sigmund Freud's work.[2] One of the many valuable legacies of the book is its analysis of testimony as a cross-generic phenomenon, in which Paul de Man's sense of autobiography as a 'figure of reading or of understanding' is applied to a variety of texts.[3] Unusually, Felman presents poetry as an exemplary instance of testimony: expositions of Mallarmé and Celan dominate the first chapter; poems can operate as testimony as they work through the effects of suffering that are not yet fully understood (p. 21). This precociousness is the 'very principle of poetic insight and the very core of the event of poetry': unlike witness statements in the courtroom, poetic language 'speak[s] ahead of knowledge and awareness and break[s] through the limits of its own conscious understanding'.[4] Nevertheless, as Gary Mole points out, many critics still assume that 'the poetic and the testimonial [are] somehow incompatible', and Sue Vice argues that 'it is not poetic testimony but prose testimony that is typical of Holocaust eye-witness, while Holocaust poetry is considered a separate and self-contained genre'.[5] World War I provides a different case study, since the poetry of Wilfred Owen and Siegfried Sassoon et al. constitutes the more popular 'eye-witness' account, rather than, say, the prose memoirs of Edmund Blunden or infantrymen. However, such poems are rarely referred to as testimony *per se*.[6] In this book, I argue that when a critical opposition is unravelled between what Sara Guyer terms 'the [supposedly] non-representational character of poetry and the representational character of testimony', poems by Holocaust, World War I, and World War II poets—amongst others—can be read afresh as testimonial performances.[7]

The poems chosen for analysis in this study all provide different insights into the function of poetry as testimony; even so, of course, the work of many other poets—such as Siegfried Sassoon, Gertrud Kolmar, and Dan Pagis—could have lead to additional chapters. However, the acute self-critique of witnessing in Owen's work provides the most pertinent entry point into a study of twentieth-century poetry as testimony. Tadeusz Borowski's poems then demonstrate how different styles of writing can function as testimony: his modernist poems written in Auschwitz testify to his experiences as do, in a different form, his journalistic pieces written after the liberation of Dachau. Borowski's work is virtually unknown in Britain and America, despite—and maybe partly because of—its controversial take on the notions of survival and culpability. Similarly, the Salamander Oasis Trust has published several anthologies of poetry written by servicemen and women during World War II, but they have been critically ignored: this book makes extensive use of the Oasis material held by the Imperial War Museum at Duxford; alongside canonical authors such as Keith Douglas, this study introduces the work of lesser-known (and unknown) writers such as Victor West, Norman Morris, and Jack Bevan. The poetry held in the Salamander Oasis archive offers proof of the proliferation of testimony in relation to World War II (rather than the Holocaust specifically) and complicates the judicial concepts of the 'victim' or 'perpetrator' witness. Charlotte Delbo's entire work is centred on the affective possibilities of witnessing; nevertheless, her books contain critiques of the 'victim' author, and potentially unreceptive audiences, fuelled by the worry that secondary witnesses may not be able to 'see' events of suffering. Primo Levi's poem 'Shemà' operates similarly to the interjections of Delbo's poems and provides a key text for the book's thesis, with its demand for hyper-attentiveness, criticisms of the civilian reader, and its function as metatestimony in relation to the writer's prose narratives. The subsequent chapter on working-class poetry demonstrates the variety of contexts in which poetry can operate as testimony, but stresses that 'singular' writing provides the most convincing testimony and poetry. Finally, my analysis of 9/11 poems emphasizes the dangers of subsuming local testimonial narratives into nationalist discourses.

Numerous anthologies and critical studies of witness poetry already exist, but they rarely engage *reflectively* with the issue of how poetry can function as testimony: this study comprises the first extended meta-analysis of testimonial poetry across different twentieth-century historical events.[8] The book proposes that accounting fully for testimonial poems entails a shift in emphasis from the way in which we read other forms of poetry, just as prose testimony demands a different response to fiction. This process is necessary due to the prevalence in such poetry of signs and issues analysed by critics of prose testimony, such as Robert Eaglestone: these concerns— which do not add up to an encompassing taxonomy—include the pressure of the metatext, the frequent demand for the reader's hyper-attentiveness, problems of witnessing, and a paradox of identification that often draws the reader towards identifying with the poet's experience, but then ultimately reminds them of its sublimity.[9] Primo Levi, for example, openly attacks the reader in 'Shemà' for their lack of knowledge about survivors' plights, ending with an impossible demand for hyper-attentiveness and a curse: readers must remember the Holocaust constantly or else their children will be blighted. Such a focus on the gulf between the testifier's horrific experience and the reader's potential for complacency dominates Charlotte Delbo's writing. In her *Auschwitz and After* trilogy, poems interrupt the poetic prose to remind the reader (and often the writer too) of the privilege, and ethical duties, of survival, as is evident in the title of the poem that ends the second book: 'Prayer to the Living to Forgive Them for Being Alive'. Many World War II poets similarly highlight the inarticulacy that scuppers their attempts to convey atrocious experiences, such as when John Jarmain—akin to Levi in 'Shemà'—bemoans the comforts of the poet-taster's surroundings; he ends 'These Poems' with both an appeal to the metatext in his reference to the Mareth line in Tunisia (1943) and a vague description of destructive things that the civilian reader cannot hope to understand. World War I poets also castigate the potential reader—perhaps most famously in Wilfred Owen's 'Dulce et Decorum Est', and also in 'Apologia Pro Poemate Meo'—but it is only during and after the subsequent war that poets give full vent to the crisis of witnessing and the difficulties of readerly identification.[10] Nevertheless, Owen's interest in critiquing his vicarious testimony on behalf of the troops, and his willingness to engage briefly with the figure of the poet as killer, mark him out as the main precursor to mid-century poems as testimony.[11]

The variety of contexts in which poetry functions as testimony illustrates that testimonial discourse has flourished in post-literate countries since the beginning of the twentieth century. In Britain, the increase of testimony is associated particularly with the decline of professional armies after the Boer War, and the subsequent prose memoirs of conscripts after the century's two world wars.[12] World War I comprises the first testimonial conflict for Britain in the sense that—like the Civil War in America—it was the first one to operate with thousands of 'citizen soldiers, including numerous well-educated and well-connected men who could record what they saw'.[13] In the twenty-first century, we are witnessing the continued increase of published testimonies in the form of memoirs, autobiographies, and 'misery literature'. Prose constitutes the dominating literary genre, and it demonstrates the inextricable link between the language of the courtroom and the development of literary testimony. The lack of critical attention to poetry—Samuel Hynes's *The Soldier's Tale* and Susan Gubar's *Poetry after Auschwitz* are notable exceptions—indicates that the formal boundaries of what are perceived to be testimonies need to be stretched beyond the important debates around how artists inscribe trauma in, for example, autobiographical prose, art, film, fiction, and photography.[14] Felman discusses poetry as a form of testimony at length in her seminal work with Dori Laub (pp. 25–40), but they do not dwell on poetry's traits in the rest of the book. An investigation of these characteristics forms the basis for this study: so far, there have been few critical responses attentive to the ramifications of Felman and Laub's groundbreaking engagement with Celan and Mallarmé's work. This book is open to an implication of Felman

and Laub's book that testimony functions primarily as a work of autonomous art, as opposed to more recent instances of testimony in the form of
victim statements in the legal process, patient responses in clinical practice,
and the advent of 'mis lit'. Testimonial poetry is resistant to the proliferation of testimony in the public sphere. Such writing celebrates an aesthetics
which may reject the temptations of mediation and its absolute integration,
defending the autonomy of the lyrical voice.

Within Holocaust Studies, critics have focussed on testimony in the form
of prose accounts of atrocity by writers such as Primo Levi, and Elie Wiesel,
rather than, for example, the linguistically-innovative, testimonial poetry
of Raymond Federman. The centrality of Levi and Wiesel in the canon of
Holocaust literature is due partly to the complexity of their broadly realist
narratives; however, this canonicity should not be acknowledged uncritically as unconnected to popular aesthetic and generic tastes in post-war
Western Europe and the United States.[15] Levi's popularity is partly an effect
of style: as well as poetry's supposed inaccessibility, a critical assumption also persists that the form complicates, embellishes, or—in a Platonic
sense—'lies' about historical events, whereas the clarity of realism gets as
close to the 'truth' of encounter as is possible in a medium which sadly
cannot prove its own authenticity in the text itself. In the following quotation from *The Soldier's Tale*, Samuel Hynes correctly notes the striking
relationship between war and realist literature, but then draws back from
critiquing this illusion of realism:

> It is striking [. . .] how little the writers of personal narratives of war
> have been affected by the literary fashions of their time [. . .] narrators
> of modern wars have not been Modernists. Whatever their dates, they
> have nearly all been realists, adopting a common style that would come
> as close as language can to rendering the things of the material world
> as they are.[16]

Hynes does not mention, at this point, modernist and postmodernist anomalies such as the work of David Jones and Federman. The prevalence of
realism is due not only to the authors' choice of style, but also to the fact
that many readers approach testimony primarily to glean the facts of the
historical experience. Realism appears to offer easier access to the metatext
(hence the popularity of *If This Is a Man*), rather than the looped, agonized,
and open-ended poetic narrative of Federman's *The Voice in the Closet*. As
Roland Barthes and Hayden White have demonstrated in relation to historical narratives, realist prose is effective in creating illusions of mimesis.[17]
Their findings apply equally to realist testimony. Prose testimony is not
necessarily 'closer' to events, and it often equally embellishes experience;
frequently—as I shall argue in relation to Levi—by making use of poetics.

Testimony can only be performed through form and genre, and poetic
forms are adept—particularly in the lyric—at conveying the epiphanic

moment, truncated traumatic recollections, silences beyond the black print, and the emotive space that need not be repressed behind the supposed objectivity of testimonial facts. Eaglestone points out that one of the most important characteristics of testimony is its focus on the epiphanic moment of witnessing, such as when Levi fishes for an icicle outside a window, and is reprimanded, in *If This Is a Man*.[18] Poetry is adept at describing such epiphanies, briefly and illuminatingly, since the lyrical tradition has always focussed on such intense moments of subjective experience. Hence I illustrate in Chapter 2 that in the neglected poem 'October Sky'—which deserves to be evaluated alongside the 'classics' of Holocaust poetry, such as Celan's 'Todesfugue' and Levi's 'Shemà'—Tadeusz Borowski intensifies experience in relation to a blockhouse window: the changes in reflection make him realize that he knows 'nothing for certain', and that his previous lyrical musings may be inadequate to the task of primary witnessing.[19] Paradoxically, these sentiments are expressed in a lyric: Borowski ends the piece by illustrating that this poetic subgenre remains as important to him as a 'wave to a shore'. Such examples of poems which display a dialectical process of working through and against, but also with, lyrical traditions form examples of Theodor Adorno's conception of the anti-lyric. Writing which does not capitulate to the conditions of its production—Adorno gives the example of Eduard Mörike's poetry during the process of industrialization—paradoxically provides the more adequate testimony to these hampering conditions.[20] Hence poetry does not have to concern itself primarily with the details of the historical metanarrative in order to qualify as testimony. Indeed, in resisting such metatextual strictures, poetry as testimony provides a barrier to commodification, and an endorsement of Felman and Adorno's defence of autonomous, testimonial art.

The time lapses, pauses, and opportunities for concentration in Borowski's poetry allow for reflection on traumatic experiences in a way distinct from prose. As Derek Attridge argues in *The Singularity of Literature*, prose—particularly modernist and postmodernist novels—can create such literary effects, too, but the extent to which they do so is precisely dependent on their use of the poetic.[21] Abrogating narrative coherence, poems can function—as Susan Gubar illustrates—as 'spurts of vision' that are effective in their engagements with baffling experiences of suffering.[22] James Young notes that, 'Upon entering narrative, violent events [. . .] seem to lose their "violent" quality'.[23] Late modernist and postmodernist poetry highlights discontinuities and ruptures in narrative form and traditional genres, and can thus—as opposed to realist prose (and verse)—appear more adept at engaging with the confusion and ineffable experiences arising from such atrocious events.[24] In *Violence*, Slavoj Žižek goes so far as to state that—contra Adorno—the Holocaust made prose, rather than poetry, impossible.[25] Prose does not 'fail', however, in this context, but merely inscribes events differently. The fragmentary openness of poetic writing contributes to—rather than negates—its testimonial function, since such language 'does not possess itself as a conclusion, as the contestation of a verdict or the self-transparency of knowledge [. . . it is] in process, and in trial'.[26] Felman and Laub discuss poetry here as an important instance of precocious testimony: the fragmented, 'breathless gasps' of such poems grapple with meaning in a testimonial process; they attempt to work through the 'ill-understood' but devastating effects of traumatic events (pp. 21–22). Unlike a judicial statement, they openly admit their shortcomings. In Chapter 4, I illustrate that Charlotte Delbo's work is particularly attuned to this notion of provisional testimony, since in *Auschwitz and After* she does not fully experience her suffering during the internment due to traumatic dissociation. Only in her post-war writing does she begin to work through 'ill-understood' events in the testimony of her remarkable prose poetry.

In her article on the Hungarian poet Miklós Radnóti, Vice illustrates the similarities between poetry and prose testimonies, but ultimately argues that they constitute separate genres. Radnóti's poems are 'not only testimony but aesthetic artefacts. An extra layer of mediation between event and reader is present, despite the poems' first-person address'. This 'extra layer' is in evidence in the image of 'pissing blood' in 'Razglednica 3', which is, as Vice argues, more effective as a trope of suffering than for its positivistic acumen.[27] Yet prose testimony too often goes beyond the reality effects of positivistic details, adding an aesthetic 'layer' of mediation. Levi's *If This Is a Man*—the most famous example of non-fiction Holocaust testimony for European readers—is full of such instances, as when he describes a musulmann as like the 'slough of certain insects which one finds on the banks of the swamps' (p. 48), or '*Muselmänner*' as 'like streams that run down to the sea' of oblivion (p. 96).[28] Levi deploys the poetic technique of simile because prose testimony does more than simply recount specific facts; these similes also illustrate that realist testimony is not adverse to the poetic flourish. Prose testimony is sometimes assumed to be beholden only to facts because of the term's origin in the judicial sense of a narrative which provides 'attestation in support of a fact or statement'.[29] Many historians often respond to testimony in this way, as it helps to verify (or not) the construction of an historical narrative.[30] In contrast, Elie Wiesel famously proposed that the Holocaust created the new *literary* genre of testimony.[31]

Initially, Wiesel's proposition appears misguided, since individual accounts of historical atrocities obviously transpired after events as diverse as World War I and the War of the Roses. In Chapter 3, I argue that World War II more widely lead to the proliferation of testimony, due to inter-war changes in the publishing industry and the rise of literacy. De Man notes that some critics of autobiography wish to elevate it 'above the literary status of mere reportage, chronicle, or memoir and [give] it a place, albeit a modest one, among the canonical hierarchies of the major literary genres' (p. 919): Wiesel's statement certainly has this intent in relation to his own writing, and that of other survivors. However, Eaglestone interprets Wiesel's polemical comment in the context of critical response: the Holocaust has precipitated an intensification of writerly and readerly activity over the last sixty years which responds to the act of witnessing (pp. 1–2). Only recently has this work been conceived as sustaining a literary genre (which has a tendency to exclude poetry) rather than being an untrustworthy adjunct to the writing of history.[32] Historians' narratives have their celebrities, whereas poetry as testimony—as General Sir John Hackett puts it in relation to poems from the ranks during World War II—comprises 'part of the structure within which the "history" was made [. . .] without which all the factual chronicles of events and all the hardware on display have little meaning'.[33] Instead of lambasting testimonies as slippery documents—in terms of their complex relationship to historical truth—Eaglestone argues that their overtly literary characteristics should be analysed afresh as specifically *generic* techniques. 'Holocaust testimony', he argues, 'needs to be understood as a new genre, in a new context, which involves both texts and altered ways of reading, standing in its own right' (p. 38). One of these 'altered ways' of receiving testimony is to insist that it should not be irrevocably entrenched in historical experience. Donald Bloxham and Tony Kushner comment that if critics focus only on the traumatic event, they add 'another form of abuse' by ignoring the lives of survivors after the advent of atrocity.[34] What, after all, is more important about an occurrence that, as Giorgio Agamben argues, 'exceeds its factual elements': to be informed that an event happened on a certain day at a specific time, or to learn about survivors' feelings of relief, shame, and guilt that persisted for a half century afterwards?[35] This question of resisting history is central to the efficacy of poetic testimony, since in many of the epiphanic poems I discuss in this book—such as Levi's 'Buna' and 'The Survivor'—the author interrupts the recounting of historical details to reflect on their ambivalent response to their own representations of, for example, former inmates.[36]

POETRY AS TESTIMONY: ANTELME'S PHOTOGRAPH

In a 1948 article, Robert Antelme argues that the 'impersonality' of genocide is compounded by the potentially chilling objectivity of photography and prose: in contrast, the discontinuities of poetry 'express experience [. . .] express reality as it is constantly lived, contested, and assumed'.[37] Over fifty years later, Julia Kristeva responds similarly to images of 'horror' as 'a monstrosity of compassionate melancholy'.[38] Antelme's link between impersonality and objectivity is registered in the superficially compassionate—but actually morbidly transfixed—gaze which, for Kristeva, is 'deprived of *intelligence*' (p. 321). Kristeva connects the 'monstrosity' of visual images with entries in history books. Even historians such as Martin Gilbert, who deploy personal testimony within their over-arching historical narratives, can only point to, rather than flesh out, traumatic blind spots within history.[39] Such entries

remain, paradoxically, de-individualized respites from the overall catalogue of disasters.

In contrast, Antelme outlines the testimonial possibilities of poetry and
contrasts them with what he regards as the drawbacks of prose testimony,
which only provides a 'photograph' that 'makes you shudder'.[40] Poems
do not 'run so great a risk of creating that naked, "objective" testimony,
that kind of abstract accusation, that photograph that only frightens us
without explicitly teaching anything' (p. 33). Antelme risks constructing
a simplistic opposition between subjective poems and objective prose and
photographs, but his focus instead is on the *reception* of the latter genres
as simplistically mimetic and as fleetingly evidential: the rubber gloves of
quotation marks indicate that he is aware that photographs are, of course,
subjectively framed. The naked accusation of the photograph refers to the
form's tendency to emphasize a specific crime in relation to the Holocaust,
as in the iconic pictures of the death pits that Janina Struk critiques as
less explicable than they appear to be.[41] In contrast to the visual stasis of
the evidential photograph, poetry encourages a multifaceted, ambiguous,
ambivalent, self-reflexive—and often unbalanced—approach to the experience of the camps.[42] Antelme's ruminations on his sense that poetry could
provide a 'true' representation of this experience were published three years
before Adorno's more famous declarations about the barbarity and impossibility of post-Holocaust poetry were first encountered in Germany. The
development of Holocaust poetry and criticism could have been very different if Antelme's comments had come to be regarded as maxims instead
of Adorno's polemics. There might not, for example, have been such an
emphasis on the resistant, modernist aesthetics of writers such as Celan.
The poetics of authors such as Borowski might not have been ignored.

The testimonial forms I engage with in this study are not, for the most
part, composed with the self-conscious and self-castigatory strategies of
awkward poetics. Adorno's maxim about barbaric poetry—and his simul-
taneous call for such modernist poetics—still haunts post-Holocaust
debates about poetry like a form of critical melancholia, and the time has
come to break the spell. The concept of awkward poetics that I explored
in my first two books on Holocaust poetry is indebted to Adorno's draconian approach to the verse of atrocity in 'Cultural Criticism and Society',
but I shall not return to such debates in this volume. Rather, I regard these
poetics as a stage of working through Adorno's admonishments in order to
reach a critical position where the importance of the anti-modernist poetics
of writers such as Levi and Borowski can be evaluated alongside the work
of, for example, Celan and Geoffrey Hill. For Adorno, writing by victims
is inherently tainted by the inscription of violence, whereas Felman's work
allows us to think about the difficulties of testimony in ways that are more
attentive to the witness's attempts at articulation. Adhering to Adorno's
thinking, James Hatley contended in 2000 that 'the writing of the *Shoah*
must involve a continuing discourse about the inadequacy of that writing',

but the danger is that such prescriptive aesthetics occlude anything that does not tally with their remit.[43] Perhaps this is the moment to argue for a cessation of such discourse about inadequacy or, at least, to accept it as taken for granted. Critical work could then begin on writing that goes beyond the paradigms of vexed aesthetics.

Poems too have their pitfalls, Antelme argues, in that they can pro-duce only a 'melodic counterpoint' to the metanarrative.[44] Yet texts which engage carefully with the survivor's experience constitute the 'poetry of truth', rather than just recounting the 'details of the horror' for possibly prurient delectation. Žižek warns of this danger of prosaic objectivity rep-licating a perpetrator perspective in *Violence*: 'Realistic prose fails where the poetic evocation of the unbearable atmosphere of a camp succeeds', because 'poetry is always, by definition, "about" something that cannot be addressed directly, only alluded to'.[45] This tangential 'evocation' works in relation to some Holocaust poems that superficially appear to be focussed on an unrelated object. Borowski's 'October Sky', for example, roots itself in the description of a blockhouse window, but this focus—and the subse-quent naturalistic details—alludes paradoxically, through its very absence, to the everyday violence occurring in Birkenau. Adorno proposes similarly in 'On Lyric Poetry and Society' that Goethe's *Wanderes Nachtlied* con-tains a dialectical air (or gesture) of consolation: 'its unfathomable beauty cannot be separated from something it makes no reference to, the notion of a world that withholds peace'.[46] The *Pathos der Distanz* ('pathos of detach-ment') in nineteenth-century German lyric poetry is at the same time a symptom of society's encroachment upon the individual and the 'unfath-omable beauty' of poetic texts. Adorno's conception of detachment, and Žižek's support of allusion, thus allow for poetry as testimony that eschews what Antelme refers to as the chilling objectivity of prosaic prose.

In reference to prose accounts depicting Nazis, Levi makes a similar point to Antelme and Žižek that documentary evidence cannot convey the 'depths of a human being [. . .] for this purpose the dramatist or the poet are more appropriate'.[47] His comment is partly applicable (although *If This Is a Man* obviously conveys these 'depths' of the witness too) to the testi-monial accounts of his own post-war existence: it is only in poems such as 'Buna' and 'The Survivor' that Levi gives full vent to his feelings of guilt and shame in relation to the musulmann and the grey zone, as opposed to the philosophical ruminations in *The Drowned and the Saved*. For Holo-caust writers such as Levi and Delbo, prose testimony, which comprises a substantial part of their work, *is still not enough*; whereas Delbo enmeshes poetic epiphanies in the main body of her non-fiction, Levi chooses to com-pose separate poems.[48] Both authors are responding to Antelme's worry that prose accounts may be all too understandable, leaving readers unaf-fected as they turn to the next book: this concern is embedded in *If This Is a Man* in that a poem, 'Shemà', comprises an epigraph, warning the recipient against a cursory reading. 'Shemà' challenges what Sarah Kofman

terms the '"idyllic" clarity of narrative'.[49] Later in *Smothered Words*, Kofman asks, 'How can testimony escape the idyllic law of the story?' (p. 36).
One answer is via 'stymied' poetic testimony, where brief, epiphanic poems
enact a blocking of extended narrative accounts.[50] Whereas Susan Gubar
contends that 'broken' poems enact a 'throttling of testimonial utterance', I
would argue that this exposition of 'throttling' is *itself* a form of testimony.
In relation to Levi's work, short lyrics engage intertextually with the prose
narratives, leading to re-evaluations of the prose testimony. For example,
in Chapter 5 I outline how the figure of the musulmann—presented as the
survivor's 'other' in Agamben's study of the *Musulmänner* in *Remnants of
Auschwitz*—sometimes refers to Levi himself.

POETRY AS TESTIMONY: THE TRACE

Writers of 'broken' poems—like all literary artists—are interested in the
selection and arrangement of words, rather than conceiving of literature
as only a utilitarian instrument of truth. As Felman and Laub indicate,
critics should celebrate, not lament, the literariness of testimony, relish-
ing its 'very messiness'.[51] In this study, I explore how the various writers
respond to this deviousness of literature. Chapter 2, for example, outlines
Borowski's distrust of poetic form in 'October Sky' and his paradoxical
exploitation of its potential for ambiguity and ambivalence. This (undated)
poem was probably written in Auschwitz in 1943 or early 1944: two years
later, he had renounced the lyrical tradition and was writing a form of
testimonial poetry that mimicked the style of prose testimony in order,
he argued, to respond quickly and diurnally to the 'fishtank of blurred
events' in post-war Europe.[52] These particular poems are antithetical to
the awkward aesthetics of Celan's allusive and elusive writing, and yet it
would be trite to argue on stylistic grounds that the Pole was therefore
less traumatized than Celan. Felman and Laub outline a teleology between
experienced trauma (what they term the 'scope of the accident'), aporias,
and disjunctions in Celan's work, and the subsequent emotional (and problematic) engagement of the reader with traumatic literature.[53] In this book,
I outline instead the variety of ways in which traces of trauma can be reinscribed in testimony as poetry, from the unperturbed, proto-Communist
journalism of Borowski's testimonial poems, to the awkward poetics of the
anti-lyrical lyric 'October Sky'.[54]

   The diversity of testimony in this book begins to look beyond Holocaust
Studies to analyse the functions of poetry as testimony in the twentieth
and twenty-first centuries.[55] As well as including chapters on Borowski,
Levi, and Delbo—poets more well known for their prose accounts rather
than testimonial poetry—this study will also investigate the formulation
of poetry as testimony from the beginning of the twentieth century, from
an analysis of the beginnings of a crisis of witnessing in Wilfred Owen's

work to an account of 9/11 poems that iterate dialectics of in/articulacy in a new context. Hence the study of poetry as testimony has repercussions within the literary history of poetry, and in poetry criticism, as well as in the fields of Holocaust and Trauma Studies. By noting the connections, and differences, in poetry as testimony in relation to twentieth-century history, this book takes a cue from the increasing consensus among cultural critics about the comparable singularity of events between 1933 and 1945 in mainland Europe, as Michael Rothberg illustrates in relation to Holocaust Studies and decolonization in *Multidirectional Memory*. This study draws the particularity of Holocaust poetry into discussion with a wider tradition of European and American twentieth-century poems, evaluating aspects of the later afresh *as testimony*. In this sense it allows for what Attridge terms the creative 're-invention of invention'.[56] Owen's outraged elegies are a form of testimony just as much as the dirges of Vietnam soldier poets; the World War II poet Keith Douglas has a desire to rid his poetry of the lyric's 'Bullshit poetics', revealing a documentary poetics comparable to those of the French writer Jean Cayrol, who provided the commentary for Alain Resnais's film *Night and Fog*.[57] In Chapter 3, I take the categories of victim and perpetrator testimony—taken from a judicial context and developed mainly in relation to the Holocaust—and apply them to the 'Oasis' poems of World War II to demonstrate how such categories are applicable to (and also similarly vexed) in a different historical context.[58]

The similarities and dissonances between different traumas and ensuing literatures explored throughout this book draw the critic into debates about the fraught relationship between language, reality, and aesthetics. In his critique of the poetry of witnessing, Thomas Vogler asserts that there is no connection between somatic trauma and literary texts: 'It would seem that only a wilful blindness to how poetry and language work could lead so many critics to make so many claims for traumatic traces in the poems they discuss'.[59] Bodily trauma is clearly not evident—in the same sense—in literary form, but such unguarded accounts of language have led to Morris Grossman's comment that he would just as soon 'think of the Holocaust as a hoax than think of it as something I can objectively grasp and behold'.[60] The irony in Vogler's statement is that he critiques the Derridean notion of the historical 'trace' in order to refute the connection between language and reality from a supposedly post-structuralist perspective. Literature obviously has an inability to register reality without the need for linguistic mediation—it constitutes Young's 'fugitive report' of events—but this does not preclude *any* relationship between the traumatic event and subsequent text.[61] As Felman and Laub make clear, testimony does not comprise a mimetic reflection of experience (which the illusion of realism encourages us to believe), but the reinscription of trauma in literary form (pp. xiii–xiv). Positivistic aspects of biography and history 'are neither simply represented nor simply reflected, but are reinscribed, translated, radically rethought and fundamentally worked over by the text' (p. xv). Contra

Vogler's comments on trauma and testimony, testimonial poetry illustrates the dialectical relationship between the text and metatext. The metatextual concerns of poetry as testimony necessarily highlight this dialectic more than conventional approaches to poetics in literary studies.

Reading poetry as testimony thus entails a shift in emphasis. Rather than perpetuate misreadings of Roland Barthes's 'The Death of the Author', and attempt to suppress any connection between the text and authors' experiences, poetry as testimony draws the reader back into an engagement with what Susan Suleiman has termed the 'conventional', the intriguing relationship between reception, autobiography, and writing.[62] War poetry has been considered as a potentially separate genre to traditional poetry because of its metatextual concerns; such views raise important questions for the study of poetry in general. Such literary separatism could be construed as a challenge to the notion of poetic singularity: metatextual issues in war poems are to be considered alongside—and, for some, perhaps on equal terms with—the poems' striving for aesthetic superiority. Some critics point out instead that metatextual issues are entwined in any notion of poetic singularity. Attridge registers this inextricability when he argues that singularity is '*constituted* by what we might call "contextual" operations [. . .] the product of a set of contexts bearing down upon a here and now' (p. 114).

In this book, I argue that the metatext does operate differently in the process of reading testimonial poems, even if they are impacted by contextual operations in a similar way to other kinds of literature. Poetry as testimony often gestures towards the metatext through the poem's title, epigraph, or concluding date, unlike in many other poems where this operation is irrelevant or rendered invisible. Attridge brilliantly demonstrates the singularity of poems such as William Blake's 'The Sick Rose' (pp. 65–72) through the events of performance—multiple readings that can be made of the poem on different occasions—but testimonial poetry often cannot perform its elusiveness so convincingly, due to the pressure of the metatext. The latter is not an excuse for literary deficiencies: the poems' aesthetic value must stand apart from such metatextual concerns; however, the danger in reading only through singularity is that this process results in Adorno's pantheon of edification (outlined in 'Commitment'), where works of art merely desecrate each other in their attempts at aesthetic supremacy. In this attitude towards literary value, I differ from Victor Selwyn's conception of war poetry: he contends that the poetry in the Salamander Oasis archive must be treated as an adjunct to the canon, in which issues of singularity and aesthetic value are suspended.[63] Rather, the difference between 'singular' poems such as 'The Sick Rose' and poetry as testimony lies in the process of reading, where links to the metatext and the issues such as hyper-attentiveness and the witness's in/articulacy demand to be addressed. Testimony focalizes Suleiman's notion of the 'conventional', which stresses the complex relationship between the reader, author and text. Biographical metatexts can be less important to readers in non-testimonial literature: in relation to false testimony—such as Gerald Kersh's poem 'A Soldier—His Prayer' about his (lack of) experience in a slit trench during World War II-they are clearly vital to critical response.[64]

Such attention in the poetry to metacontextual issues does not preclude the mendacity of false testimony: when reading poems for the first time, the reader can only respond to words that cannot evidence their own veracity. Following Wiesel and Eaglestone's arguments about prose testimony, this metatextual emphasis comprises one of the reasons that these testimonial poems require us to think through de Man's concept of autobiography as 'a figure of reading or of understanding' that may occur, 'to some degree, in all texts' (p. 921), but which is heightened in these poems. Such poems require a different approach to reading than the traditional lyric, which is not to say that the lyric itself cannot operate in testimonial form. As in other forms of testimony, the text often demands increased affectivity. This readerly hyper-attentiveness contains the trace of the judicial: like an addressee in court, the reader of testimony is bound, as Derrida argues, by 'a promise [of witnessing the truth] whose performativity is constitutive of the testimony and makes it a pledge [*gage*], an engagement'.[65] As Eaglestone emphasizes, a paradox of identification also then distinguishes testimony. The reader is drawn into the text at the same time as it reminds them of the testimony's radical alterity and resistance to assimilation. Ultimately, however, poetry as testimony is not beyond aesthetic considerations: it is inseparable from the performance of form, genre, and subgenre. As a form which requires a distinct 'figure of reading or of understanding', it can still be critiqued within Adorno and Attridge's 'pantheons' of singularity. Journalistic poems about the Holocaust, such as Borowski's post-Munich pieces, are not as unsettling, resonant, or singular as the modernist poems about Auschwitz written earlier by the Polish poet. Despite the sentiment that some non-professional poetry about World War II in the Salamander Oasis archive can induce in readers, the detached, well-wrought, and callous texts of Keith Douglas are ultimately more satisfying as war poems and as testimony. Simplistic rallying calls in the protest poetry of magazines such as *Voices* cannot overshadow Arthur Adlam's sensitive engagement with poetic tradition in his poem 'Ode to Winter', which I discuss in Chapter 6. Although sometimes conceived as antithetical to life-writing, linguistic complexity comprises—as writers such as Felman and Jorge Semprun, amongst others, have recognized—the most effective form of testimony.[66]

TESTIMONIAL POETRY: N. T. MORRIS'S 'MOLISE 1943'

In the final section of this introduction, I wish to look briefly at Norman T. Morris's poem 'Molise 1943' as an example of a testimonial poem which illustrates some of the themes I have discussed above, including the issue of the metatext and Antelme's criticisms of prosaic and photographic testimony. Morris was an army recruit who only started writing poetry during World War II: his work was then published in *Poems from Italy: Verses Written by Members of the Eighth Army in Sicily and Italy July 1943–March 1944*, and later in one of the Salamander Society's anthologies, *From Oasis into Italy*.[67] One of Morris's archives is held in the Imperial War Museum: it reveals that Morris was a technical adjutant's clerk in the Fiftieth Battalion Royal Tank Regiment (Twenty-Third Armoured Brigade); he was involved in the campaigns in North Africa, Sicily, and Italy (July 1942–May 1944) and in Greece (November 1944–June 1945).[68] The files held in the War Museum also illustrate that 'Molise 1943' was one of the few formal pieces—registered in the blank verse—that Morris wrote during the war. His style is primarily satirical, and is epitomized in the pantomime 'Sandarella'—which he wrote for the Eighth Army in Christmas 1942—and a 'desert alphabet', which he includes in a letter to his wife (August 1942): 'D' stands for 'Desert', 'A large area of sand, entirely surrounded by sand'.[69]

Despite the aesthetic frame of the pentameters, Morris registers the provisionality of testimonial poetry in the Salamander Society's archive of his work (held in the Imperial War Museum at Duxford). His poems written in Italy received 'little polishing: there wasn't time'; 'On the whole I tried to be immediate and spontaneous [. . .] I tried to describe it as it was, not as I thought it ought to be, or requiring a special sort of poetic voice'.[70] As in many such testimonial poems from the Salamander and Oasis Trust's archive, the metatext is registered in the title: Morris's poem records the massive destruction of characteristic medieval hill towns during World War II in this southern region of Italy after the Allies landed at Termoli in September 1943. In this context, the first line of the poem is disconcerting: set in the medieval period, it depicts an abbot instructing a painter. Yet it illustrates my argument that testimonial poetry is not—following Felman and Laub—beholden to the historical metatext: the Imperial War Museum archivist notes that 'reference is seldom made [in Morris's work] to particular events'.[71] 'Molise 1943' illustrates Felman and Laub's point that testimony reinscribes traces of memory as it works over traumatic experience in literary texts. For Morris, the process of witnessing is inextricable from the memory trigger of the medieval painting:

> What gallery? The Louvre? That placid light
> Pours on the banks to silhouette the trees,
> Cypress, and guardians of the plain. The painter?
> My brain will fidget till I call his name,
> Some limb of the Renaissance . . .
>
> The front rolls on. The gunners and the tanks
> Have all passed through. The hill-top town is dead.

Its wall is pock-marked: there is a door smeared
By flame-thrower. The houses naked lie,
Truncated by the artifice of war;
The towers I knew, unpinned and like to fall.
This place is dead, save for a dozen birds
Picking for bits amid a ruined house:
Robin and chaffinch, wren. This ancient quiet
    Is full of ghosts . . .

If testimony is primarily concerned with historical facts, then the fourth stanza only in the Morris poem (quoted above) should provide the focus for this introduction, and the basis for an historicist reading. But what is particularly striking about this poem is that, rather than make sense of a war experience through positivistic data, it does so through an aesthetic paradigm that precedes the testimonial act. Poetry comprises testimony here in the sense that the poem depicts an act of witnessing through the aesthetics of a half-remembered painting. Aesthetic contemplation is bound up with personal history through reflection on the origins of the Renaissance painting, its subsequent viewing of the picture in a gallery, and then the third 'painting' of the ruined village.

The phrase 'the artifice of war' in the fourth stanza highlights the poem's engagement with the testimonial dialectic of aesthetics and artistic truth. The original painting is 'True' only in its witnessing of the village and the 'common touch' of the birds, and yet the town is still '*Posed* on a hill-top', and inconsequential compared to the centrality of the Virgin and Infant.[72] Similarly, the description of the ruined town appears 'true' in its (presumably) positivistic details of the precarious towers and absent gunners, but as soon as the poet comes across the landscape, he interprets it as a posed, aesthetic 'view'. Instead of the 'pattern' of the land being figured through the military discourse famously parodied in Henry Reed's sequence *Lessons of the War* (including 'Naming of Parts'), the town 'hangs' on its slope like a painting and a door is 'smeared' as if with paint as well as a flame-thrower.[73] The 'artifice of war' has turned the town—in the artifice of the poem—into a surrealist painting: the 'houses naked lie' as surreal equivalents of classical nudes. The town is full of the 'ghosts' of absent people, but also the 'ghost' of the aesthetic frame that encapsulates the entire poem. One of the most obvious connection between the two pictures is that the 'Robin and chaffinch, wren' picking in a ruined house cannot help, for this poet, but recall the 'common touch' of the birds in the original Renaissance painting.[74] Of course, as well as constituting a third painting in the poet's imagination, the ruined town also subverts the classical harmony of the Virgin and Infant in the original picture. Testimonial poetry demands a historical metanarrative (even if it is not subsumed by it), and Morris's poem forms no exception with its gestural title. In a sense, the 'true' background of the town in the classical painting *becomes the metanarrative* in the last stanza; religious icons give way to secular destruction. The 'human touches' in the classical painting become, in an unintentional paronomasia, the human torch of the flamethrower smearing the door. And the wall is 'pock-marked', in contrast with the 'exquisite' light in the earlier painting.

Antelme's photograph 'that only makes you shudder' becomes, here, an ekphrastic depiction of barbarism painted with words. However, Antelme's account of evidential photography and its obsession with positivistic detail does not apply to this testimonial poem. Unlike a conventional photograph or unreflective prose narrative, the poem succinctly allows for three time frames in order to try and make sense out of the process of witnessing. The reader moves from the voice of an abbot and a gallery guide to the poet's in order to appreciate the present scene more fully through a particular 'chord'—as Morris puts it here—in the writer's memory. The poem cannot constitute testimony in the sense of an adequate historical narrative: the aesthetic framework of the painting would be irrelevant in this context. But this is not the point. What the poet does is to try and make sense of his own *process* of witnessing, whereby he records the disturbing destruction of the town via Nabokovian memory triggers. For Morris, this means reacting 'truthfully' to the process of witnessing by recording how, for him, the experience is bound up with the aesthetic framework of the elusive classical painting. Despite the artistic authority of the aesthetic frame, memory work is still fraught at the end of the poem: he registers an incompleteness in the witnessing with his use of ellipsis. The inability of the poet to fully recall the picture mirrors the fallible process of recollection outlined in many of the testimonial poems I discuss in this book and of witnessing in general. In the following chapter, I analyse how this fraught process of witnessing is bound up with Owen's worries about representing his troops' experiences.

1 Who Are 'You'?
Addressivity and Vicarious Testimony in Wilfred Owen's Poems

Wilfred Owen was the first poet in the twentieth century to engage at length with some of the key themes examined throughout this book: poems such as 'Insensibility', 'Apologia pro Poemate Meo', and 'Spring Offensive' illustrate the ways in which poetry as testimony inscribes historical events, often berates the reader in fraught processes of addressivity, and grapples with the in/articulacy of the witness. World War I was the first testimonial conflict to involve British forces in the sense that (as noted in the introduction) it eschewed small, professional armies and operated with 'a huge army of citizen soldiers, including numerous well-educated and well-connected men who could record what they saw'.[1] Moreover, the ensuing abundance of testimony in poetic form has become central to our understanding of World War I, to the extent of parody: Captain Flasheart sums up the war in the British television series *Blackadder* as 'the mud, the blood, the *endless* poetry'.[2] More than any other World War I writer, however, issues surrounding addressees and witnesses persist in Owen's poems, from the worries over the representation of fellow soldiers, killing and conflict in 'Insensibility', 'Strange Meeting', and 'Spring Offensive', to the berating of the reader in 'Dulce Et Decorum Est' and 'Apologia pro Poemate Meo'. The development of poetry as testimony is only at a nascent stage in Owen's work: his concerns about, for example, the inscription of infantrymen in 'Insensibility' emerge at the beginning of the poem, but are then quashed by elegiac conventions. Only in the later work of Holocaust poets such as Charlotte Delbo and Primo Levi does the fraught recollection of fellow sufferers—and those that died in the camps—reach the point of a crisis of representation. Yet Owen's work is important to this book as a precursor to ensuing critical debates in memory studies about dialectics of in/articulacy, the inscription of the metatext, and the transmission of memories.

In the introduction, I outlined the demand for hyper-attentiveness often encountered in poetry as testimony: this process is highlighted in poems I discuss later in this book, such as Primo Levi's scathing poem 'Shemà', which promises to curse the reader if they do not constantly remember the poet's suffering. Redressing the complacent reader in mid-century testimonial poetry has its origins in Owen's work, where the civilian in 'Insensibility' and—as in Delbo's Auschwitz trilogy—the author himself (in 'Apologia pro Poemate Meo') are targets for the poet's ire. Moreover, Owen's awkward poetics in the final stanza of 'Spring Offensive'—when attempting to describe the processes of killing and fraught survival—anticipate the perpetrator aesthetics of World War II poetry that I analyse in Chapter 3. James Campbell's influential essay on World War I poetry interprets such passages as instances of 'combat gnosticism', where the poet closes off experiences from civilian readers; a process that critics then replicate when they argue for the persistence of the ineffable in such work.[3] Such 'gnosticism', a key problem for potentially affective memory, is common in other testimonial texts.[4] In Owen's work as well as Holocaust testimony, '[w]e, as an audience are asked' to empathize, but we are also often told, implicitly or not, 'that we *can't* understand' through our own irrelevant experiences.[5] Campbell's thesis could fruitfully be applied to Holocaust testimony, and criticism in Holocaust Studies: I have wondered elsewhere how long dialectics of in/articulacy can be iterated in relation to the former.[6] However, in this chapter I argue differently to Campbell that—if read through the proclivities of twentieth-century poetry as testimony— Owen's 'gnosticism' provides (as in Delbo's trilogy) a necessary resistance to the reader's potential over-identification with suffering.[7] Campbell's critique of an epistemological gulf between survivors and non-survivors risks the reader's imaginative colonization of World War I poems, just as Pierre takes over the Auschwitz experiences of his wife, Marie-Anne Louise, in Delbo's *The Measure of our Days*.[8]

DULLARDS VERSUS THE POETIC: 'INSENSIBILITY'

Like Robert Antelme, who argued that poems express 'reality as it is constantly lived, contested, and assumed', Owen believed that poetry has a testimonial function 'capable of a truth beyond the range of other media': in 1917 he wrote to his sister stating that Siegfried Sassoon's work was more 'perfectly truthfully descriptive of war' than '[c]inemas, cartoons, photographs, tales, plays'.[9] In his own poems, however, such as 'Insensibility' and 'Apologia pro Poemate Meo', Owen is sometimes not so sure about the efficacy of poetry as testimony. 'Insensibility' opens with criticism of his own poeticisms, and, by proxy, those of other war writers. In the discussion that follows, I illustrate that—despite his initial reservations—poetry's right to represent war experience is ultimately reinscribed. Owen's work is thus central to the development of poetry as testimony, since it constitutes the first (extensive) self-conscious engagement with problems of representation in World War I poetry. Owen takes the first step towards the depicted crisis of witnessing, awkward poetics and 'aesthetics of agitation' in the work of Holocaust poets such as Delbo and Paul Celan.[10]

In 'Insensibility', testimony comprises the response to the event rather than a historical delineation of the event itself, just as 'Strange Meeting' is 'less a rehearsal of the horrible realities of war than an interpretation of what the war means to those who find themselves victims of it'.[11] 'Insensibility' focusses on providing vicarious testimony for infantrymen for forty-nine lines, before addressing the famous 'dullards' at the closure. In the first stanza, some troops practise insensibility as a response to, in a memorable and disturbing image, the trenches 'cobbled' with their dead comrades:

> Happy are men who yet before they are killed
> Can let their veins run cold.
> Whom no compassion fleers
> Or makes their feet
> Sore on the alleys cobbled with their brothers.
> The front line withers.
> But they are troops who fade, not flowers
> For poets' tearful fooling:
> Men, gaps for filling:
> Losses, who might have fought
> Longer; but no one bothers.[12]

The simple diction here might dupe the reader into thinking that Owen has no qualms about his poetics, but the end of the stanza proves otherwise.[13] In the introduction, I critiqued Samuel Hynes's conception of realism when he contends that war writers as 'realists, [adopt] a common style that would come as close as language can to rendering the things of the material world as they are'.[14] Owen is aware of the impossibilities of a purely mimetic language and an authentic discourse to represent the troops; he begins to self-critique his representation in the seventh line. 'The front line withers' is immediately undercut by the next two lines: 'But they are troops who fade, not flowers | For poets' tearful fooling'; 'flowers' (akin to Isaac Rosenberg's poppies in 'Break of Day in the Trenches') and 'fooling' are emphasized with the hypercatalectic metre that dominates the first stanza.[15] This shift is akin to the subversion of the poetic in Owen's poem 'Miners', where, instead of the coals providing a 'tale of leaves [. . .] steam phantoms [. . .] From Time's old cauldron', they murmur about the tribulations of miners, the 'moans down there | Of boys', and men 'Writhing for air' (p. 186). However, even the word 'fade' in the line from 'Insensibility' perpetuates the poetic diction that Owen simultaneously critiques. He then accuses poetic language of being culpable in a similar way to military discourse when failing to provide a 'true' representation of the troops: just as the phrase 'the front line' evades the presence of 'troops', 'men' are merely 'gaps for filling' and 'losses, who might have fought | Longer' (pp. 189–90). Nevertheless, the very first line deploys 'men' not as potential 'gaps', but to provide vicarious testimony about what it means to become an insensible veteran (p. 189). 'Insensibil-ity' ultimately undermines military discourse: as I outlined in the intro-duction, General Sir John Hackett argues that war poetry comprises 'part of the structure within which the "history" was made [...] without which all the factual chronicles of events and all the hardware on display have little meaning'.[16]

This critique of the poetic in Owen's first stanza chimes with Shoshana Felman and Dori Laub's endorsement of testimony as a form of writing which 'does not possess itself as a conclusion'; however, the rest of 'Insen-sibility' then begins to undermine the initial uncertainty and closes with the generic characteristics of the elegiac tradition.[17] As the poem develops, Owen reinscribes the poet's right to provide vicarious testimony for the troops. By stanza four, their 'many sighs are drained' (p. 190): metonymy without censure replaces the self-critique in the first stanza. This return to the certainty of representation has problematic repercussions in the fifth stanza for the vicarious testimony of the 'ordinary' soldiers, who could easily be misread as the 'dullards' of the last stanza (p. 191), since they too—according to the poem's logic—must now be unaffected, as insensible soldiers, by the stunning canon:

> We wise, who with a thought besmirch
> Blood over all our soul,
> How should we see our task
> But through his blunt and lashless eyes?
> Alive, he is not vital overmuch;
> Dying, not mortal overmuch;
> Nor sad, nor proud,
> Nor curious at all.
> He cannot tell
> Old men's placidity from his.[18]

In contrast with his sympathetic engagement with forgotten labour in 'Miners', 'Insensibility' implicitly depicts the troops in the same way as his letters, where Owen feels the 'weight' of his men, who are 'expression-less lumps' akin to the soldiers in Bruce Bairnsfather's war cartoons.[19] The poem enacts the letters' dichotomy wherein Owen, as the 'thinking being', marooned on a '[c]rag of superiority', praises the infantrymen as durable, but also criticizes them (more discreetly in 'Insensibility') as 'loutish [...] coarse, ungainly'.[20] One of this author's relatives, Charles Rowland, was one of these rough 'dullards'; in a letter in the Emory archive, the poet Ted Hughes writes about his father as, in contrast with Owen's poem, an intel-ligent infantryman with reservations about peculiar officers.[21] At least the class distinctions and vicarious testimony in 'Insensibility' avoid the awk-ward and Kiplingesque representation of working-class voices in Owen's poems 'The Letter' and 'The Chances'. Yet the brief return to a critique of poetics in the following lines is disingenuous: 'We wise [...] How should we see our task | But through [the insensible soldier's] blunt and lashless eyes?' (p. 191). The latter phrase denotes a stubborn will to witness, but also indelicacy. 'How should we see our task [...]?' is answered by the poem itself in the final stanza, with the poetic tradition of the elegy, not the articulacy of infantrymen. Owen may have been 'comforted by the thought' that his poems were providing vicarious testimony on behalf of 'the inarticulate soldiery', but infantrymen were articulate in other ways than poetry as testimony, such as the popular songs that Brian Murdoch refers to in *Fighting Songs and Warring Words*, and post-war prose testimony, as in Charles Rowland's account of his tribulations on the western front.[22] Unlike the exaggerated dichotomy in the poem, Owen sometimes presents himself as rather like the insensible infantry: in a letter to Susan Owen (7 January 1917), he cannot tell her 'any more Facts. I have no Fancies and no Feelings. Positively they went numb with my feet' (p. 424); in a letter to Sassoon (10 October 1918) he has become taciturn, 'having let [his] brain grow dull' (p. 664).

Along with its testimony on behalf of supposedly inarticulate infantrymen, 'Insensibility' could be criticized for its vague addressivity. As I argued in the introduction, appeals to addressees are one of the key aspects of poetry as testimony. Here, the readers' attention is drawn to the fact that they—amongst other recipients—are the targets of 'combat gnosticism'; they are (partly) the civilian 'dullards whom no canon stuns' (p. 191). Owen's attack on the reader rather than the enemy in 'Insensibility' anticipates the more ferocious assault on readers in the camp gnosticism of Levi's 'Shemà', which I discuss in Chapter 5. Criticisms of Germans in Levi's poem may be implicit, but—as in Owen's work—the main target of the poet's anger is not the enemy but the civilian reader, who is cursed in 'Shemà' because they cannot think constantly about atrocity. In 'Insensibility', Owen berates readers who do not even think about the war in the first place: in stanza one, 'no one bothers' (p. 190) about the 'brothers' (p. 189). '[N]o one' is frustratingly non-specific for critics such as Campbell; however, readers should be responsive to the deliberate ambiguity of address in Owen's poems. The phrase 'dullards' may not refer primarily to civilian readers, but to senior army staff far behind the front line, just as Sassoon attacks the safely ensconced in poems such as 'The General' and 'Base Details'.[23] Or maybe—as the letters and manuscripts suggest—the elderly in general are the main targets. '[D]ullards' replaces the crossed-out 'these old' in the manuscript; in a letter to Susan Owen (4 April 1917), Owen admits: 'I hate old age' (p. 448).[24] (These denunciations cement the link between the elderly and 'dullard' soldier, particularly since the latter 'cannot tell | Old men's placidity from his' in the penultimate stanza.) Owen's criticisms of the elderly and complicit appear in other poems, such as 'The Parable of the Old Man and the Young', where 'Abram' slays his son '[a]nd half the seed of Europe, one by one'

(p. 42) rather than accept the sacrificial offer of the ram.[25] Similarly, in Sassoon's 'The Fathers', 'impotent old friends' who brag about the war are '[g]ross, goggle-eyed, and full of chat'.[26] Non-conscripts may also be the target of the poet's ire: in a letter to Susan Owen (25 April 1917), he feels bitterness 'towards those in England who might relieve us, and will not' (pp. 452–53). 'War-profiteers' concern Owen in a letter to his mother (10 August 1918) (p. 568) rather than the aggressive militarism of the Central Powers: Germans, Austrians, or Turks are rarely the targets of Owen's and Sassoon's poems; Owen's 'Sonnet: On Seeing a Piece of Our Artillery Brought into Action' forms a rare exception.[27] Indeed, in a letter to Susan Owen (27 August 1916), Owen repeats the phrase 'Fritz, whom I did not hate' (p. 408): Dominic Hibberd asserts in his biography that it was 'Wilfred's [ahistorical] belief that the Germans were no more to blame for the war than the Allies' (p. 334).

The problems of ambiguous address and vicarious testimony discussed so far should not overshadow the singularity of 'Insensibility'. The poem ends with a brilliantly affective—if generically conservative—neoclassical reinscription of the elegy:

> But cursed are dullards whom no cannon stuns,
> That they should be as stones.
> Wretched are they, and mean
> With paucity that never was simplicity.
> By choice they made themselves immune
> To pity and whatever moans in man
> Before the last sea and the hapless stars;
> Whatever mourns when many leave these shores;
> Whatever shares
> The eternal reciprocity of tears. (p. 191)

Charles Hamilton Sorley's anti-elegiac 'When You See Millions of the Mouthless Dead' rejects platitudes of mourning in lines such as: 'For, deaf, how should [the dead] know | It is not curses heaped on each gashed head?'[28] In contrast, Owen chooses the neoclassical diction of 'the last sea' and 'hapless stars', and the well-timed dimeter ('Whatever shares') before the grandeur of '[t]he eternal reciprocity of tears' (p. 191). In *Owen the Poet*, Hibberd contends that such imagery 'lacks substance' (p. 140), but the ending self-consciously refers back to the earlier self-critique of poetics: the 'poets' tearful fooling', criticized in stanza one (p. 189), is reinstated as the only adequate response to '[l]osses', since the 'dullards' and insensible infantrymen who feel no compassion or pity have already been rejected as potential sources of mourning. As with the earlier metonymy of the sighs, the poem here ultimately writes against itself, but—unlike other World War I poets—Owen is willing to engage, at length, with these problems of representation and vicarious testimony.

WHO ARE 'YOU'?: ADDRESSIVITY IN 'APOLOGIA PRO POEMATE MEO'

'Insensibility' provides anti-sacred testimony for survivors who '[c]an laugh among the dying, unconcerned' (p. 190): this process continues in 'Apologia pro Poemate Meo', but with a much more open critique of the poet's representation of the troops. Since testimony can portray individual suffering (rather than focussing on the metatext), this poem emphasizes the laughter of the troops amongst traumatic circumstances. As Todman notes, 'Laughter, drunkenness and camaraderie were as much a part of the war, for many men, as terror, violence and obedience' (p. 5), and some veterans were determined 'to commemorate their more positive version of the war', 'from the inter-war years through to the 1960s' (p. 194). In the fourth stanza, Owen connects this 'godly' laughter of the troops to the poet-officer, who, momentarily celebrated after an action, is greeted with their 'passion of oblation' (p. 187).

However, the poem then distinguishes between the poet-officer and troops in the last two stanzas. Owen demands that readers refrain from trusting his vicarious testimony in diction similar to Levi's meta-testimonial poem 'Shemà', and John Jarmain's 'These Poems' (which I discuss in Chapter 3). Levi and Jarmain's opening lines—'You who live safe | In your warm houses' and 'You who in evenings by the fire . . . '—are anticipated in Owen's scathing stanza:

> You shall not hear their mirth:
> You shall not come to think them well content
> By any jest of mine. These men are worth
> Your tears. You are not worth their merriment. (p.188)[29]

The last sentence means that readers are not 'worth' laughter in the sense that the soldiers' merriment—as in the first stanza—is sacred, or that they are so 'worthless' in contrast with the troops that they are merely risible. Infantrymen are worthy of readers' tears, but, as 'Insensibility' outlines, an abstract account of the 'eternal reciprocity of tears' (p. 191) proves necessary when the dullards are absent. For critics such as Campbell, combat gnosticism is evident here in that, even if they try hard, non-combatants will never 'hear' the soldiers' mirth. However, this stanza—as in the opening lines of 'Insensibility'—contains self-critique, since the men may actually not be 'well content', as the author presents them in the 'jest' of his vicarious testimony.

Moreover, it is not just that—as in many testimonial poems, such as Levi's and Jarmain's—readers are implicitly criticized for being non-survivors, but (as in Delbo's work) the accused 'You' in the final stanza encompasses the poet himself as well as the reader. The 'you' in the penultimate stanza, who shares '[w]ith them in hell the sorrowful dark of hell' could refer to the 'I' (the poet) of the previous stanza. After all, Owen also shares the iconography of hell with the soldier's world, which is 'but the trembling of a flare': he specifically refers to battle as 'hell's upsurge' in 'Spring Offensive' (p. 202). Sassoon's 'Aftermath' (p. 143) makes similar use of this ambiguity of address: the 'you' repeated *passim*, who must not forget the war's events, refers to the poet as much as civilian readers. Owen is concerned that his celebrations of the troops' laughter might be akin to the impressionistic writing of the journalist in Sassoon's 'Editorial Impressions', who hopes he has 'caught the feeling of "the Line"' | And the amazing spirit of the troops' (p. 89). The epistemological gulf in understanding outlined in the last stanza thus falls not only between civilians and soldiers, but also, potentially, between the troops and the poet-officer. Contra Campbell— and if read via Holocaust poetry as testimony—'Apologia pro Poemate Meo' constructs necessary protection against over-identification between the three parties of infantrymen, civilians, and officers. As in Delbo's work, the reader will never 'see' exactly what happened, but rather than valorizing gnosis, the stanza suggests that the reader should be aware of colonizing the victim's experience, as Pierre does in *The Measure of Our Days*.[30] Ultimately, the poem upholds a final self-critique (unlike 'Insensibility') of the vicarious representation of fellow sufferers: such censure is virtually absent in other World War I poems. After World War II, such critiques of testimony are developed into a critical paradigm in Holocaust Studies: worries over the representation of fellow sufferers in Levi's work result in the philosophical ruminations about *Musulmänner* and 'bare life' in Giorgio Agamben's work.

Owen's critique of his own testimonial representations links with his assertion in his famous 'Preface' to his poems that he is not concerned with 'Poetry'.[31] Attracted to what he correctly perceived as the anti-iconoclastic nature of Owen's remark, Philip Larkin comments in a letter to Monica Jones (31 August 1963): 'Isn't that a marvellous thing to say [about poetry]'?[32] Owen's poems are forging a new kind of poetics, which grate with contemporaneous ideas as to what poetry might be; one of which was that it should not engage with war, as Robert Graves stated (paradoxically, as a soldier poet) when he wrote to Owen that he should 'have a spirit above wars'.[33] Owen's letters to the aesthete poet Leslie Gunston emphasize his conviction that poetry must be responsive to modern experience, rather than outmoded notions of the aesthetic. Hence the ironic apology for his poems in the title: in 'Apologia pro Poemate Meo' we have 'beauty' in the soldiers' 'hoarse oaths' (p. 187); such poetry foreshadows Theodor Adorno's notion of 'barbaric' poetics, in which—if applied to this poem— the aesthetic sibilance of 'shell-storms' spouting 'reddest spate' arises out of atrocious events.[34] As Tim Kendall—Owen's shrewdest critic—puts it, 'Owen wants a new poetry which is fighting fit and able to brave the war' (p. 50). Such representations will have to include awkward representations of fellow soldiers, whose friendship, in 'Apologia pro Poemate Meo', is 'wound with war's hard wire whose stakes are strong' (p. 187). The opening lines of 'Exposure' form examples of this new, testimonial poetry:

> Our brains ache, in the merciless iced east winds that knive us . . .
> Wearied we keep awake because the night is silent. (p. 180)

The depicted inaction of soldiers 'in action' is unsettled with the awkward metre of the first line, with metrical breaks on 'ache' and 'east' as Owen emphasizes the troops' discomfort. '[S]ilent' exemplifies Owen's frequent use—as in 'Insensibility'—of hypercatalectic metre, which draws attention to the dissonance of the pararhyme (as in 'brambles | rumbles' in 'Exposure'). Whereas Graves accused Owen of 'metrical outrages', Kendall rightly defends the latter's aesthetics: 'What is sometimes criticised as failure of technique [. . .] is an ambitious and forceful new poetry which, attuned to its historical circumstance, necessarily affronts the old harmonies' (p. 59).[35]

KILLERS IN 'HELL'S UPSURGE': 'SPRING OFFENSIVE'

These awkward poetics persist in 'Spring Offensive', which dwells on soldiers, who—as in the second stanza of 'Apologia pro Poemate Meo'—can slash 'bones bare' but not 'feel sickness or remorse of murder' (p. 187). Unlike World War II poetry—as I outline in Chapter 3—World War I poets rarely engage with their culpability in enemy deaths: Owen's 'Strange Meeting' and 'Spring Offensive' form rare exceptions. As Kendall points out in an article on Ivor Gurney, 'Great War poets' may be eloquent 'about suffering and being killed', but they 'keep their counsel when it comes to the business of killing'.[36] The last stanza of 'Spring Offensive' comprises instead a fraught attempt to present the testimony of soldiers as killers, and the Owen in the letter to Susan Owen (4 or 5 October 1918) who 'shot one man with [his] revolver', and then 'took' the rest 'with a smile' (p. 580).[37]

Awkwardness begins in the third stanza, with the archaic diction of 'begird', the apostrophe and the deferred personal pronoun ('these') in '[m]ightier than his whose bounty these have spurned' (p. 201). At the beginning of the final stanza, the strained syntax and diction continue:

> But what say such as from existence' brink
> Ventured but drave too swift to sink
> The few who rushed in the body to enter hell,
> And there out-fiending all its fiends and flames
> With superhuman inhumanities,
> Long-famous glories, immemorial shames—
> And crawling slowly back, have by degrees
> Regained cool peaceful air in wonder—
> Why speak not they of comrades that went under? (p. 202)

Rather than regard the first two lines as the poor work of an overrated poet—as critics such as Craig Raine might have it—I would argue that this is the testimony of an author struggling in an unfinished poem to articulate the role of the killer as witness.[38] These lines are particularly stilted: 'say such' (in other words, 'those soldiers who ventured . . . ') constitutes the awkward subject of the sentence; it is no accident that a metrical break occurs on the word signalling an attempt at articulation ('say'). The strange possessive ('existence' brink') then avoids the extra syllable of 'existence's'; the archaic 'drave' is also distracting. Instead of wilfully obscuring his experience by indulging in a moment of combat gnosticism, however, Owen then goes on to present an early version of Levi's 'grey zone' in admitting the 'inhumanities' that soldiers may be required to perform.[39] Arthur Brock (Owen's tutor at Craiglockhart) celebrated the 'superhuman sanity' 'in acts of [. . .] self-abnegation', whereas the poet alludes here to survivors' 'super-human inhumanities'.[40] Such phrases enact the testimonial problem, as Paul Fussell describes it, of 'the collision between events and the language available—or thought appropriate—to describe them'.[41] The phrase does, and does not, describe the action, since we learn of the inhumane act of killing without the further specificities that World War II poetry will dwell on at length. Unlike 'Insensibility', 'Spring Offensive' does not critique its own poetics, yet the abstract language does appear to obscure the action in the last stanza. Instead of contending, like Caesar, that Owen 'still implicitly resists a bald recognition of the violence man is capable of' (p. 166), I would argue that the stanza comprises an awkward attempt, in a new, testimonial poetry, to engage with perpetrator aesthetics, a process which is taken further in World War II poetry—in, for example, Keith Douglas's 'How to Kill' and 'Vergissmeinnicht' and Jack Bevan's 'Ubique'.[42]

The final line of this stanza ('Why speak not they of comrades that went under?') criticizes other survivors as inarticulate, but the poem itself cannot completely rebuff that inarticulacy. Owen is not (following Campbell) stubbornly insisting that World War I experience is incommunicable, but—as in Holocaust testimony—the stanza reflects the fact that writers are often not sure what exactly constitutes this experience in the first place. As I discuss further in Chapter 4, Delbo questions her own testimony when she escapes a selection in *None of Us Will Return* and when she attempts to remember washing in a stream in *Useless Knowledge*. The SS forces her to sprint during the selection: afterwards, she 'had no idea whether [she] reconstituted this whole scene after the fact or if [she] had an overall concept from the start' (p. 36). In *Useless Knowledge*, Delbo begins to fictionalize her imagined experience, since she has 'no memory of it. I only recall the stream' (p. 153). Survivors such as Delbo are also often unsure of how to assimilate this experience into post-war life, as the various women's testimonies in *The Measure of Our Days* attest, and as David Jones indicated with the title of his World War I poem *In Parenthesis*. Owen's diction is also maybe self-censoring: poets may wish to spare readers the worst atrocities, unlike Dan Todman who—like Daniel Goldhagen in *Hitler's Willing Executioners*—has an unsettling tendency to quote the visceral.[43] Sassoon's trooper sides with such censorship in 'Remorse', whilst paradoxically describing 'inhumanities' such as an assault when '[o]ur chaps were sticking' Germans—who were attempting to surrender—'like pigs' (p. 118). Such 'immemorial shames' provoke embarrassment, as in Owen's shame of success in his poem 'With an Identity Disk'. In addition to this awkwardness of articulacy and embarrassed self-censorship, the language is also opaque in the last stanza of 'Spring Offensive' because Owen is trying to make his experience of 'inhumanities' universal: all '[l]ong-famous glories' in warfare are daringly exposed as simultaneously shameful (p. 202), rather than acts of untainted heroism. This abstractness reflects the stage of development in poetry as testimony. Owen's abstract titles, such as 'Insensibility' and 'Spring Offensive'—rather than 'Beaumont Hamel' or 'Fayet'—contrast with the specificity of testimonial utterance in World War II poems which openly engage with the metatext, such as Jarmain's citation of 'Tunisia 1943' in 'These Poems' (p. i). Owen also semi-fictionalizes the historical narrative in order to suit his artistic purposes: 'Spring Offensive' is based on his experience at Fayet during the assault on Savy Wood in April 1917, but the month is changed so that summer can ooze 'into their veins' with a 'May breeze' (p. 200). Such aesthetic tweaking is much less likely in the testimonial poetry of World War II.

Owen's end-line—simultaneously the final line of his *oeuvre*—challenges other post-war survivors (the 'undying dead', as he puts it in 'Smile, Smile, Smile') to confront problems of witnessing and ethical responsibility. Of course, poetry as testimony does reply to this concern in numerous World War I poems, such as Ivor Gurney's 'To His Love', which exposes a 'red wet | Thing' on a fellow soldier that Gurney feels a duty to represent, but must also 'somehow forget'.[44] Even during the war, Sassoon was outlining survivors' 'cowed | Subjection to the ghosts of friends who died', in poems such as 'Survivors' (p. 97). However, this pressure for vicarious testimony on behalf of 'comrades that went under' does not take into account the problems of representation that Owen has already outlined in 'Insensibility' and 'Apologia pro Poemate Meo'. Hence the awkwardness of the final stanza partly answers the rhetorical question posed in the last line: many comrades do not speak of the dead precisely because of the difficulties of witnessing their experience and finding a diction and syntax adequate to represent the act of 'superhuman inhumanities'. In Chapter 5, I analyse Levi's similarly fraught attempts to engage with his fellow sufferers in poems such as 'Buna' and 'The Survivor'. Owen's attempts to confront such problems of articulacy, vicarious representation, and address mark him out as the progenitor of twentieth-century poetry as testimony.

2 Culpability and the Lyric in Tadeusz Borowski's *Selected Poems*

Our era hurts too much to write poems about the setting of the moon.[1]

The Polish writer Tadeusz Borowski was a poet long before he turned to prose, but in Britain and America he is more widely known as the author of the short story collection *This Way for the Gas, Ladies and Gentlemen*.[2] When I interviewed Tadeusz Pióro about translating Borowski's work, he explained that the latter's short stories are still taught in Polish high schools, and that students study his poems at university.[3] The lack of knowledge outside Poland about Borowski's substantial poetic output—before he gave up writing poetry in 1946—indicates that canons of Holocaust literature are bound up with the availability of translations as well as (if not as much as) literary value. In contrast with Primo Levi's poetry (which is more commonly read in Britain due to the Faber and Faber collection), only three Borowski poems are readily available in English translation: 'Night over Birkenau', 'The Sun of Auschwitz', and 'Farewell to Maria' appear in Hilda Schiff's anthology *Holocaust Poetry*.[4] A few more poems feature in the English translation of Adam Zych's anthology *The Auschwitz Poems*, but this edition is now out of print.[5] In 1990, Pióro produced a whole volume of Borowski's work, published by a small press in California.[6] I wish to make three claims in this chapter for the importance of Pióro's translations. Firstly, Borowski is an unjustly neglected figure in British and American debates about Holocaust and post-Holocaust poetry. Poems such as 'October Sky' (as I stressed in the introduction) deserve to be read alongside the 'classics' of European and American Holocaust poetry, such as Paul Celan's 'Death Fugue', Nelly Sachs's 'A Dead Child Speaks', and Primo Levi's 'Shemà'.[7] Secondly—and most importantly for this book—Borowski's anti-lyrical pieces are symptomatic of an overlooked genre in Holocaust Studies: the testimonial poem which mimics the style of prose testimony. Less prosaic poems such as 'October Sky' illustrate that—as I argue throughout this book—lyrical poems can function as a form of testimony, which (in this case) demonstrate a specific link in Borowski's work between the lyric form and complicity. Thirdly, Borowski's measured, 'testimonial' poetics indicate an alternative way in which to discuss how trauma is potentially inscribed in testimony. Whereas Shoshana Felman and Dori Laub focus on the 'scope of the accident' in Holocaust literature (the ways in which diagnostic, traumatic criteria are registered in the texts), Borowski's shockingly unperturbed narratives resist this teleology of trauma.[8]

Borowski's testimonial poems written in 1945–46 anticipate Theodor Adorno's later concerns in 1949 with 'barbaric' poetry.[9] The Polish poet's awkward poetics also connect with contemporaneous writers' suspicion towards the European legacies of the lyric, or what the British poet Keith Douglas termed 'Bullshit'.[10] As I outline in Chapter 3, in a letter to J. C. Hall (1943), Douglas admits that he fails as a lyric writer, but not as a poet: the 'lyric form and a lyric approach' to the events of the war 'will do even less good than a journalese approach', he argues. 'To write on the themes which have been concerning me lately in lyrical and abstract forms, would be immense bullshitting.' 'Bullshit', he explains, is an army word which signifies 'humbug and unnecessary detail'. Similarly to Douglas, Borowski's testimonial poetry is partly driven by his suspicion towards the 'lyric approach' in his poems composed between 1943 and 1946. By Borowski's 'anti-lyrics' I do not mean poems that reject the lyric form entirely, but poems that display a dialectical process of working through and against, but also with, lyrical traditions. In other words, anti-lyrical lyrics enact what Adorno termed 'hating tradition properly', in narratives of survival.[11] However, Douglas's 'Bullshit' and Borowski's 'hating' are more specifically concerned with the anti-lyric than Adorno's more general comments about 'barbaric' poetry. Adorno's original statement in 'Cultural Criticism and Society' is sometimes misread as targeting the lyric in particular, but he writes about *ein Gedicht*, a poem, not *die Lyrik*.[12] This misconception sometimes arises out of the misconception that Adorno is engaging with Celan's agonized, lyrical aesthetic, but Adorno had not read Celan by 1949.[13]

This chapter argues that Borowski's 'hating' results in two very different artistic responses to the lyric. In contrast with the self-questioning poetics of his early poetry, Borowski changes stylistic direction after his experiences in Auschwitz-Birkenau, Nazweiler-Dautmergen, and Dachau. As opposed to the agonized, epiphanic poetics of poems such as 'October Sky', Borowski develops a more accessible, testimonial *style* of poetry after his internment in a displaced persons' camp at Freimann near Munich after the liberation of Dachau (which, in a bitter Borowskian irony, just happened to be a former SS barracks).[14] The first kind of poem—the self-conscious lyric epitomized by 'October Sky'—comprises an example of the awkward poetics I discuss in my first two books on post-Holocaust poetry (in relation to, for example, Celan and Geoffrey Hill), but in the second half of this chapter I wish to outline an alternative tradition to this late modernist form of poetry.[15] In the 1940s and 1950s there was an upsurge in prosaic testimonial poetry—as opposed to testimonial poems more generally—as evidenced in the work of European and American poets such as Borowski, Charles Reznikoff, and Alan Ross. In the context of this kind of writing, it is questionable whether the late modernist poetics of Celan, Hill, et al., are, stylistically, the most innovative post-Holocaust forms of poetry. Instead, the anti-lyrical poetics of many of Borowski's Munich poems are symptomatic of a new, post-Holocaust form: the testimonial poem that mimics the stylistics of prose testimony. Post-Romantic lyrics tend to focus on the extraordinary, the epiphanic, whereas anti-heroic testimonial poetics form the invisible middle ground in poetry's narratives of survival.

'OCTOBER SKY' AND THE ANTI-LYRIC

'October Sky', on the other hand, is an anti-lyrical poem which struggles with vexed aesthetics in the context of the camps:

> October was beautiful. As if it were yesterday I remember
> the strangely clear, strangely deep sky
> shimmering in the noon heat as a leaf shimmers in the wind,
> empty and unreachable. I am oddly melancholy
> telling you about this, for what do words mean?
> I saw the lines of smoke the wind traced on the elusive sky
> and I waited for the moment
> when this unreachable sky would lean toward them
> to absorb them. After that there is nothing but
> the poet's sadness and a subject for a poem.
>
> And once I saw the sky through window panes.
> We had just been ordered to open the windows in the blockhouse
> and walking by I saw the sky in the glass,
> unexpected and wonderful, as if it were
> a great camp. Posts stapled with wire,
> roads I know so well, were suspended in air
> and the grass sparkled in the glass of the window pane
> dark green, as from the bottom of a lake. A red flame moved
> across the sky and glistened on the grass in a russet stream.
> Above this sky, a sky covered with smoke,
> another sky hung clear and empty
> and the smoke of the first sky drowned in the second.
>
> And I realised that I didn't know anything for certain,
> that the earth and all that happens around me
> are only a glass pane for someone else's eyes.
> Then someone blurred the picture and closed the window.
> A moment long gone. The earth is real, and now I know
> how real human suffering is.
> But as a wave to a shore, a moment of doubt returns
> still, today, it still pierces me,
> and always when I look at the December clouds
> I see above them the October sky.[16]

One of the reasons that this poem has not been encountered more is due to the lack of metatextual specificity in the title, as opposed to Borowski's more commonly anthologized pieces, 'Night over Birkenau' and 'The Sun of Auschwitz'.[17] Testimonial poetry (as I outlined in the introduction) demands a metanarrative, but 'October Sky', because of the title's topographical elusiveness, both is and is not an Auschwitz poem. Borowski holds the more horrific details of everyday camp life at bay, as if it would be inappropriate—at this point in his writing—for them to intervene in, and interfere with, the lyrical form. For example, the Polish *bloku* in the original poem is not specific to Auschwitz-Birkenau and could refer to any blockhouse; the 'red flame' in stanza two might refer to flames from the crematorium (the same phrase is used in *This Way for the Gas*), but it could just denote the sun.[18] The lack of exact topographical detail means that the metanarrative of Auschwitz can only undercut the naturalistic poetics from outside the text. However, the singularity of the 'lyrical approach' in the first stanza is clearly inseparable from the context of the camp.[19] Celebrations of the aesthetic are, for Borowski at this stage, more painfully necessary (and fraught) in Auschwitz-Birkenau. Frieda Aaron contends that poetry written in 'the shadow of gas chambers' is not concerned with aesthetics, but if Pióro is right that 'October Sky' was composed in Auschwitz, then she is wrong in this specific case: the poem is a complex anti-lyrical poem, self-consciously grappling with the possibility of the aesthetic inside the camp.[20]

The lyrical form is already fraught in stanza one: awkward poetics interrupt the celebration of the pastoral after only four lines to ruminate on the impossibility of entirely capturing epiphanic moments and rendering them meaningful to the implied reader. 'I am oddly melancholy', the poet writes, 'telling you about this, for what do words mean?' (p. 17).[21] In the English translation, the contamination of the unblemished sky with lines of smoke also puns on the corruption of now 'blemished' aesthetics in the lines of the poem as a whole. The sadness of the poet at the end of stanza one results from both a traditional contemplation of the sublime and the obscenity of a poetic 'subject' in the context of the metanarrative. Rather than give up on the lyric form, however, Borowski paradoxically stresses the preciousness of aesthetic moments in the camp, particularly in relation to memory and personal recollection. 'October Sky' constantly puts pressure on the lyrical tradition, traditional poetic forms, subject matter, and genre in the context of Auschwitz. For the moment, the anti-lyric remains dialectical, maintaining the ghost of the lyrical among the agonized self-questioning.

Hence the epiphany of the window image—and the poem as a whole—suspends and manipulates the metanarrative of camp life for a moment; the end of the stanza seems to enact a Platonic triumph of the aesthetic, as the uncontaminated sky 'drowns' the crematorium's smoke. However, the opening line of the third stanza ('And I realised I didn't know anything for certain') subverts the (relatively) stable naturalistic poetics.[22] Mirroring Antelme's worry—noted in the introduction—that poems could be just 'melodic counterpoints' to the metanarrative, the anti-lyric registers here a distrust of artifice that can turn Auschwitz-Birkenau into a 'great camp'.[23] Our world is a 'glass pane' for someone else (other writers, prisoners, guards, God, or readers): for Borowski, the aesthetic can always distort reality to encompass individual taste. The metanarrative then momentarily enters the poem in abstract form, as the poet admits 'how real human suffering is'. However, 'October Sky' retreats from rejecting the lyric entirely, since 'a moment of doubt returns' about the appropriateness of the aesthetic at the end of the poem. The temptation for the survivor poet to aestheticize, and remember, remains too potent, even amongst the suffering: lyricism is—at this point—as enmeshed in Borowski's writing as 'a wave to [the] shore'. Indeed, 'October Sky' closes with the irresistibility of the utopian thrust of the lyric, and its 'restorative impulse', as the poet imagines the glorious October sky when he looks at the December clouds heavy with snow.[24] Hence, according to Keith Douglas's criteria, 'October Sky' is still, ultimately, a dissenting example of 'Bullshit' poetics.[25]

THE CULPABILITY OF THE LYRIC

Another reason why Borowski rigorously examines the aesthetic processes of poetry and re-memory in 'October Sky' is that lyrical moments also comprise potential poetics of distancing, avoidance, and culpability. ('Poetics of complicity', as I first wrote, is, perhaps, the wrong phrase, since writing an evasive lyric in Auschwitz is obviously not a 'partnership in evil' in the same way as the narrator's unloading of the transports in *This Way for the Gas*.[26]) In 'Night over Birkenau', the 'blameworthiness' of culpability is openly registered in the metaphor of the 'lead foot' crushing the poet's chest, an admittance of his specific guilt as well as an overall lament for all those murdered in the camp.[27] In contrast, culpability or complicity is not overtly discussed in 'October Sky'. Critiques of the lyrical moment are more explicit in *This Way for the Gas*. In a review of an early book about Auschwitz, Borowski argues that representations of the camp—including those in the lyric form—can be evasive if they avoid questions about *how* the writer survived. '"Tell, then," Borowski writes, "how you bought places in the hospital, easy posts, how you shoved 'Moslems' [. . .] into the oven [. . .] [unloaded] the transports"'.[28] In his 1994 memoir *Beyond Lost Dreams*, J. N. Siedlecki refers to the bond of 'old numbers' in the camp that became a kind of Polish 'mafia', 'gaining positions of responsibility in the camp hierarchy. They supported and promoted their friends and soon most functionaries were the prisoners with low numbers'.[29] *This Way for the Gas* is thus an important example of one of the first 'anti-sacred' responses to the Holocaust that Matthew Boswell analyses in *Holocaust Impiety*: rather than writing the 'myths' and 'legends' of perpetrators and victims, Borowski explained that 'we fought for a bowl of soup, for a place to sleep, for women, for gold watches from the transports [. . .] we often renounced our humanity because we wanted to survive'.[30]

Pióro revealed that the notoriety of Borowski's short stories in Poland arose partly from his attack on any notion of the sacred survivor:

> Other fictional accounts—that is, short stories in odd books about the death camps—embellished the truth: there were the good victims, and the bad torturers and executioners. Borowski exploded this distinction, and showed how it was meaningless in the world of the concentration camps, and for that he was bitterly criticised. (p. 46)

For Borowski, the 'you' in the previous quotation appertains to all survivors (since he was not a member of the *Sonderkommando*): *all* camp narratives of survival for the Polish poet are bound up at some level with culpability. One of the problems with this universality is that there is no distinction made between different kinds of prisoners: Polish political prisoners such as Borowski could receive food parcels and eat bacon, onion, and evaporated milk for breakfast, as opposed to less fortunate inmates.[31] Borowski argues that survivors should acknowledge a moral code specific to the camps: in a preface to one of his early stories in *We Were in Auschwitz* (not reprinted in *This Way for the Gas*), he describes the *Sonderkommando* as 'not *bad* people', but 'simply *accustomed*'.[32] As opposed to the narrator's unloading of the transports, the 'accustomed' forms one end of the camps' continuum of complicity. Borowski is struggling with an adequate discourse of ethics to describe everyday acts in the camps. Levi illustrates these problems with the 'grey zone' when he steals a spoon in *If This Is a Man*: is this an act of complicity, culpability, being accustomed, or none of these, since these words—as Levi argues in relation to 'good'—are specific to a world outside the camps?[33]

To be 'simply accustomed', however, is, for Borowski, to be potentially complicit; this connection is manifest in the language of *This Way for the Gas*, as opposed to the lyrical evasions of 'October Sky' and other poems written about the camp, such as 'The Sun of Auschwitz'. For example, in *This Way for the Gas* the inmate Henri speaks in the language of the guards as he runs gleefully towards the transports; '*Keine Angst*' ('no fear'), he says.[34] The more lyrical passages towards the end of the eponymous story evoke a sense of aesthetic distancing inextricable from complicity: cries from the transports are repeated 'like a late showing of the same film' (p. 47). By reading the horrific incidents in *This Way for the Gas* alongside Borowski's poetry, the lyrical epiphany in 'October Sky' can be seen to comprise a similar moment of aesthetic distancing, in which the lyric form, like the vodka in the story, attempts to block out the everyday life of the camp. As the utopian, redemptive thrust of 'October Sky' illustrates, the lyric in Auschwitz is a form of forgetting, as opposed to the testimonial style of Borowski's post-Holocaust poetry, which is more beholden to historical facts.

'The Sun of Auschwitz' is an undialectical love poem in the midst of Dachau that similarly avoids the metanarrative.[35] Auschwitz becomes the locus for romantic yearning, where the lover's smile was

> [. . .] as elusive
> as a shade of the color of the wind,
> a leaf trembling on the edge
> of sun and shadow, fleeting
> yet always there.[36]

Memory, aesthetics, and the lyrical form are inextricable in this poem: Borowski concentrates on 'remembering' the lovers' dissolution into 'the green of the distant meadows' (a form of displaced escape) and blots out the details of everyday life in Auschwitz. Syntax and line sense vie in the opening lines, illustrating the utopian thrust of the whole piece: surely it is impossible to remember the sun of Auschwitz 'lightly' (*lekko*).[37] There is no 'evoking [of] evil' in this love poem, as Borowski claims he is doing in his Auschwitz letters to Maria in *This Way for the Gas*.[38] In these letters, he explains that the lovers have unavoidably become part of the 'great camp's' machinery. Aesthetic moments in the previous section ('The People Who Walked On') are castigated as a form of evasion: a camp elder tells the women inmates to dance, sing, and recite poetry, but then angrily interrupts the participants to inform them that their families have been gassed (p. 91). She ends her tirade with the challenge: 'Now go on and sing' (p. 92). The story reflects Borowski's grappling with the efficacy of the lyric in the midst of the camps: in 1949, Adorno targeted the philosophical equivalent of her outburst at poetry more generally.

In both 'The Sun of Auschwitz' and 'October Sky', the reflective, lyrical moment cannot help but register momentary survival, and therefore, for Borowski, be bound up with the 'accustomed'. This is made clear when the narrator of the first story in *This Way for the Gas* comes back from the transports, returns to his 'cool, kind' bunk, and, on reflection, suddenly sees 'the camp as a haven of peace' not unlike the 'great camp' in 'October Sky' (p. 48). The second story in *This Way for the Gas* reverses the narrative structure of the first by opening with a reflective moment in which the chestnut trees 'rise up in sea-green cupolas scented with the morning freshness'; this lyrical contemplation is subsequently undercut by the details of the following story (p. 50). In 'Auschwitz, Our Home (A Letter)', Borowski directly satirizes such aesthetic moments: 'we marched to Auschwitz', he writes, 'along a very beautiful road, observing some *very interesting* scenery en route' (p. 99; my italics). Similarly, in a letter to Halszka Bodalska (2 February 1946), he ruminates on his reservations about ahistorical aesthetics in relation to Germany:

Please believe me when I say that some parts of Germany (Dresden, Wüttemberg, the Alps, for example) are as beautiful as the landscapes in the novels of bygone centuries. But when we walked across them in prison stripes, we did not extol the beauty of this country. The beauty of an enemy land? We developed our own criteria for beauty: the most beautiful city? Frankfurt reduced to rubble. And in sonnets the poet praises beauty as though he were completely free. Reality—next to the poet stands a gendarme.[39]

Three days later, Borowski wrote to Zofia Świdwińska that 'our era hurts too much to write poems about the setting of the moon'.[40] Due to this pressure of history, lyrical composition for Borowski had already become a potentially outdated habit a year earlier in the camps, as opposed to his time in Pawiak prison, when he used to pace up and down the cell, composing hexameters to the rhythm of his steps. And yet, in *This Way for the Gas* as in 'October Sky', the paradoxical preciousness of the inappropriate lyrical moment remains. When he describes the violence of his own transport, the narrator notes, 'You have no idea how tremendous the world looks when you fall out of a closed freight car [. . .] [the sky is so] blue', even though 'the S.S. men surrounded us on all sides, holding their automatics' (p. 126).[41] Whereas the elder's fable silences the aesthetic earlier in *This Way for the Gas*, here the deportation ends in the triumph of the lyrical despite, and due to, the interruption of history.

'HOMECOMINGS' AND TESTIMONIAL POETRY

In addition to historicized aesthetics and subverted lyrical forms in 'October Sky' and *This Way for the Gas*, another result of Borowski's resistance to the lyric is his development of anti-'Bullshit', testimonial poetics.[42] All poetry that recounts traumatic experience—such as 'October Sky'—is testimonial. Testimony—like witness statements in court—is, in general terms, considered to be a form of evidence. This (assumed) primary function—as I outlined in the introduction—has proved useful for Holocaust historians, many of whom have nevertheless (and rightly) distrusted the form as a supposedly uncompromised access to 'true' reality. In contrast, Robert Eaglestone (following the work of Elie Wiesel and Felman and Laub) has argued that testimony should not be the preserve of historians, since it constitutes a previously unrecognized literary genre.[43] As Felman and Laub contend, 'the essence' of testimony may seem to be 'the historical [. . .] its function [. . .] to record events and to report the facts of a historical occurrence', but it is also important to explore its performed *literariness*, and the generic characteristics of (in Borowski's case) written testimony.[44] The most common (so common as often—problematically—to be unnoted) generic characteristic of this testimony is that it is generally written in the

tradition of nineteenth-century realist prose.[45] 'October Sky'—like prose
testimony—recounts an incident, but one bound up with the generic characteristics of the anti-lyric and post-Romantic epiphany, rather than the
Victorian novel. Prose could be argued to be the more natural form for
writers to convey the gist of an occurrence, as opposed to poetry, but prose
is only, in this literary context, a formal convention. Indeed, once testimony is prised away from its juridical origins, and its primary function as
evidence, paradoxical poetry such as 'October Sky' can be read as another
testimonial form in which to register complex human experiences, which
resist the illusions of mimesis. Poetry, however, is clearly a different kind of
testimony, usually focussing on one epiphanic experience, rather than the
(normally) variegated experiences in prose testimony. Borowski's poems
written in 1945–46, for example, frequently recount reactions to a specific
incident, such as the liberation of Paris in 'Homecomings'.[46]

During this period, Borowski was developing a journalistic, testimonial
style at odds with the complex, vexed aesthetics of 'October Sky'. Pióro
argues that these poetics arose out a tension between the poet's classical
training and his experiences in the camps:

> When he found himself in the camps, he was still writing using the
> models that he'd been studying in his secret, underground university
> courses on literature, where old professors, philologists, told him how
> to write alexandrines and so on. He would continue with that for a
> while, but then I think—and, of course, this is speculation—we see the
> results of what must have been a process of revaluation of his poetics.
> Such formal models as he was using made little sense in the environ-
> ment where he was, and the things he was writing about, so the jour-
> nalistic approach to the immediate, historical detail must have been
> much more sensible than his previous modes of writing. (p. 51)

These poetics also arise out of his conviction—expressed in a letter to
Helszka Bodalska (2 February 1946)—that 'we are going to experience a
renaissance of Positivism' in European writing.[47] The following excerpts
from 'Homecomings' and 'A Walk through Munich' form examples of
these testimonial poetics:

'Homecomings'

The broad snout of the Marseillaise
'allons
enfants de la patrie'
the Parisian crowd
from even the best circles
floods the boulevards even in Montmartre
hundreds of thousands roar 'Vive la France'

Streets passionate as a steam bath
brothels exploding with democratic enthusiasm
banners waving from houses
wrapped in patriotic vapours

At the airport
long known as Le Bourget
on a plane called 'Liberator'
(belonging to L'Armeé de l'Air)
arrives the millionth Frenchman
a convict named Garron

The crowd sang idiotic songs
as the minister for Prisoners
pinned a medal to his chest
leaned forward and kissed him
straight
on his snout, unshaven for a week
and said 'vive la patrie'
(shamefaced he promptly added 'pardon')
the minister was called Fresnay
and the convict (the same)
was known as Garron [. . .]

'A Walk through Munich'

In the beautiful city of Munich
girls are out for a stroll [. . .]
I walk straight out of Allach
to take the city in my hands as a text [. . .]
There go the pliable girls [. . .]
in little batiste blouses [. . .]
stolen from *Zauna* [. . .]
young, pretty SS men
from crematorium *eins*
as well as *zwei, drei, vier,* and *fünf* [. . .]
there go the beautiful girls [. . .]
they smile tenderly
and sink their eyes into a Negro [. . .][48]

'Homecomings' and 'A Walk through Munich' are illustrative of Borowski's
post-liberation poems that reject the 'Bullshit' of the lyrical form in favour
of a journalistic style that conveys the urgency of recounting (and embellish-
ing) what Borowski terms in another poem the 'fishtank of blurred events'

in liberated Europe (p. 89), a 'time of limbo, a time without structure or form, a time of uncertainty, fear, and loss'.[49] 'My [new] style is lousy | alas', the poet claims in the poem 'New Deal' (p. 79): testimonial poetics in this context encompass sparse, prosaic diction, anti-aesthetic reportage, irregular rhyme and metre, chopped rhythms and line length, breathless pace augmented by the lack of punctuation, and an overall sense of the urgency of witnessing daily events at odds with the immanent ruminations on the aesthetic in 'October Sky'.[50] This immediacy is often evident in other forms of testimony, such as *If This Is a Man* (where the effect is compounded by the lack of semicolons). The following sentence is illustrative: 'Kraus is clumsy, he has already been kicked by the Kapo because he is incapable of standing in line: and now he is beginning to gesticulate and chew a miserable German, listen, listen, he wants to apologise for the spadeful of mud, he has not yet understood where we are, I must say Hungarians are really a most singular people'.[51] As I argue in Chapter 5, the 'accustomed' Levi here begins to speak not unlike the more cynical narrator of *This Way for the Gas*.

As opposed to the classical rhetoric and form of Borowski's early poems, his testimonial poetics value an anti-aesthetic immediacy and accessibility. The Munich poems written in this way are certainly not examples of complex, allusive metatestimony (such as Jorge Semprun's *Literature or Life*). They eschew the metapoetics of 'October Sky', although they are still self-conscious pieces of writing in that they encompass references that only survivors (in 1945–46) would recognize, such as *Zauna* in 'A Walk through Munich', which refers to a specific area in Auschwitz-Birkenau.[52] As Felman and Laub argue in relation to Celan's work, the poet is 'freed [to a certain extent] from the "aesthetic project"' in such poetry, but here in a radically different way to the elliptical, modernist aesthetics of Celan.[53] The irreverent, realist satire of *This Way for the Gas* increasingly pervades Borowski's Munich poems: the poet clearly did not think the lyric was a suitable form for savage irony. The satirical, anti-lyrical, and anti-redemptive poem 'Homecomings' rails in particular against simplistic liberatory narratives; in this case, the unreflective Parisian celebrations of liberation. A testimonial style arises partly out of Borowski's sense that his antipathy towards the French (which is in evidence throughout the Munich poems) would not be suitably expressed in the anti-/lyrical poetics of the earlier poem.[54] Anger, revulsion, and nationalistic jealousy in 'Homecomings' all grate against the lyrical balance of 'October Sky'. As opposed to the lyrical evasions of 'October Sky', the metanarrative engulfs the poem in Borowski's testimonial accounts of survival in a displaced persons' camp.

How can this testimonial poetry attain singularity in the same way as 'October Sky', or Celan's elliptical writing? For Borowski, this is not an issue in the Munich poems, since he relents from the lyrical idealism of earlier pieces which attempt to 'recreate the world [. . .] anew | struggle to shape words' (p. 23). Poetry is not 'magic' anymore, as it is in 'Rain Is

Lashing the Mud', a poem Borowski composed in Nazweiler-Dautmergen before his transfer to Dachau in April 1945 (p. 25).[55] Indeed, many of the Munich poems openly discuss his sense of poetic failure.[56] In a letter to Zosia Świdwińska (6 October 1945), Borowski notes that the publisher Anatol Girs—who established a family tracing service in Munich—'is currently publishing my poems for me, a little against my better judgment because they are neither particularly artistic nor intellectual achievements'.[57] There is a poignant link between the testimonial poetry, Borowski's decision to stop writing poetry altogether, and his subsequent (and notorious) political journalism in *Nowa Kultura*. In *The Captive Mind*, Czesław Miłosz notes that the journalist Borowski would take a 'snapshot' of an event, and turn it into an impressionistic political article for the Communist authorities.[58] 'Homecomings' is the equivalent 'snapshot' of liberation scenes, but without the political gloss of the later 'journalese'. However, this poem—like the Communist journalism—is a testimony of displaced self-loathing. In a letter from Paris (and unlike in the poem) Borowski admits that he too lux-uriated in the celebrations: 'I plunged into hypocrisy as into the current of a mountain stream', he writes, 'I drank wine with hired women [. . .] I don't feel well in Paris'.[59] As William Hitchcock notes in *Liberation*, 'France for a brief moment was awash in the explosive and heartbreaking sweetness of *le Retour* [. . .] [Yet] amidst the happiness was also longing, sadness, frustra-tion, anger, alienation, and a host of complex, contradictory emotions that welled up in many of those who survived captivity' (p. 264). 'Homecom-ings' and the Paris letter demonstrate that Borowski was one of those who suffered in a 'mountain stream' of 'contradictory emotions' in spring 1945. Liberation had become, as Hitchcock puts it, a 'liberation deferred' (p. 5).

The testimonial poetry's capitulation to the commotion of the survivor's post-war life clearly grates against Adorno's wish for a committed, autono-mous art along the lines of the high modernist aesthetics of Kafka, Celan, and Beckett. Yet Borowski's Munich poems deserve more attention in that they form part of a new style of writing responding in a different way to post-Holocaust pressures on the lyrical form. This testimonial style is anti-modernist, but only in a dialectical sense: rather than an absolute repu-diation of modernist poetics, the writing comprises a more recent version of the early modernist, symbolist, and Imagist desires to rid poetry—in Ezra Pound's terms—of the 'emotional slither' of neo-Georgian writing.[60] Felman and Laub's groundbreaking study of testimony explores trauma within Celan's deployment of, for example, aporia, but it leaves untouched the question as to why a modernist lyric open to fragmentation and disjunc-tion in his work might fit all too easily with the machinations of trauma theory, and what they term the traumatic 'scope of the accident'.[61] Testi-mony leads to existential crises for the authors and readers of Felman and Laub's examples of witnessing, but Borowski's unperturbed, testimonial poetics are noteworthy in that they resist this teleology of trauma, in which avoidance strategies and diagnostic, traumatic criteria are registered in the text. As Borowski puts it bluntly in a letter to Zosia Świdwińska (16 October 1945), 'I survived, it was awful, but no matter'.[62] Borowski's Munich poems link instead with a new testimonial form of poetry in evidence across Europe, in which the urgency to record overcomes the lyrical urge, as in the British poet Alan Ross's journalistic accounts of post-war life in verse.[63]

Borowski's testimonial poems are, however, markedly different from contemporaneous poetry in Poland, such as Miłosz's symbolist and allegorical verse, or Różewicz's 'naked', abstract lyricism.[64] Nevertheless, Miłosz, Różewicz, Ross, and Borowski were all responding in different ways to an anti-lyrical turn in Europe during World War II: in 1942, the Polish writer Trzebinski contends that 'the lyric died in September 1939', and with the death of the Polish lyrical poet Czechowicz.[65] And in 1943, Douglas begins his tirade against the lyric's 'Bullshit' poetics. The 'Bullshit' of Borowski's 'October Sky' satisfies in traditional, aesthetic terms, yet there is also a critical need to explore testimonial poetics that do not privilege ellipsis, aporia, and vexed aesthetics. Ultimately, however, 'October Sky' comprises the more singular piece of writing, an extraordinary lyrical—and anti-lyrical—outburst in the midst of Auschwitz-Birkenau, as Borowski toiled in Canada and Zauna. Registering the culpability of all survivors, the poem grapples with inherited poetic forms as Borowski's faith in the lyric begins to wane. It deserves to be read alongside Levi's 'Shemà', Celan's 'Todesfugue', Nelly Sachs's 'O the Chimneys', and Douglas's 'Vergissmeinicht' in schools and universities outside Poland as one of the exemplary poems of the Holocaust and the Second World War. However, as well as arguing for this adjustment to the canon of Holocaust and World War II poetry, I have stressed in this chapter that the critic should not forget the important anti-lyrical turn towards more accessible, journalistic, and anti-canonical poems. In the next chapter, I discuss such poems from the archive of the Salamander Oasis Trust.

3   The Oasis Poets
Perpetrators, Victims, and Soldier Testimony

The Armed forces are not conducive to the creation of contemplative verse.[1]

In *Dimensions of the Holocaust*, Elie Wiesel famously commented that the Holocaust produced the new literary genre of testimony.[2] As I related in the introduction, many critics—such as James Young—have pointed out that testimonial accounts abound in relation to many other wars and atrocities, but studies of testimony over the last forty years have (following Wiesel) mainly focussed on the Holocaust.[3] In this chapter, I analyse British soldiers' poetic accounts of World War II as a kind of testimony, and look in particular at the Imperial War Museum's vast collection of material on the 'Oasis' poets. This archive has the potential to change our perceptions of World War II, particularly in relation to notions of the 'good war' and post-war trauma, and the (post-Vietnam) conception of the soldier as victim. The concepts of victim and perpetrator testimony that have been developed mainly in relation to the Holocaust are both relevant and problematized in the context of soldier testimony. Clearly, the origin of the terms 'victim' and 'perpetrator' lie in a judicial context, but with the development of critical discussions about testimony outside the courtroom—as in the notion of literary testimony—the efficacy of these terms has been questioned. For Primo Levi, the trace of legal discourse is important, since it allows us to distinguish his tormentors from his fellow prisoners.[4] However, Levi himself introduced the notion of the 'grey zone', where the guilt of, for example, the *Sonderkommando* does not sit easily with legal notions of criminality. In Tadeusz Borowski's work, political prisoners of Auschwitz are (as victims) not guilty in judicial terms when they become complicit with the machinery of the camp, but this does not stop him admitting the moral ambiguity of unloading the transports and sending others to the gas chambers.[5]

In relation to soldier testimony, these categories are also vexed, since—as the variety of writing in the Oasis archive attests—an Allied recruit as a reluctant conscript, or subsequently traumatized individual, or even a violator of the Geneva Convention, could be considered a victim. Sometimes the categories blur within an individual poem, as when Oasis writers celebrate the killing of German soldiers, but then also engage with troubling memories that surface in relation to such events after the war. Who is a perpetrator in the context of soldier testimony (as opposed to a perpetrator of genocide), and what W. H. Auden described in 'Spain' as the 'conscious acceptance of guilt in the necessary murder'?[6] Should the term only be used in a legal sense, or should critical discussions of literary testimony draw on the dictionary definition of a perpetrator as an instigator of (potentially heinous) acts, which may include—whatever the pertinent definition of criminality—the killing of others in combat?[7] Is the Allied soldier never a perpetrator by mere dint of the term 'Allied'?[8] Is he only ever a victim (a common descriptor of soldiers after Vietnam and the advent of PTSD in 1980), or something between these two testimonial categories? And—most pertinent for this chapter—is there such a thing as a perpetrator voice, perspective, or aesthetic when the poet dispassionately records enemy deaths, or—as in Keith Douglas's 'Elegy for an 88 Gunner'—voyeuristically mulls over the corpse of an enemy soldier?

In this chapter I address such questions in relation to the canonical writer Douglas and other, relatively unknown, writers in the Oasis archive. The Salamander Oasis Trust was established in 1976 to collect testimony from World War II, primarily in the form of poetry. Appeals in newspapers such as the *Daily Mail*, *Daily Telegraph*, and *Daily Mirror* resulted in an archive of nearly twenty thousand manuscripts by two hundred authors, which is now held in the Imperial War Museum at Duxford.[9] The advent of the Trust was partly a response to an approaching post-testimonial age: one of the appeals appeared in *Yours*, the magazine of Age Concern; some of the potential contributors had already died when the Trust was inaugurated, requiring surviving family members to submit their work. A standard letter in the Salamander Oasis Trust Archive file of the poet Philip Whitfield (8 May 1996) indicates that the Imperial War Museum wrote to the executors of deceased contributors to inquire whether any extra material might be available, since personal papers 'are all too quickly lost to posterity if prompt action is not taken to secure their permanent retention in a suitable repository'.[10] These precarious attempts to collect soldiers' testimony are crystallized in the circumstances surrounding the submission of *The Oak*, a magazine published by the 46th Division: the editor, David Morgan, died only two weeks after he posted a whole set of the magazine to the Trust.[11] After the commemorations marking the war's fiftieth anniversary, when the Trust had been collecting manuscripts for twenty years, the collection 'was finally wound down, continuing to accept only very occasional contributions'.[12] Since the archive is not well known, in the first section of this chapter I shall outline the Trust's serendipitous collection of soldier testimony and examine what kind of witness literature the trustees were particularly interested in amassing.

The origins of this remarkable, but critically ignored, repository of soldier testimony lie in the *Oasis* anthology of 1943, which collected poems from those on active service in the desert.[13] When the book was nearly abandoned due to the dispersal of the editors on military service, the Salamander Society in Cairo stepped in, and the anthology subsequently made a profit for the Red Cross. After 1976, several new collections appeared: *Return to Oasis* (1980), *From Oasis into Italy* (1983), *Poems of the Second World War* (1985), *More Poems of the Second World War* (1989), *Schools Oasis* (1992), and *The Voice of War* (1996).[14] The conditions in which the testimony was written and collected compounded the fraught publishing history of the original *Oasis*. In a letter to the editors (10 July 1990), Clifford J. M. Fidler recounts the variety of compositional materials: 'In the first instance [poems] were usually scribbled on the back of "fag" packets, letters from home, or even "Army Form Blank" (toilet paper) if nothing else was available' (p. 1).[15] Ernest Court's book of poems and illustrations was buried under a manure pit in Italy and only retrieved a year later after the line had moved up to the depositing area.[16] Other stashes were never recovered: Frederic Gale wrote to the Trust (23 September 1981), explaining that his 'greatest regret [was] that lying buried somewhere in the Western Desert is a fat exercise book almost filled with poems written by me over many months'; Michael Cooney lost a poem 'blown up at Arnhem'.[17] In *From Oasis into Italy*, John Brookes recounts how poems were written on toilet paper in Japanese POW camps, bound into books, and kept from endless searches.[18] Brookes's own poem, 'Thermopylae 41', was kept in a shoe box under the stairs until his wife persuaded him to submit it to the Trust.[19] In a letter to Victor Selwyn (18 October 1983), Captain S. John H. Durnford notes that 'Japanese security forbade us to keep pens or notebooks. So most of the poems were written on scraps of paper. Secreted in hollow bamboo bed-rafters. Or even in the soles of my wooden sandals' (pp. 2–3). In an undated letter to the Imperial War Museum, Victor West explains that he kept a microscopic diary (against orders) during his service and after his capture: it survived over ten searches, including two conducted by the Munich Gestapo.[20] Some of West's early poems were even written in handcuffs; his own survival is miraculous, since he fought during the invasion of Crete, nearly succumbed to pneumonia as a POW, and later escaped (in April 1945) from a march away from a German camp only to confront (and confound) the Commandant in a wood only hours later.[21]

Even the infamous storm of 1987 threatened the Trust's 'precious debris', since letters and manuscripts were lost when the severe weather conditions hit the South of England.[22] Aside from (and as a repost to) this precariousness, one of the most striking features of the archive is its abundance of manuscripts, written primarily by non-professional authors. Testimony has been regarded (following Wiesel) as inextricable from survivors' recollections of the Holocaust, yet the Oasis archive makes a case for World War II in general establishing the form, due to inter-war factors such as the rise in literacy, the expansion of the publishing industry, and the vast number of those affected (and thus writing and reading) during the 1939–45 conflict.[23] However, the trustees were determined to collect only a certain kind of testimony. Introductions across the anthologies repeat the policy that poems must have been written in action, rather than by, say, civilians or correspondents: *Return to Oasis* begins with the question 'What did the poets in uniform write?' (p. xx).[24] The figure of the soldier poet inaugurated during World War I is thus promulgated in a later conflict where it took many more workers behind the lines to keep one soldier active at the front. The deputy to the keeper in the Department of Documents at the Imperial War Museum also emphasizes the Trust's desire to 'publish writings as they were written at the time': post-war editing was discouraged, since technical deficiencies were perceived as part of the testimonial frisson of 'action' poems.[25] The deputy's letter (1 November 1982) was sent to a potential contributor, G. W. Canham, who replied:

> If the Trust wants to publish material exactly as it was written some 40 years ago, and is unwilling to have the writer edit his own work in the sense of removing some of the verbiage, slackness, etc. etc . . . then I have misunderstood [the Trust's] aims . . . No *writer* worth his salt publishes stuff containing glaring weaknesses. If they're simply looking for contemporary documents to reproduce, warts and all, then they can't have mine till after my death.[26]

As a reviewer of *From Oasis into Italy* spelt out, the policy of ostensibly ignoring post-war testimony and editing in relation to World War I would have resulted in the disqualification of 'perhaps the greatest war poem in English', David Jones's *In Parenthesis*.[27] David Gerard submitted his poem about the Foggia Plain in Italy (1943) to the Trust but freely admits it was written after the war. The editors chose not to anthologize 'Piano Forte', yet it contains some of the most arresting poetry in the archive: on a 'terret of a leading chain' the soldier confronts 'the rust of battle' and 'cheap walls above a quaking earth [. . .] the peeling space'.[28]

What exactly 'in action' meant during World War II is also debatable, given that *More Poems of the Second World War* contains Mary Harrison's poem 'My Hands' (p. 186): it depicts the guilt of a modeller in England viewing subsequent photographs of the devastation of Cologne; the poet wonders 'How many people have died through me | From the skill in my finger tips'.[29] In contrast, Sheila A. Gregg is outraged that Selwyn has rejected her poetry because it does not 'smell' of war: 'So you DO want your wretched war poems go smell [*sic*] of Gun Smoke I thought as much HOW DARE YOU I served my country as 2099186 in WAAF World War Two'.[30] The editors' hope, as stated in *From Oasis into Italy* (p. xix), was that the focus on soldier testimony would instil 'an added quality of immediacy and authenticity'. In a letter to Selwyn (30 September 1979), the contributor Jack Bevan praises the 'air of reality' about the anthologies, but such an effect depends on style rather than contemporaneity.[31] This 'air' and 'quality' are often illusions of simultaneity: as Vernon Scannell points out in *Not without Glory: Poets of the Second World War*, 'The soldier in action in the Second World War quite simply did not have the opportunity to write anything at all'.[32] Similarly, Norman T. Morris writes in a letter to an editor (SOTA Box 26 M) that 'I note you emphasise "especially poems in action". That for me was the time when poetry seemed most remote' (30 September 1979).[33] 'In action' thus actually meant, more accurately, 'in contemporaneous reflection'. M. Mackinnon-Pattison satirizes this paradox in 'Written at the Time':

> Cassino—1944
> I crouched in my slit trench scribbling
> They wanted poems 'written at the time'
> While all around me was hell let loose
> I struggled to find a good rhyme [. . .]
>
> His bayonet point pressed on my collar
> I said: 'What word rhymes with throat?'
> As he plunged the steel through my gullet
> I heard him say: 'Why not try TOT!!' (*German for dead*)

> Sent by:
> Obergruppenfuhrer Hans Kniescheibe Bumpfs Von Ganseblumchen
> in honour of: M. Mackinnon-Pattison[34]

Perhaps understandably, the editors did not select the poem for an Oasis anthology. In a final irony, the compiler of the archive's catalogue clearly failed to detect the satire, since the submission is filed under Obergruppenfuhrer Ganseblumchen. A further note states simply: 'Relationship to author unknown'.

The reviewer of *From Oasis into Italy* could have also pointed out in his critique of the editors' policy that it should have disqualified many of the testimonial poems actually included in the anthologies. In 'Ubique' (singled out for praise in the review), Bevan asks where his 'indestructible metal | charge boxes' are: 'some [are] in junk shops on Merseyside still' and 'one in the garage at my last address'.[35] Clearly, the poem's composition could not be contemporaneous with the Italian campaign: the version of 'Ubique' in Bevan's collection *My Sad Pharaohs* suggests it was written in the 1960s, since it refers more specifically to the present as 'two decades later'.[36] Similarly, Scannell's 'Walking Wounded' refers to 'remembering after eighteen years'.[37] Letters to contributors such as Mainka Das (20 August 1990) and Commander W. E. Grenfell (5 January 1987) reveal that the editors were aware of such anomalies.[38] Selwyn writes to Das, explaining their policy: 'Strictly speaking we only consider poetry written *during* World War Two by those serving at the time—but we may stretch a point' (p. 1). By 1990, Selwyn admits to Grenfell that some poems written shortly after the war are still considered to be 'action' poems: 'We understand that you wrote this shortly after the War. Could you please let us know when.

We can stretch a point—in fact have had to do this once or twice before' (p. 1). Some of the typescripts held in the archive indicate that—despite many anomalies—the editors still did reject many post-war testimonies. For example, Bevan's 'Kaput' does not feature in any of the anthologies, possibly because it starts with the 'hissing names' of all the death camps which the poet could not have known about during action.[39] Alec Fieber sent poems to the archive, but they were not included in the anthologies, maybe due to his admission in the accompanying letter (16 February 1987) that 'I cannot say that they were written in the heat of battle on the edge of a slit trench. They have been written over the past five years whilst I was engaged upon writing my memoirs of the Normandy campaign'.[40] One of the reasons for the editors' desire for supposed simultaneity was their understandable wariness of false testimony: they checked the contributors' service records, and 'rejected poems […] we suspected from a professional source'.[41] In *Return to Oasis*, they note the mistake of the contemporaneous anthology *Poems from the Desert: Verses by Members of the Eighth Army*, which purported to contain a poem which—according to General Sir Bernard Montgomery's 'Forward'—'fluttered into the hands of a soldier sheltering in a slit trench during a heavy bombardment' (p. 5).[42] 'A Soldier—His Prayer' (pp. 45–46) does indeed contain an epigraph which explains that '[t]his anonymous poem was blown by the wind […] at El Agheila' (p. 45), but Selwyn reveals that the poem is an example of false testimony in *Return to Oasis* (p. xx). The professional author Gerald Kersh actually wrote the poem: in a letter to Ivan Henson (3 August 1988), Selwyn complains, 'We really are tired of having this bogus poem sent to us by so many. It was not written by an unknown soldier, but from the comfort of a Guards Mess a long way away'.[43]

This wariness towards possible false testimony resulted in revised drafts and skewed meanings of particular testimonial poems, however. Correspondence between the editor Victor Selwyn and the poet Philip Whitfield (SOTA Box 43) reveals that Whitfield updated his poems before submission in 1987, but then returned to his first drafts. In a letter to Selwyn (11 March 1987), Whitfield mentions a previous submission (23 December 1986) of poems for 'Oasis Four' (*More Poems of the Second World War*), and adds:

> At the risk of seeming tiresome I am sending you updated versions. I am in the process of publishing some of my work privately and have therefore been doing some revising. Just in case you should think of considering any of these suitable for OASIS FOUR, I would be sorry to allow some of the clumsy writing in the earlier versions to see the light of day! (pp.1–2)[44]

In a subsequent letter (19 March 1987), Whitfield backtracks and accepts Selwyn's policy of simultaneity:

Many thanks for [...] your good advice about my poem on Belsen.
I entirely agree, the poem is much improved by omitting the fourth
stanza, as well as sounding more contemporary with the event [...] I
never 'finished' the Belsen one and I have only recently tried again [...
the fourth stanza] was an attempt to explore this difficulty [of assimila-
tion], but it is not really relevant to the event itself and the four stanzas
as they now remain are substantially close to the first drafts. (pp.1–2)

These 'substantial' changes affect the entire meaning of the testimonial
poem 'Day of Liberation'. A typescript of the poem in the archive (SOTA
Box 43) reveals the cut stanza:

Belsen was long ago
and now it is evening,
already there are stars
in the shrinking circle of darkness,
the jewels to which we cling.[45]

The revised poem emphasizes the tribulations of primary witnessing rather
than belated trauma. In a moment akin to Jorge Semprun's encounter with
Allied soldiers in *Literature or Life*, Whitfield witnesses his distress '[i]n
the faces of other people' as he tends to the sick and dying in Belsen.[46] The
next stanza would have stressed the poet's inability to banish the involuntary memory of 'piled [...] flesh-pits' in the present. Its omission makes
the final stanza read as (or, as he puts it in the letter, 'sound' like) a contemporaneous inscription of the traumas of primary witnessing: the poet
closes his eyes in 1945 and sees 'ten thousand wasted people | still' rather
than in 1987. Subsequent and disturbing memories are not, in the final version, considered 'really relevant to the event itself'. The opening line of the
final stanza ('I close my eyes') can be interpreted in the final version as a
failed, momentary attempt to avoid witnessing the Belsen scenes in 1945,
rather than a willed evocation of traumatic memories. 'Day of Liberation'
occludes the possibility of subsequent trauma.

　Whitfield's revisions illustrate that the main problem with the editorial
policy is that it conflated testimony with the contemporaneous, rather than
extending it to encompass belated trauma, as examined in the work of
many of the writers included in this book. The disqualification of post-war
writing about the conflict ties in with Selwyn's statement in *More Poems
of the Second World War*—not long after the official recognition of post-
traumatic stress disorder in 1980—that 'those who came out were not subject on release to the trauma and claims of later conflicts [by implication,
Vietnam] [...] Sufficient to stop Hitler, Germany and Japan and go back
into civilian life with least fuss' (p. xvi). His assertion should be placed in
the context of contemporaneous medical discourse: as Roger Luckhurst
points out in *The Trauma Question*, shell shock was not recognized in

World War II and was replaced with '"battle fatigue" or the deliberately vague "exhaustion"'.[47] However, Selwyn's claim is contradicted not only by historians such as Nafsika Thalassis (and her work on Northfield Hospital), but also by soldier testimony such as Colin Rushton's *Spectator in Hell* and—again—by close readings of the Oasis poems and archive.[48] Bevan's memoirs are riddled with the traumatic sign of the ghost; Victor West's testimonies repeatedly return to an episode in which he may have mistakenly killed a Greek policeman, and his later depression and nervous breakdown; Whitfield's 'Day of Liberation' refers to the trauma of witnessing a camp inmate clutching wheat grains, even though 'Belsen was long ago' (SOTA Box 43). Ralph Dargue sent Selwyn a poem entitled 'Unquiet Peace', which was about 'finding difficulty in my adjustments following demobilisation', but it was returned to the author.[49] In one of the most poignant letters in the archive, Mrs E. Hayden writes about her brother, who was shot down over Belgium and joined the Resistance: when he returned to celebrate VE Day he committed suicide at the age of twenty-one; 'The verdict was "owing to his war experiences"'.[50] Again, Selwyn's offhand comment has to be read in the wider context of the momentous effort in compiling—and the difficulties of dealing with—a vast archive: at least the emphasis on supposed simultaneity allowed for a concentration on non-professional writers of testimony; in contrast, Linda Shires's account of World War II poetry has a tendency to divert into tales of literary Oxbridge.[51] Yet ultimately the editors' conception of testimony is opposed to literary-critical or psychoanalytical approaches, which allow for belatedness in witnessing.

The editors' tribulations in compiling an archive of nearly twenty thousand entries impact on the critic's (lesser) problem of how to engage with a body of testimony containing two hundred authors. SOTA manuscripts are written in a variety of styles and are of varying quality, but the archive as a whole does have discernible themes, concerns, and implications. I focus on three aspects in the next section: the way in which the ambivalent soldier testimony shuttles between categories of victim and 'killer' testimony; the reaction to traditional lyric poetry in the form of soldiers' supposed 'anti-poetry'; and critical reactions to the poems centred around notions of literary value and singularity.

VICTIM–KILLER TESTIMONY

The editors complain repeatedly in the anthologies that World War II poetry has been neglected in comparison with the space allocated to World War I poets in the literary canon.[52] One reason for this occlusion is the focus on the unsettling shifts between victim and killer perspectives in many World War II poems.[53] In Holocaust Studies, the judicial categories of perpetrators, victims, and bystanders are well established: Raul Hilberg's *Perpetrators Victims Bystanders: The Jewish Catastrophe 1933–1945* is split into these three eponymous sections; he argues that the 'groups were distinct from one another and they did not dissolve in their lifetime'.[54] Holocaust testimony, however, sometimes blurs the categories from within, as in Levi's famous account of the 'grey zone' in *The Drowned and the Saved*. At the same time, Levi warns against too much blurring: ultimately, 'to confuse [perpetrators] with their victims is a moral disease or an aesthetic affection or a sinister sign of complicity'.[55] Hilberg defines a perpetrator as someone who 'understood his function, and he ascribed it to his position and duties. What he did was impersonal. He had been empowered or instructed to carry out his mission' (p. ix): in a different context, such a description can be applied to Allied soldiers. Bevan's 'Ubique' and 'Kaput' form examples of discomforting perpetrator perspectives, with their celebration of the aesthetics—and deadly results—of long-range artillery and the latter's description of abject Italian peasants, killed and piled like 'forked parsnips'.[56] Keith Douglas's scathingly ironic depiction in 'Elegy for an 88 Gunner' of a German soldier's corpse that has just been looted is a more famous example.

Such testimony is clearly not coterminous with such perpetrator testimony as Hoess's *Commandant of Auschwitz*, which Levi famously criticized as packed with mendacity and attempts at self-exculpation.[57] An Oasis writer is obviously not a perpetrator in the sense of a 'supreme architect' of war, as Hilberg describes Hitler; as Selwyn bluntly puts it, 'A soldier goes where he is sent'.[58] Indeed, as opposed to Hoess's clumsy attempts to deceive his readership, the Oasis poems are striking in their open celebration of killing machinery and enemy deaths: G. C. Norman's actions in 'Night Raid' even flout the third article of the Geneva Convention as he recounts shooting German officers attempting to surrender. One of the reasons for this openness is ideological: many poets—and the editors—repeat the mantra of 'the just war' to defend their actions and writing (as opposed to the occlusions in Hoess's memoir).[59] Historians and literary critics are only just beginning to come to terms with the Allies' perpetrator behaviour, such as rape and the shooting of prisoners: as R. W. Johnson stresses in relation to Antony Beevor's *D-Day: The Battle for Normandy*, one of the 'surprising conclusions' of the book (published in 2009) is that 'the Allies shot many prisoners and committed all manner of atrocities'.[60] William I. Hitchcock notes in his book *Liberation* that these atrocities included the mutilation of corpses and playing football with a severed head.[61] Johnson goes on to note that, on the other hand, 'very little of this would come as a surprise' to anyone teaching in the Military Academies of Sandhurst or West Point.[62]

In contrast to such behaviour, the archetypal soldier poet in World War I poetry is a version of the compassionate and pacifist narrator of Wilfred Owen's 'Strange Meeting', who is willing to treat the enemy as a potential friend. As Tim Kendall points out in an article on Ivor Gurney (which I quoted in Chapter 1), 'Great War poets' may be eloquent 'about suffering and being killed', but they 'keep their counsel when it comes to the business of killing'.[63] World War II poetry introduces instead the more disturbing figure of the soldier as a scathing, dispassionate killer: Paul Fussell argues in *Wartime: Understanding and Behaviour in the Second World War* that such figures are anathema to the 'sanitized' versions of the war in popular culture.[64] Peter Hopkinson's poem 'Execution' from the Oasis archive is representative: the enemy is a 'fat Italian bastard'; 'for shooting bloody rabbits', he contends, 'I'm [. . .] born and bred'.[65] Charles McCausland ruminates dispassionately on soldiers' corpses in 'Dead Japanese', complaining, 'Why do you stink so, fouling the air [. . .] No other animal stinks so in putrefaction'.[66]

Such poetry has caused considerable discomfort in liberal custodians of the literary canon. Ian Hamilton and Bernard Bergonzi react with distaste to Douglas's uncompromising anti-elegies in *A Poetry Chronicle* and *Wartime and Aftermath*.[67] An irony persists that many anthologies of war poetry perform an act of anti-war sentiment: such politics are easier to justify in relation to Owen rather than Douglas. To argue for the inscription of perpetrator perspectives in World War II poetry might seem to chime with Hamilton and Bergonzi's distaste towards literary accounts of violence. On the contrary, such an argument attempts to respond soberly to writing about the many acts of (in context) necessary violence and the dissonances, and similarities, between soldier testimony and victim testimony. Nevertheless, comparisons between Holocaust and Second World War testimony are not entirely satisfactory due to the contextual, ideological, and ethical differences between the perpetrators in question. Nor should the perpetrator perspectives in the Oasis archive be overemphasized. The archive as a whole, and especially the poems about post-war trauma, corroborates Shoshana Felman and Dori Laub's sense that testimony confronts the victim's 'radical human condition of exposure and vulnerability'.[68] Even so, the shuttling perspectives still demonstrate that categories of victim, perpetrator, and bystander testimony developed in relation to the Holocaust do not entirely pertain in the context of soldier testimony. These categorical difficulties also highlight the fact that, in contrast to attempts to sanitize the events, testimony can show us—as Felman and Laub argue—that we do not yet understand historical events which are so central to our sense of our own historicity, and are thus not, in that sense, over (p. xx). I have argued elsewhere that the current turn to perpetrator testimony in Holocaust Studies marks a stage of remembering in order, ultimately, to forget such mendacious memoirs as *Commandant of Auschwitz*.[69] This process distinguishes Oasis poems from perpetrator testimony, too, since the complex literary engagements with memory and warfare in, for example, Douglas's and Bevan's poetry deserve to be studied beyond the point of our own historicity.

If the victim–perpetrator model does not suffice, then what would a taxonomy of soldier testimony look like in the context of Oasis poetry? As with survivor testimony (and less so, as Robert Eaglestone argues, with perpetrator testimony), the Oasis poems are frequently positivistic in their accounts: for Bowen, they evidence a 'scrupulous cataloguing of the bric-à-brac of the war'[70] . They often gesture directly towards a metatext: John Jarmain's 'These Poems', West's 'Drumhead', and Morris's 'Molise 1943' are all examples of where metatextual details are referred to in the title or at the end of the poem (as in Jarmain's 'Tunisia, 1943').[71] The archive frequently deploys the illusion of mimesis to testimonial effect: Bevan's 'Ubique' contains a section in which guns 'fire!' across the line to 'recreate' the timing of artillery.[72] Many poems are understandably sentimental as they recall 'Georgian vistas' or homosocial bonds during the war; Bowen harshly decries the latter as 'Kiplingesque laments for "Archie, Johnnie and me"' (p. 11a). Unlike perpetrator testimony, they are often strikingly self-critical, as in 'My Hands' and 'Chindit': the latter poem appears to be a wounded soldier's lament as his friends leave him under a tree; a devastating twist reveals the real culprit to be the poet, who guiltily dwells on the necessary departure.[73] As in perpetrator testimony (as Eaglestone argues, p. 9), but for less self-exculpatory reasons, the Oasis narrators espouse a double identity: the voice of the soldier acting in the poem is often filtered through that of the veteran. Unlike survivor testimony, the military successes of the war years are celebrated (records of particular defeats are rarer). Aesthetics of killing machines are unquestionably lauded (as in Bevan's work), but these are counterbalanced by confrontations with belated trauma (as in 'Ubique' and West's 'Drumhead'). Such melancholic attachments to previous events distinguish the poets from perpetrators; as Eaglestone writes, 'unlike survivor testimony, which is told and retold, with new versions appearing over and again, testimony by perpetrators often seems to be the end of the matter for the authors' (p. 7). On the other hand—as in perpetrator testimony—there are paradoxically confessional blind spots in the Oasis narratives. Norman confesses to murdering the surrendering German officers and justifies his actions as avenging '[s]ome ghastly crime | In Poland'.[74] The likelihood, of course, is that the officers had nothing directly to do with the camps (which were virtually unknown during the war); even if—as Norman implies—they have to take some form of collective responsibility for Nazism.

Oasis poets' commitment to testimonial truth—however disturbingly close to a perpetrator perspective that might sometimes prove to be—connects with Douglas's plea in a letter to J. C. Hall for an excision of lyrical 'Bullshit' in World War II poetry:

> [Y]ou say I fail as a poet, when you mean I fail as a lyricist [. . .] A lyric form and a lyric approach will do even less good than a journalese approach to the subjects we have to discuss now. I don't know if you have come across the word 'Bullshit'—it is an army word and signifies humbug and unnecessary detail [. . .] To write on the themes which have been concerning me lately in lyrical and abstract forms, would

be immense bullshitting. In my early poems I wrote lyrically, as an innocent [. . .] I see no reason to be either musical or sonorous about things at present.[75]

Other Oasis poets have reflected on 'Bullshit': in a letter to Selwyn (30 September 1979), Norman T. Morris deploys the same word to describe morale-boosting journalism during the desert war.[76] The Morris archive—held separately at the Imperial War Museum in London—also indicates that the author reacted to the 'Bullshit' of a 1942 army competition about 'My Most Exciting Desert Adventure' by writing a reflective piece about a grave at El Daba after the Battle of El Alamein. Morris recounts that he met the German youth buried there in 1935 during a holiday in Switzerland.[77] For Douglas, 'Bullshit' comprises not just journalistic or army activity, but, as for Tadeusz Borowski, the lyric tradition. In Douglas's letter to Hall, he objects to a critical supposition that the lyrical form denotes poetic sensitivity, musicality, and aesthetic transcendence. Such a priori judgements allow for an occlusion of the poet as killer in the critical reception of World War I poetry. Instead, Douglas implies, war poets must be able to present themselves as killers in a modulated, harsher and—as he puts it in another letter to Hall—'extrospective' poetry.[78] Just as Borowski produces anti-/ lyrics such as 'October Sky', Douglas responds with dialectical war poetry that—in an Adornoian sense—'hates tradition properly' by critiquing as well as drawing on literary tradition.[79] Jarmain similarly upholds traditional poetic forms whilst being attuned to lyrical 'humbug': in 'The Innocent Shall Suffer'—the last poem he completed before his death in action—the 'clipped and careless phrases' of military discourse (when describing a bombing raid) are compared to the aesthetic lies of lyrical phrasing, where '[l]ike a gold rose the beaten cities burn [. . .] No rose in all the earth was blossomed so'.[80] In his memoirs, Bevan often deploys juxtaposition to contain his lyrical urge: corpses of Italian peasants have the 'emerald Arno smiling beyond them'; the 'mirage' of Naples bay is soon countered with 'dirt and squalor' and 'filthy urchins' prostituting their sister.[81]

Some soldier poets respond less ambivalently, however, than Douglas, Jarmain, and Bevan to 'Bullshit', and—as in Borowski's later, journalistic poetry—reject the lyrical tradition entirely: West draws on the critical work of Michael Hamburger in *The Truth of Poetry* to argue that his texts are 'anti-poems'. For Hamburger, anti-poems reject 'technical terms, foreign phrases, literary and vernacular borrowings', and contain 'plain, bare, minimal diction'.[82] This taxonomy chimes with Douglas's anti-lyric:

The new anti-poetry—a product of the Second World War [. . .] arose from an acute distrust of all the devices by which lyrical poetry had maintained its autonomy [. . .] [poetry] should also be capable of communicating as directly as prose, without resort to a special language mainly distinguished by its highly metaphorical character. (p. 220)

Hamburger notes that for the Polish poet Tadeusz Różewicz, the notion of the aesthetic strikes him as a 'harmless but ludicrous and childish occupation' (p. 249). The critic notes that Britain has produced few anti-poets, without making a connection with Douglas; his later correspondence with West suggests an acceptance that, for him, some British World War II poets may have indeed fulfilled his criteria for the anti-poem. West's unpublished critical article 'Apology for Lateness' in the Oasis archive reveals that his anti-lyrical stance results partly from a distrust of the melodic in the form of songs he heard as a POW: 'I had listened to four years to the regimented, measured, Nazi marching songs [. . .] the primrose path of soft, poetic diction was not for me'.[83] A biographical note in Box 44 states that West did not consider the writing he produced during the war as poems at the time, and it was only 'some time before he realised that eminent critics [meaning Hamburger] accepted them as valid [. . .] Perhaps, they were anti-poetry'.[84] In the essay most indebted to Hamburger—'Anti Poetry' (Box 44)—West asks his readers to contact him if they find a metaphor in his poems, and he will then strike it out. However, his redeployment of Hamburger's argument about mid-European post-war poetry is, I would argue, a case of misrecognition. Różewicz is an anti-poet (following Hamburger's thesis) in that he responds to Adorno's complaint about potentially 'barbaric' poetry by writing terse, minimalist poems which—like Douglas's, Jarmain's, and Bevan's work—are still not adverse to the lyrical flourish.[85] In contrast— and as a SOTA letter from Jacqueline Simms at Oxford University Press indicates (4 March 1992)—West's prosaic testimony in poetic form has weaknesses of structure (and a flatness of tone) which 'can't be subsumed under the "anti-poetry" heading'.[86]

The rejection of West's manuscript links with other critical evaluations of Oasis poets; some (like Simms's) are justified, but others fail to respond to the attempts at testimonial poetry and dialectical anti-lyrics. Bergonzi dismissed the Oasis authors in *War Poets and Other Subjects* as populist amateurs, effectively arguing that war poetry was an oxymoron in the context of the anthologies: 'The pressure of experience is often apparent and the poems may have value as human documents [. . .] rather than contributions to the difficult art of poetry'.[87] His stance is not dissimilar to Hall's in its failure to think outside the boundaries of the traditional lyric: for Bergonzi, testimony cannot be art, compared to the complex musings of professional poets, written—as Jarmain states in 'These Poems'—behind 'placid curtains'.[88] More recently, in *The Oxford Handbook of British and Irish War Poetry*, Hugh Haughton lauds instead the 'quality' writing and 'dazzling record' of the Oasis anthologies.[89] As well as unsettling critics because of its various testimonial perspectives, World War II poetry—and war poetry more widely—constitutes an *unheimlich* intervention in, and challenge to, the literary canon. Bergonzi's and Haughton's opinions typify the polarity of critical reactions to war poetry. Due primarily to the pressure of the metatext, war poetry is valued as either the highest form of poetry (as Selwyn contends) or as testimonial trash.[90] In *More Poems of the Second World War*, Selwyn signals the generic instability of testimonial poetry when he argues that war poems should be regarded as a different kind of art to the poetry of 'placid curtains'. '[T]he poems' in the anthology, he argues, 'have to be judged not just as poems—but as *war* poetry, a genre on its own' (p. xv). In the following sections on individual poems, I discuss such fraught issues of the metatext, as well as the shuttling victim–killer perspectives.[91] One poet who concurs with Selwyn's analysis of war poetry is John Jarmain, and it is to his poem 'These Poems' that I now turn.

JOHN JARMAIN'S 'THESE POEMS': METATESTIMONY AND THE WAR POEM

'These Poems' functions as metatestimony in that it comprises a poetic preface for *From Oasis into Italy* (and, symbolically, the anthologies as a whole), as well as starting Jarmain's own collection entitled *Poems* (p. 17). The poem partly fulfils the editors' criteria of simultaneity: metatextual data offered at the closure reveal that it was written in March 1943, when the British army opened its assault on the Mareth line in Tunisia; Jarmain was an officer with the anti-tank unit of the Fifty-First Highland Division. However, since the poem was written by candlelight in a doover (a dugout and tent), it was not strictly composed 'in action', but—as I argued above—in contemporaneous reflection. 'These Poems' does comply, however, with Selwyn's sense that war poetry constitutes a separate genre. The poem commends the anthology's (and Jarmain's) readers to think about the differences between war poems and literature written behind 'placid curtains' (p. i):

> You who in evenings by the fire
> May read these words of mine,
> How let you see the desert bare
> In the print-smooth line?
>
> Listen! These poems were not made in rooms,
> But out in the empty sand,
> Where only the homeless Arab roams
> In a sterile land;
>
> They were not at tables written
> With placid curtains drawn,
> But by candlelight begotten
> Of the dusk and dawn.
>
> They had no peace at their creation,

No twilight hush of wings;
Only the tremble of bombs, the guns' commotion,
And destructive things.

Mareth, Tunisia, March, 1943

The didactic pressure of the metatestimony forms part of a striking correlation between Jarmain's text and Levi's more well-known poem 'If This Is a Man'. Written only three years apart, both poems address the relevance of poetry to the war's destruction and atrocities. Lexical similarities initiate bitter assaults on the recipients of testimony (primarily civilians and other non-survivors). Jarmain's opening lines ('You who in evenings by the fire | May read these words of mine') link with initial words in 'If This Is a Man':

You who live safe
In your warm houses,
You who find, returning in the evening,
Hot food and friendly faces[92]

Like Levi, Jarmain courts the hyper-attentiveness of readers before the testimonial aspects of the poem can begin. However, the placement of the irate 'If This Is a Man' before the measured prose of Levi's book betrays the Italian author's specific worry that his testimony will be misunderstood, or elicit a prurient response. Jarmain is concerned instead with the falsifying aesthetics of the 'print-smooth line'. He is also preoccupied with the radical difference of war poetry in general; unlike 'If This Is a Man', 'These Poems' does not actually reveal subsequent testimonial details in a positivistic sense.

Jarmain's poem nevertheless shares the problems of readerly identification that ensue from testimony. 'How let' reveals the poet's desire to convey his experiences to civilians at the same time as he worries that the 'print-smooth line' will prove inadequate to the testimonial act. Charlotte Delbo—as I illustrate in Chapter 4—similarly muses about the impossibility of 'seeing' the victim: readers can only dwell on false signifieds, at the same time as the urgency of witnessing and reception remains.[93] As Margaret-Anne Hutton puts it in relation to Delbo's work, an 'epistemological abyss' exists between the camps—and, in the context of Jarmain's work, desert warfare—and the receiver of testimony.[94] Holocaust testimony, and Oasis poetry, often dwells on the problems of confronting the family in relation to Hutton's abyss. Levi's recurrent nightmare in Auschwitz is that his family will not understand his oral testimony and turn away from him; Bevan's prose testimony ends with him feeling 'like a newly arrived visitor from outer space' when he returns home (p. 384). 'These Poems', like many instances of testimony, attempts to use an imperative to elicit the hyper-attentiveness of family and other civilians. 'Listen!'—the opening word of the second stanza—connects with Douglas's demand that the reader 'look' at a corpse in 'How to Kill', and Levi's more chilling address in 'If This Is a Man': 'I commend these words to you'.[95] The imperatives betray the authors' concerns about the 'epistemological abyss' between the survivor and civilian that Owen dwells on in poems such as 'Insensibility': Jarmain contrasts the readerly identification possible with 'room' poetry compared with poems composed in the 'empty sand'. For Jarmain, 'poems [. . .] made in rooms' have a freedom of expression denied to the war poet weighed down with metatextual pressures.

The poet's robust defence of his writing provides *From Oasis into Italy* with a valuable, meta-testimonial account of war poetry as a separate genre, but the didactic deployment of 'These Poems' occludes the regretful tone of the poem. As the forward to Jarmain's *Poems* stresses, 'it was not martial action which primarily appealed to his spirit, but silence and solitude'.[96] The Jarmain letters held separately in the Imperial War Museum reveal that the poet envisaged a different creative path only a few months before the composition of 'These Poems'. By March 1943, Jarmain presents himself as an encumbered war poet, whereas in an earlier letter (30 June 1942), he ruminates on the artistic freedom symbolized in 'the inviting sheets of a notepad, clean and unwritten' and 'the very emptiness of the days'; 'What shall I write poems about?' he asks, 'War? or Flying Fishes? or English fields?'[97] Jarmain's poetic mentor was not Wilfred Owen, but Rupert Brooke: the archives contain a manuscript poem which praises the latter's ability to 'love the common and familiar things', but by 1943 English fields (and flying fishes) had been replaced with the metatextual pressures of the 'destructive things' that end 'These Poems'.[98] In a letter written only a few days after the poem's completion, Jarmain complains about the same writing conditions portrayed in 'These Poems'. 'Room' poetry is contrasted with the conditions of testimony scribbled by candlelight at dusk and dawn:

> My handwriting has not really become as spidery as this. But although we are no longer in action we are still living in desert fashion in 'doo-vas' [*sic*] (dugouts, with a low sloping tent for roof) in the sand of the foreshore. We still have no chairs or tables, none of the necessities of life save bread, bed and wine (yes, wine!): therefore I am still writing on my knee by candlelight, with a map case to stiffen the writing-pad.[99]

Jarmain's account of these conditions hampering his writing—and the regretful tone of 'These Poems'—is poignant in the context of the poet's fate. Denied the opportunity to return to a Brookian contemplation of nature, Jarmain died in Normandy after being hit by shrapnel on 26 June 1944, and was buried in the Sixth Airborne cemetery near Caen.[100]

'These Poems'—standing as an epigraph for the Oasis anthology as a whole—argues that the testimonial poems are also not 'drawn' with 'placid curtains' in the sense of hiding the reality of atrocious events. 'These Poems' and 'If This Is a Man' both imply that the civilian reader may not wish to confront such testimonial evidence or, as in Levi's poem, think deeply about its ramifications. However, Jarmain's text (unlike Levi's) appears to eschew finally any possible identification with the reader: the last two lines seem to promise a positivistic account of war events, but only present the abstractions of bombs, commotion and destruction. The closure, quoted below, may thus appear aesthetically, and conceptually, deficient:

> [These poems] had no peace at their creation,
> No twilight hush of wings;
> Only the tremble of bombs, the guns' commotion,
> And destructive things.

Readers might well ask why the 'tremble of bombs' and 'the guns' commotion' are not 'destructive things', as registered in the conjunction before the final phrase. However, 'destructive things' is located in the final line's effective recourse to dimeter (as in the previous stanzas): after the metrical breaks of the poem's only Alexandrine, the sparse syllables emphasize the litotes. Instead of the Hopkinesque 'twilight hush of wings' that might produce impassioned nature poetry, the rhyming link emphasizes that, in Jarmain's reluctant war poems—and war poetry as a whole—the 'creation' is in the 'commotion'. The (non-)image of 'things' actually appears to protect the reader (as with Owen's 'inhumanities' in 'Spring Offensive') from this 'commotion', as if a more detailed account might deepen the 'epistemological abyss' even further. Indeed, the phrase 'destructive things' reads precisely like the discourse of a civilian unable to 'see'—in Delbo's sense—the victim's signified experience. In this sense (and unlike 'If This Is a Man'), 'These Poems' is an unusual case of poetic metatestimony that then draws back from providing any testimony itself.[101]

JACK BEVAN'S 'UBIQUE': THE AMBIVALENCE OF SOLDIER TESTIMONY

In contrast to the terseness of 'These Poems', 'Ubique' forms the epitome of the testimony in the Salamander Oasis archive that dwells at length on soldiers' experience. The poem provides a veritable barrage of positivistic details: the second sentence—framed with the hypotyposis of 'I can see'—comprises an eighty-three-line account of Bevan's experiences as an artillery officer during the Italian campaign.[102] As the epigraph explains, the title is the motto of the Royal Artillery (given by King William IV in 1832); 'Ubique' ('everywhere'), also refers hyperbolically to Bevan's journey in the ninety-seven-line poem from Naples to Como. 'Ubique' also gestures towards Rudyard Kipling's eponymous poem about the Boer War, but

Bevan replaces the affected voice of the lower orders with an extended and erudite account of the Italian campaign which makes up one of the most aesthetically successful Oasis poems.[103] Felman and Laub's sense of the provisionality of testimony is embodied in the poem's excitably jumbled recollections: as opposed to Bevan's prose memoir *Through the Donkey's Ears* (published in 1997), the incidents do not occur in chronological order, but as if the testimony is unfolding for the first time.[104] In *Through the Donkey's Ears*, he apologetically comments that 'for almost a year my memories are a series of impressions, out of sequence, and muddled by the almost day-to-day advances we made' (p. 245). In 'Ubique', poetry as testimony allows instead for an abrogation of narrative coherence as the memories—in the words of the memoir—'jumble and jostle, refuse to assemble themselves in order' (p. 246); Bowen's review of *From Oasis into Italy* singles out the ensuing 'verbal energy' for especial praise. This fragmentary openness contributes to—rather than negates—the poem's testimonial function, since, as Felman and Laub argue, such 'language [. . .] does not possess itself [as in historical narratives] as a conclusion, as the contestation of a verdict or the self-transparency of knowledge . . . [it is] in process, and in trial'.[105] In 'Ubique', this 'contestation' partly consists—as I shall illustrate in this section—of a confrontation with the figure of the Allied soldier as both a victim and killer.

Throughout the poem, the soldier testimony remains ambivalent: memories prove to be both nostalgic and traumatic. Rather than provide a case study for a teleology of trauma where aporetic poetry inscribes previous harms (as in Felman and Laub's critique of Paul Celan's work), 'Ubique' maintains its exuberant 'verbal energy'. And unlike Levi's lament for the overall lack of homosocial bonds during his internment, Bevan celebrates the adaptability of 'Archie, Johnnie and me', such as when 'David made a suspension footbridge' over the 'deeply snowed' Serchio (p. 175). However, the camaraderie and cherished repetition of artillery discourse is interlaced with more troubled images of 'grey | shapes [. . .] rumbling away to the cemetery' (pp. 175–76), and a gun explosion which leaves Gunner Lea burning and his crew dazed (*Through the Donkey's Ears* reveals that he died days later from shock (p. 294)). In response to this ambivalence, 'Ubique' displays distrust towards the aesthetic, but—unlike West's 'antipoems'—Bevan does not reject the 'primrose path of soft diction' entirely, but chooses to counterbalance (and undercut) nostalgic and traumatic memories. The line beginning 'and the summers' might seem to promise a laudatory account of Italian pastoral, with the 'scissor sharpeners [cicadas] busy all night in the quincunx | olive ranks' (p. 176). However, the exactitude of the five trees' layout is immediately linked to precision artillery: in the next line, the 'musk smell of dusk' is subverted with the 'sudden flash-bang of the high-velocity | guns, dragged on the edge of dark'. Nevertheless, as in Borowski's poems, the celebration of the aesthetic remains as much a part of the testimony as traumatic experience.

The ambivalence of soldier testimony is immediately captured in the poem's opening metaphor:

> The long barrel of the past is pointing towards me;
> I peer down its spiral rifling, reflecting those times
> so many mortgages, lectures, removals,
> so many bombards, ranging rounds ago. (p. 175)

Peering 'down [the past's] spiral rifling' allows the former officer to work through the relative boredom of 'mortgages' and reach his beloved 'five-fives with the vertical horns'; unlike many instances of victim testimony, the past offers aesthetic succour rather than Felman and Laub's uncompromised 'wound'. Even so, the image is akin to Levi's favourite testimonial metaphor of the albatross, since the barrel is constantly 'pointing towards' the poet, suggesting an iterative compulsion to testify rather than the potential pleasures of what Lawrence Langer terms 'common memory'.[106] Bevan's return to the metaphor at the end of 'Ubique' inscribes this testimonial entrapment into the poem's structure. *Through the Donkey's Ears* refers to repeated dreams in which Bevan still receives fire orders: 'For many months I woke in the night to spring out of bed [. . .] and for years—even decades—I would see the long five-fives in fallen tree trunks, and dream that the war was still on' (p. 384). Bevan fuses the nightmare's iconography with his metaphor for the past in the penultimate lines when he asks (rhetorically) whether the guns can 'still fire such long-range salvos' (p. 177).

'Ubique' then ends with two, apparently contradictory, answers. Initially, the poet appears to have mastered his ambivalent memories given his apparent belief in the agency of common memory: 'The soul saves what it needs | from the waste, halts time at its will'. However, the poem then subverts these lines by alluding to the threat of that 'waste' returning from 'deep memory': 'Those gun positions, those faces, those parallel pieces | are ranging on me still'. Bevan thus replaces the enemy as the guns' (and the past's) primary target. Rather than cancelling each other out, the two answers embody the paradox of memory that Anne Whitehead outlines in relation to Plato: the process 'seems to be uncertainly suspended between that which we wish to retain, making a conscious effort to do so, and that which impresses itself upon us so that it is more passively experienced or undergone'.[107] In a more modern sense, they also depict the successes and failures of repression. In *Through the Donkey's Ears*, the mental 'carapace' that protects Bevan from traumatic memories is sometimes intact: Bevan can 'save' certain memories, and has 'acquired the technique of closing [his] mind and imagination' to less pleasant recollections (p. 357). At other times—such as during his suicide attempt—the ghosts of the 'grey shapes', 'the sound of the screams, the shock of those bursts, the human things flying in the air' prove irresistible, and 'emerge unexpectedly [. . .] when [he is] for the moment unoccupied'.[108]

As in victim testimony, the paradox of memory encompasses a conscious and unconscious return to the sites of trauma. Nevertheless—and despite the traumatic memories inscribed in 'Ubique'—the poem also shuttles between the perspectives of victim and killer. Adam Piette argues convincingly that the archetypal soldier of World War II was not the infantryman (as in the previous war), but the artillery officer, who, in contrast, 'with the help of elaborate technical skills killed at such distance that their victims could have no reality for them except in the imagination'.[109] In contrast to Bevan's prose testimony, where he describes 'unspeakable remnants of limbs and heads, with tatters of grey uniforms', his poetry seldom describes the enemy except in the vague form of 'grey shapes'.[110] Piette adds that this detachment meant that '[m]inds were swept clean of responsibility by the war's smooth displays of technological power over distances' (p. 219), and that engagement became 'a cerebral war of calculation of range, trajectory, velocity, altitude, deflection, with allowances for wind and gravity—a classroom exercise in maths, a war-game science' (p. 215). Bevan's prose testimony affirms these assertions: 'Throughout the chaos of the Italian campaign the logic of the principles of deployment of gunnery, fire orders and ballistics offered a cool aesthetic, a stable norm to rely on'; the 'cool precision of shells' offered a 'consolatory satisfaction', and Bevan 'felt no guilt, realising perhaps that it was a form of escape' (p. 179).

Throughout his training and active service, Bevan embraced this aesthetic complicity. During live shoots, he 'quickly caught a sense of the aesthetics behind the whole business of deployment, gunnery, ballistics and communications' (p. 51), and he comments later that '[t]hose without a basic sense of rhythm could never acquire the skill of producing the right "quantities" in the prosody of Morse [. . .] An obsession with poetics and a classical education made it easy for me' (p. 102). Hence in the typescript of the poem 'Battery Target' (SOTA Box 2), the rhythm of firing guns is likened to 'stichomythia' (a dialogue of alternating single lines common in classical drama). In 'Ubique', perpetrator aesthetics encompass Bevan's celebration of the guns' 'loving response' to his commands (p. 177). Personification—and the reduction of the enemy to 'miniature toys' (p. 177)—deflects attention from the piles of 'limbs and heads' ensuing from this 'response' and the inevitable destruction meted out to Italian villages. (As *Through the Donkey's Ears* reminds the reader, to many villagers Allied forces were perpetrators in the sense of the second, more recent invaders of Italy.[111]) Eight lines later, the complicity of 'a cool aesthetic, a stable norm' returns with the revealing and nostalgic celebration of 'those ithyphallic barrels, always exactly parallel'. (The classical reference is to the phallus carried in Bacchic festivals.) The guns embody a potency that Bevan denied himself during the war: as *Through the Donkey's Ears* reveals, he associated sex primarily with dangers of venereal disease (pp. 227–28). In the typescript poem 'Battery Target, Italy' (SOTA Box 2), the guns openly 'love' their commanding officer, who 'thrills' to his 'all-obedient | instantly acting pack', and the text ends with a 'message of love' in which he chides 'Number four' for 'dropping [shells] short'. However, whereas the amorous discourse dominates in 'Battery Target, Italy', the typescript poem 'Kaput'—in the same way as 'Ubique'—highlights his ambivalence towards the guns: they are 'dutiful', but their 'gleam' embodies a perpetrator aesthetic, a 'truth winking malign | as the orders go out enlarged | in the hot panoramas of doom'. This ambivalence is symbolic of the shifts between killer and victim testimony in the Trust's archive as a whole, and 'Ubique' is the most successful aesthetic engagement with such conceptual shuttling in the anthologies.

VICTOR WEST'S 'DRUMHEAD': TRAUMA AND EMBELLISHED TESTIMONY

Victor West's poetry initially appears distinct from Bevan's in that this 'anti-poetry' focusses on soldiers purely as victims, and the suffering of prisoners of war, rather than perpetrator aesthetics. However, the structure of 'Drumhead' and 'Ubique' similarly emphasizes traumatic recollection. Just as 'Ubique' circles back to the opening image of the threatening 'spiral rifling', 'Drumhead' figures the return of the past with the opening and final image of disconcerting hospital tables:

> Four trestle tables in the sand
> covered with issue blankets taken
> from the tented hospital . . . The forms
> pushed back, as though in hasty decision,
> standing a solitary still-life
> group in early morning sun.
>
> The scene rises before me
> and I people it in my mind. [. . .]
> 'Three more Greek bandits shot
> for committing unspeakable atrocities' . . :
>
> The scene has unfolded itself
> and the figures vanish before my eyes . . .
> only the horror remains
> and that I cannot paint:
> Four trestle tables in the sand.[112]

Metatextual information relayed at the end of the poem ('29th May, 1941 "The Galatos Cage", formerly 7th British Tented Hospital, Calibes, Crete') situates 'Drumhead' as a response to Nazi atrocities following the invasion of Crete. In *Inside Hitler's Greece: The Experience of Occupation*

1941–44, Mark Mazower recounts that in May 1941 General Kurt Student, commander of XI Air Corps, was outraged at the part the islanders had played in resisting invasion and attacking German paratroopers and ordered 'Revenge Operations'.[113] Student insisted, 'All operations are to be carried out with great speed, leaving aside all formalities and certainly dispensing with special courts [. . .] These are not meant for beasts and murderers'. A handwritten note in West's 'Nazi Justice and Nazi Terror' (held in the Oasis archive) attests to such outrage: he 'saw the body of a German parachutist on a pink hillside near Galatos, trussed like a chicken. I asked a feldwebel [*sic*] what had happened to that man. . . . He grew [. . .] vehement—but I did not understand his reason for such anger'; later in the poem, West stresses that '*parachutists formed shooting parties*'.[114] In 'Drumhead', West emphasizes the horrific irony that the 'bandits' and 'murderers' were probably innocent villagers, including an old man in his *vraka*; the Germans were the ones committing 'unspeakable atrocities'. West's memoirs of his experiences in Crete and as a POW (held separately in the Imperial War Museum in London) reveal that he was interned in Galatos: the British Tented Hospital 'stood on a sandy field that led down to the sea, a sleazy reminder of its short period as the pride of the Medical Corps [. . .] like a vandalised circus'.[115] These memoirs indicate that West came across the poem's tables on arrival in the makeshift camp: Felman and Laub's sense of the provisionality of testimony is registered in the fragmentary phrases in the first stanza. Here, the ellipsis registers the difficulties inherent in Proust's concept of 'voluntary memory': the poet struggles to move from the recalled image of the tables to that of the forms; this difficulty is registered with the lack of a main, active verb in the entire stanza.[116] The repetition of the tables in the final stanza marks a different reason for ellipsis. This time, the latter registers the familiar testimonial sign of the incommunicability of traumatic experience, the 'abyss' in understanding that Owen was concerned with in poems such as 'Spring Offensive' and which Jarmain grapples with in 'These Poems'. The condemned figures vanish just as the sentence is about to be carried out, as if the 'horror' that West recalls cannot be rendered linguistically or, as he indicates, with a visual image ('and that I cannot paint').

If 'Drumhead' is read in this way as an instance of positivistic testimony, then the potentially 'barbaric' aesthetics build up towards the expected execution; West subverts this possibility with his appeal to the ineffable.[117] The '[f]our trestle tables in the sand' remain as both a conventional elegiac sign for the murdered Cretans and an indication of West's apparently traumatized inability to confront the scene. By deflecting attention onto the tables rather than the execution, West also highlights their effectiveness as a sign of atrocity. Their surreal incongruity in the sand registers their congruency with the uncaring bureaucracy of war: as the second scene of *Schindler's List* succinctly conveys (as makeshift tables are set up at a railway station to record incoming refugees), many atrocities began with a typewriter and table.[118] In Spielberg's film, these signs are ambiguous, however, since the salvation of the Jewish inmates of Płaszów relies on Stern's counter-deployment of the same objects in order to create Schindler's famous list. In contrast, in 'Drumhead', the 'hasty decision' quickly demonstrates that the court martial has complied with Student's command to leave aside 'all formalities and [dispense] with special courts'. West's unsettling pun on 'still-life' in the first stanza stresses his compulsion to keep the condemned 'alive' in the main part of the poem, and he describes the participants for thirty-three lines.

'[S]till-life' constitutes more than a pun, however, since the ekphrastic poem paradoxically refers to a painting which does not, and cannot, exist. The tables, blankets, and forms appear to the poet-painter as a potential 'still-life', but 'Drumhead' ends with the emphatic statement that he 'cannot paint' the atrocity. As with the last four lines in 'Ubique', there seems to be a potential paradox here: West cannot paint the picture, and yet, if 'painting' is read as the wider artistic process of inscription, then at least the poem itself is completed and the tables do endure as signs of the ineffable. A letter to Selwyn (1 September 1990) reveals, however, that the discussion of the visual image constitutes more than an ekphrastic metaphor: West writes that as a POW, 'They gave me a studio [. . .] to paint the picture of a Nazi "court martial" on Crete. I never have been able to paint this picture. My hand shake [*sic*] so much with emotion'.[119] West's inability to complete the picture in the past and present functions as a resistance to complicity and a refusal to glorify the atrocity with 'barbaric', perpetrator aesthetics. Inscribing the atrocity with the written word—but at the same time denying the reader and perpetrators text about the moment of execution—allows the poet to testify to the murders without actually depicting them.[120]

So far, I have read 'Drumhead' as an effective poetic response to witnessing a traumatic event, but if literary testimony is to be judged solely on its positivistic acumen, then West's memoirs reveal that the poem is a sham. Shortly after the description of Galatos as a 'vandalised circus', West encounters the four tables:

> covered by regulation grey blankets . . . an old hand explained there had been a courtmartial earlier that morning; three Greeks had been accused of atrocities—mutilation. We remembered the unburied corpse [of the parachutist] we had passed. The impatient way the wooden forms had been pushed back told us the verdict had been reached. Yes, the old hand confirmed, the firing squad had been drawn up ready on the beach . . . waiting.
>
> Whether the actual perpetrators, or hostages taken from the nearest cottages, it made no difference . . .
>
> They had been shot. (p. 196)

West repeats 'had been' six times in the passage above: the 'old hand', not the poet, witnessed the sentence and execution. 'Drumhead' is thus arguably an example of false testimony in a similar way to Gerald Kersh's fabricated poem about a slit trench, since West can only imagine the condemned characters he describes for thirty-three lines. However, this categorization only appertains if the reader interprets the first two lines of the second stanza as a (false) act of voluntary memory rather than fabrication: West has not seen the 'scene' and peoples it not in the sense of remembering, but of imagining a potential painting. Nevertheless, the lines appear ambiguous, and they can certainly dupe the reader unaware of the memoirs into thinking that 'Drumhead' is a positivistic account of a witnessed atrocity. Hence the poem is closer to Sue Vice's category of 'embellished testimony'.[121] Vice asks why a writer such as Martin Gray—with firsthand experience of the Warsaw ghetto—should have to pretend that they were at Treblinka. West is clearly not open to such a charge of gross deception, but the lines' deliberate ambiguity still begs the question as to why someone who had seen the death of fellow soldiers during the invasion of Crete—and who narrowly avoided death himself due to pneumonia and a subsequent escape from a German camp—should wish to focus on an event he did not witness.

There are several possible answers to this question evident in the memoirs and poetry. 'Drumhead' wishes to testify for those who are not allowed to give adequate testimony at the court martial: a *dolmetscher* (interpreter) badly translates a 'last, eloquent plea' (p. 232). West also engages here with a central moment in his own war experience, as he moves from an active participant to, as Hynes puts it in *The Soldier's Tale*, 'the overriding, dominant feature of POW life: constant anxiety, and utter powerlessness' (p. 233). West has only just been captured when he enters Galatos, and, after viewing the tables, he collapses due to a septic wound, breaking—as his memoir recounts—a table of 'precious medical supplies' in the process (p. 196); the Cretans' fate thus figures the potential endpoint of his own new 'powerlessness'. In *British Writing of the Second World War*, Mark Rawlinson demonstrates that the war 'was being restaged in POW novels and memoirs of the 1950s as heroic adventure' (p. 204): prison was a site of 'unquestioning defiance' (p. 204) and 'a place of recuperation, contemplation, and education [asserting] liberating disciplines' (p. 176). West's memoir provides a corrective to such heroic narratives: he describes the 'first shock of being taken prisoner' as a 'trauma' (p. 347), since he has become 'a disarmed nonentity with no orders, no future' (p. 348); he goes on to recount how his fellow prisoners 'keeled over, with dysentery, typhoid and polio' (p. 217). Shortly after beginning work in the Imperial War Museum on 'documents of low-level origin' on the invasion of Crete, West suffered from acute depression and had to give up his career in teaching; in his memoirs he laments 'a course on the same drug that they feed to Russian dissidents' (p. 374).[122]

Hence 'Drumhead' testifies to the beginning of West's suffering as a POW; however, this autobiographical explanation still does not adequately account for the reason why he chose to write potentially embellished testimony, rather than, say, provide a positivistic account in poetry of his near demise from pneumonia. The poem's depiction of summary justice provides a potential answer, since elsewhere in the memoirs and poetry West describes his own guilt at summarily killing an unidentified man during the invasion who may have been a Cretan policeman. In his memoirs, West spots:

> a figure, spreading out a red swastika flag on the road, who had started up and ran to the ditch at our approach. Someone in unfamiliar uniform, like a Greek policeman? Can't be. Looked scared. This one's mine at any rate. I lie in the ditch waiting for his reappearance and he pops up to see if we're still there. And again. Foresight on forehead, I squeeze gently. A cloud of dust arises where he has fallen back. (p. 126)

As in 'Drumhead', a potentially mistaken identity leads to the death of a villager. As a sign of guilt, West returns to this moment several times in his work: the poem 'Crete 20th May, 1941' depicts the event, as does 'Encounter', a poem (held in the Oasis archive) which was written fifty-six years after the event in 1997. At the bottom of the manuscript of 'Encounter', West writes, 'It doesn't pay to be over-curious'; the same logic (in a different context) appertains to the Germans' desire to dispose of the Cretan villagers. Ultimately, however, definitive reasons for the potentially embellished testimony remain opaque. What can be ascertained is that West intertwines the imagined 'horror' at the end of 'Drumhead' with the act of the killing of the Cretan and his capture and subsequent suffering as a POW. The poet's inability to paint a picture at the end of 'Drumhead' can be read as a sign of West's own failure to come to terms with his traumatic experiences over fifty years after the war.

KEITH DOUGLAS'S 'ELEGY FOR AN 88 GUNNER' AND PERPETRATOR AESTHETICS

In the final section of this chapter, I propose to read 'Elegy for an 88 Gunner'—which features in three of the Oasis anthologies—in the light of the testimonial poetry discussed above, particularly in relation to the concept of perpetrator aesthetics.[123] Whereas 'Ubique' and 'Drumhead' engage with the fraught inscription of trauma, Douglas's poetry proves more akin to the scathing poetics of Tadeusz Borowski in his shockingly unperturbed responses to desert warfare. Critics such as Ian Hamilton and Adam Piette decry the 'tight lipped insensitivity of the officers' mess' and the 'officer class poise' that they detect in 'Elegy for an 88 Gunner', but the lack of 'Bullshit' precisely highlights the poem's veracity as an example of soldier testimony.[124] Hynes demonstrates that Douglas's focus on looting in *From Alamein to Zem Zem* 'deflects the tone from mourning and makes [the tone] tough and ironic, like a good soldier of that war'[125]. Similarly, 'Elegy for an 88 Gunner' marks an elegiac shift towards a dispassionate soldier's voice, rather than attempting to poeticize the recoil of a civilian response amongst the horrors of mobile warfare. Douglas's detractors often read his work as if it were that of a World War I poet; more specifically, as if the poetry might comply with the comradely exchanges of Owen's 'Strange Meeting'. By requesting the intervention of a subjectivity unaffected by war, they wish for Keats in a Sherman tank rather than a 'tough and ironic' narrator who regards Germans and Italians not as potential friends, but as decaying corpses. Instead, 'Elegy for an 88 Gunner' constitutes the most famous example of perpetrator aesthetics in English poetry: the poet returns to a battle site, immediately engages—as Tim Kendall emphasizes—in looting, and regards the enemy corpse 'almost with content'.[126]

Linda Shires reads 'Elegy for an 88 Gunner' as a version of 'Strange Meeting' when she contends that the poet is 'identifying himself with the enemy' (p. 130); he 'becomes that German' (p. 135), and the poem proves to be a 'culmination of [a] development towards a greater humanity' (p. 135). On the contrary, Douglas's poem embodies the turn to 'killer' testimony in World War II poetry with its absolute refusal to identify with the enemy. A souvenir picture of a dead soldier with the skull and uniform visible is held among Douglas's photographs in The Brotherton Library; the German's helmet has been placed on the remains of his back.[127] Janina Struk has analysed the perpetrator poetics of such photographs: this particular one is symptomatic of an unashamedly voyeuristic interest in the dead enemy that persists in Douglas's work.[128] It has often been noted that the preoccupation with the dead in *From Alamein to Zem Zem* is reflected in the poetry, but it is less often remarked that the representation is strikingly different in 'Elegy for an 88 Gunner'. Whereas the narrator views the corpses with 'reverence' and admires their 'triumphant silence' in his prose memoir, in this poem he emphasizes the dead soldier's indignity.[129] 'Elegy for an 88 Gunner' maps out a process of dehumanization: as the poem unfolds in the first stanza, the reader can be tricked into thinking the 'soldier' in the fourth line is animate, 'sprawling in the sun'; any Owenesque sense that the enemy constitutes a fellow 'combatant' is dispelled in the voyeuristic description of the 'decayed' corpse that so displeases Hamilton. Finally, the German soldier loses even the identity of a corpse: whereas Steffi implores him on the back of her looted photograph to '*Vergissmeinicht*', Douglas 'forgets' him by turning him into a poetic abstraction, a 'lover' and 'killer' marked out by 'Death'. Following Kendall's reading, it is noteworthy that the reader only confronts the unsettling depiction of the corpse after the narrator has engaged in looting in the 'gunpit spoil': as Bernard Gutteridge notes in the Oasis poem 'The Enemy Dead', 'The dead are always searched', because, as

Douglas Street recounts (ironically) in 'Love Letters of the Dead', 'There's a lot of good stuff to be found there'; Commando intelligence believes that '[l]ove letters are specially useful [. . .] It's amazing what couples let slip'.[130] Douglas indicates that the 'tough and ironic' soldier is more interested in the spoils of war than pondering the potentially 'greater humanity' of an incidental corpse. Not only is the poet 'content' to regard the enemy as humiliated ('abased'), but Douglas also carefully builds up to the 'barbaric' aesthetics of the penultimate stanza. Initially, the civilian reader is protected with the deliberate poeticisms of the 'swart flies' and 'paper eye', but then, in the stanza's final line, Douglas deploys the testimonial *coup de grâce* of the 'burst stomach', which he emphasizes with a metrical break on 'burst'. Hamilton objects particularly to 'swart', but—apart from the aptness of its German derivation—it also registers the radical otherness of the corpse. As in Thomas Aird's poem 'The Devil's Dream on Mount Aksbeck' and Henry Alford's 'The Gypsy Girl', it usually denotes the 'swarthy' skin of colonial subjects: Douglas probably came across the word in Keats's 'On the Eve of St Agnes', where it refers to 'swart Paynims' (pagans).[131]

Rather than engaging in a process of 'identifying [. . .] with the enemy', then, 'Elegy for an 88 Gunner' maintains a perpetrator perspective in which the humiliated enemy has unremarkably 'paid' his dues. In *The Holocaust and the Postmodern*, Robert Eaglestone argues that the literary genre of testimony is distinguished by a process of identification in which the reader attempts to align their experience with the witness (p. 16); the latter subsequently rejects this possibility. Testimony's paradox of identification is thrown into especial relief in 'Elegy for an 88 Gunner': unlike the sympathy-inducing, liberal perspective of, for example, Primo Levi's testimony, Douglas's poem presents the reader with the impossibility of identifying with a dead enemy, and the difficulty—for civilian readers—of engaging with the perspective of the 'tough and ironic' soldier in World War II. Steffi's imagined reaction ('she would weep') comes closer to the secondary witness's response (A. Banerjee concludes that, 'in reality', the scene must have been 'disgusting and revolting'), but Douglas gently mocks even Steffi: her Gothic script is 'copybook', in other words, tritely conventional.[132] Douglas's ironic tone persists throughout: just as the poet is 'amused | to see the centre of love diffused' as he kills someone in 'How to Kill', he points out that the dead soldier is 'mocked'—as in Douglas's war sketches—by the 'durable equipment' that endures (and is, by implication, looted) as the corpse decays.[133] Indeed, the title of the poem itself contains an irony, since 'Elegy for an 88 Gunner' is not really an elegy. Elegies do not perform a straightforwardly testimonial function: as in Drummond Allison's elegy for Hedley Verity (the England spinner who died after action in Italy), the genre is normally concerned primarily with the experience of the deceased, not that of the witness poet. In contrast with the familiarities of 'Verity'—including Allison's reference to Hedley's heroics in a 1934 Test against Australia—Douglas's poem steadfastly refuses to engage with any (imagined) experience of the German soldier. 'Elegy for an 88 Gunner', with its 'refusal to mourn in the poetry of mourning', ultimately comprises one of the most devastating anti-elegies of the twentieth century.[134]

Unusually for World War II poetry (as I outlined at the beginning of this chapter), 'Elegy for an 88 Gunner' does not vacillate between victim and perpetrator perspectives. One of the reasons that some critics respond with revulsion to the poem is that it refuses to diverge from its 'tough and ironic' stance. The anti-elegiac tone complies with Hilberg's definition of a perpetrator (someone who 'understood his function [. . .] What he did was impersonal. He had been [. . .] instructed to carry out his mission'); only the adverb in 'almost content' intimates that the narrator might be more perturbed by the incident than the surface details admit. Unlike 'Ubique'— which presents the poet as a traumatized victim of war as well as the perpetuator of the 'cool' aesthetics of murderous artillery—'Elegy for an 88 Gunner' pitches the nursery rhyme rhythm of (primarily) iambic tetrameter and the simple rhyme scheme against the disturbing subject matter, as if to stress the narrator's uncomplicated resilience in the face of potentially traumatizing events. Douglas's anti-elegy is ultimately closer in tone to G. C. Norman's 'Night Raid'—with its refusal to see the enemy as anything else but the enemy—than West's agonized inability to come to terms with his own perpetrator act of killing a Cretan. Unlike 'Ubique' and 'Drumhead', Douglas never drops the guise of the 'tight lipped' ironist: such differences emphasize the difficulty in generalizing about Oasis poetry in the anthologies and archives.

Nevertheless, the refusal to mourn in Douglas's poem epitomizes the fresh persistence of the 'tough' soldier-narrator in Oasis poetry, alongside the more familiar figure of the traumatized combatant. Close attention to the Trust's archive challenges such familiarity (established after World War I), and other popular perceptions of the Second World War, which, for example, occlude the Allied soldier as injurer and killer and the helpless POW. The 'myth' (to deploy Hynes's phrase) of the 'just war'—in which soldiers cleanly dispose of Germans and then return unaffected to civilian life—gives way in the context of the archive to a series of texts engaging with victim and perpetrator behaviour; sometimes (as in 'Ubique') within the confines of a single text.[135] This 'myth' is also subverted with the amount of Oasis material which attacks Allied politicians rather than German expansionism: Frederick Horn's 'Conscript' proves illustrative with its depiction of a dead Allied soldier; it concludes that it was 'a pity [. . .] | his life should run, like bright oil down a gutter | to implement some politician's brag'.[136] As William I. Hitchcock argues in *Liberation*, 'More than half a century later, we now have the evidence, and perhaps the critical distance, to develop a richer, more complex history of the "good war" that incorporates both its glories and its misfortunes' (p. 373). The lack of critical attention to the Oasis material is troubling in the context of persistent myths about World War II—and Hitchcock's point about 'critical distance'—as if fulfilling Pierre Nora's indictment that archives are concerned with the for-getting, rather than the perpetuation, of collective memory. By not paying attention to the archive in the Imperial War Museum, potential secondary witnesses 'delegat[e] the responsibility for remembering': British society is subsequently able to discard memories of its participation in the central event of the previous century 'as the snake deposits its shed skin'.[137] In addi-tion to Selwyn's worry that literary critics and poetry readers were stub-bornly forgetting poems about World War II (in contrast to the canonicity of Owen and Sassoon), the editor still remained concerned that he was himself failing to collect a lost classic of war poetry. Hence his perturbed response to the 1987 storm: an advert in the *Legion* (May/June 1990) states that the editors are 'seeking some very good material indeed that was sent to us for our last anthology but unfortunately was lost in the storm [. . .] This involved about 20 manuscripts including some powerful poetry from a former member of the Royal Air Force' (p. 27). I began this chapter with an account of the precariousness of such testimony, but rather than dwell on the possibility of lost masterpieces, Selwyn should instead have congratu-lated himself—and other members of the Trust—in ultimately amassing a remarkable testimonial archive. The discarded memories that lie among the twenty thousand manuscripts are tangible evidence that the history—and literary history—of World War II is not yet over.

4 Provisional Testimony in Charlotte Delbo's *Auschwitz and After*

Charlotte Delbo's testimony is more sophisticated than the work of any other writer discussed in this book, yet it has been neglected in French literary studies because of the association of war writing with male authors and the dominance of the Resistance in representations of World War II in France.[1] Delbo's modernist poetics distinguish her work from testimony analysed in other chapters, such as Tadeusz Borowski's later texts, Primo Levi's work, and the amateur verse in the Salamander Oasis Trust and *Voices* archives. As noted in the introduction, Samuel Hynes demonstrates that most war narratives are not modernist; yet the more memorable forms of testimony—such as David Jones's *In Parenthesis* and Delbo's books—do not rely on the illusions of realism.[2] Delbo's work chimes with Jorge Semprun's sense—also outlined in the introduction—that the most successful forms of testimony are those which are linguistically sophisticated. By 'successful' I do not mean in the sense of imparting information about historical events: as Shoshana Felman and Dori Laub have argued, testimony is concerned with more than the substantiation of facts; literature 'becomes a witness, and perhaps the only witness, to the crisis within history which precisely cannot be articulated, witnessed in the given categories of history itself'.[3] Delbo's writing is exemplary in that, as a form of life-writing, it still achieves—as Derek Attridge would put it—singularity; a level of aesthetic sophistication and ethical engagement which can, initially, baffle the reader. Her books display an:

> extraordinary ability to grip the reader in proceeding from sentence to sentence and from page to page, to move intensely with their depictions of cruelty, suffering, longing, and love, to give pleasure even when they dispirit and disturb, but also in the way they raise and illuminate questions of immense practical importance to all of us. These include the relation between ethical demands and political decisions, the human cost of artistic creation, the exactingness and uncertainty of confessional autobiography, and the difficulty of doing justice to others in a violent society.[4]

The quotation above comes from Attridge's account of J. M. Coetzee's novels, but it could equally apply—on every count—to Delbo's work, from the 'gripping' fusion of poetry and prose, and its ability to 'move intensely with [. . .] depictions of cruelty', to her interest in ethics and praxis, the problems of autobiography, and the links between historical and contemporaneous events. Her writing has attracted excellent criticism from a range of writers in Holocaust Studies: I refer to their work throughout this chapter, but I still do not feel that we have been attentive enough, as yet, to the form of her 'singular' writing and the ways in which her books demand several re-readings in order to come to terms with the subtle connections, differences, and modulations between each text, particularly in terms of her self-conscious engagement with the aesthetic. Hence I make no apology for the close readings that follow in this chapter: it is only through attention to detail that her readers can appreciate the aesthetic sophistication of the testimony, and its wrestle with 'the exactingness and uncertainty' of autobiography.

Delbo deploys an unsettling testimonial style that juxtaposes, and often merges, poetry and prose.[5] This generic instability is not uncommon in Holocaust testimony: in Chapter 2, for example, I illustrated how Borowski produces an awkward compromise between poetry and literary journalism in his later poems. Whereas Borowski's journalistic style endeavours to react faithfully to diurnal events, however, Delbo's blend of forms results in a more tentative form of representation. Rather than exploit the illusion of mimesis in testimony written in the style of nineteenth-century realism, her prose poetry works towards the impossibility of the reader (as she often puts it) 'seeing' the traumatic events she endured. This tentativeness abounds in *None of Us Will Return*, the first volume of the *Auschwitz and After* trilogy, where sections of prose poetry give way to prosaic poems isolated typographically on separate pages. In contrast, the second volume (*Useless Knowledge*) gradually adopts the evidential realism more familiar in Holocaust testimony after the poems at the beginning of the book.[6] Delbo utilizes poetry as testimony in *None of Us Will Return* partly because of the rhetorical attentiveness of the verse line and its ability to draw the reader into thinking about the signified events (if not the impossibility of 'seeing' the referent). The first volume gives the impression that prosaic prose is not sufficient, for Delbo, to emphasize the slow time of Birkenau or the endured pain.[7] Hence the 'Daytime' section fragments finally into verse (p. 48) with the spacing of line breaks and anaphora, creating a pastiche of scripture for the inscription of her suffering.[8] Delbo also switches to poetry after the repeated, prosaic 'try and see' sections (pp. 84–86), as if the generic switch might fulfil her assertion in an interview that '[o]nly the language of poetry enables one to make people see and feel'.[9] However, the provisional nature of her testimony undercuts this claim: Delbo sometimes presents herself, as well as the reader, as unable to 'see' her experience. Later in this chapter, I argue that this problem of representation leads to a re-evaluation of the aesthetic, which, for Delbo, still remains important to her understanding of Birkenau and Ravensbrück during and after her internment. Such aesthetics sometimes metamorphose into parody, such as when she discusses the presence of music in the camps.

These problems of 'seeing' link with Felman and Laub's concept of provisional testimony, which has 'not settled into understanding or remembrance'. These testimonial acts:

> cannot be constructed as knowledge nor assimilated into full cognition [. . .] What the testimony does not offer is [. . .] a completed statement, a totalizable account of those events. In the testimony, language is in process and in trial, it does not possess itself as a conclusion, as the contestation of a verdict or the self-transparency of knowledge.[10]

Similarly, Delbo insists that her life-writing does not provide the 'truth' of, or 'conclusion' to, events in Birkenau and Ravensbrück. I analyse her contestation not of the 'verdict' of history, but the relationship between *vrai* and *véridique*; in other words, what is 'true' in the sense that she offers testimony that might approximate to, but not fully capture, the victim's experience, and 'truthful' in that her writing connects with the metanarrative of history but does not encapsulate historical events. Felman and Laub begin with but then work beyond the idea that the signified referent of testimony is history: Delbo also highlights the importance of the lyrical voice, but she nevertheless compares the 'truth' of history with the 'truthfulness' of subjective experience. Delbo's language may be 'in process and in trial' but it does not—as in a judicial context—lead to the 'conclusion' of a verdict: her provisional testimony is, paradoxically, 'final' in that it is not written to be superseded, or treated only as a minor, initiatory process that leads towards ultimate enlightenment. (Famously, Delbo wrote her first book soon after her return from Ravensbrück, but she worried that it may not contain any literary value: after languishing in a drawer for nearly twenty years, she read it again and—convinced of its achievement—decided to publish her work.) It could be argued that the permanently 'provisional' is not actually provisional in any meaningful sense, but the term is important in relation to Delbo's work in that it allows me to stress her awareness that her testimonial poetry—like historical narratives—can never depict the 'truth' and complexity of individual suffering and the unfolding of events. Her poetics emphasize the problems of grasping what was experienced (indeed of *feeling* that it was experienced), and appreciating the event's traumatic repercussions in the present. Delbo's metatestimony is only 'final' in its provocative grappling with the radical uncertainty of testimonial accounts: hence the aptness of her prosaic poetry and poetic prose. Delbo eschews the prosaic prose of the courtroom in order to point to the inevitable blind spots in her testimony;

it does not lead to a 'transparency of knowledge' about Ravensbrück and Birkenau. Nevertheless (and unlike prosaic prose), her poetics provide the reader—and Delbo—with a necessarily compromised ability to 'see and feel' her previous suffering.

Delbo's acute sense of the frailties of testimony contrast with the way in which Levi establishes the role of the witness in *If This Is a Man*. In the afterword to his book, Levi argues that his will to survive was partly bound up with the 'precise purpose of recounting the things we had witnessed and endured': his 'need to tell the story was so strong in the Camp that I had begun describing my experiences there, on the spot, in that German laboratory'.[11] In *None of Us Will Return* this idea of surviving in order to witness—common in Holocaust testimony—is rejected: during the agonizing roll calls, the narrator 'thought of nothing' and 'could not account for what had taken place' (p. 64). The difference in the titles of the testimonies is instructive: whereas Delbo writes partly from the perspective of an inmate who cannot imagine anyone's survival, or surviving unaffected, Levi's stubborn interest remains, 'which has never flagged, in the human spirit' (p. 398). That 'none' in Delbo's title clearly precludes any humanist sense of post-war redemption; on the contrary, following the title of her second book, anything learnt in the camps is 'useless knowledge'. For Levi, his 'brief and tragic experience as a deportee has been overlaid [by] that much longer and complex experience as a writer-witness, and the sum total is clearly positive: in its totality, this past has made [him] richer and surer' (p. 398). Levi's interest in 'the human spirit' manifests itself in his expositions of various characters in the camp, such as Elias and Kraus: these confident character sketches of the 'old stable ego' dominate *If This Is a Man*, whereas Delbo often does not even name the people she encounters. Instead, in passages such as the description of the woman climbing a bank in *None of Us Will Return* the 'she' poses only a series of unanswerable questions: 'What does she want me do? [. . .] Why does she stare at us?' (p. 26). 'She' demands a witness, but rather than respond heroically, the narrator turns away, for a while, to 'look elsewhere' (p. 26). Lacking confidence, the witness then worries not about a burning desire to testify, but the possibility of the narrative turning into a pleasurable account.

The writers' different conceptions of the witness are bound up with the style of the testimonies. Levi has commented that his first book was written like a factory report: it assumes 'the calm, sober language of the witness, neither the lamenting tones of the victim nor the irate voice of someone who seeks revenge' (p. 382).[12] He evokes the judicial origins of testimony in a further statement that unemotional and objective witnesses thus 'in matters of justice perform [their] task, which is that of preparing the ground for the judge. The judges are my readers' (p. 382). In contrast, Delbo judges the reader, as is indicated in the title of the poem 'Prayer to the Living to Forgive Them for Being Alive', and engages instead with the 'lamenting tones of the victim'. In *None of Us Will Return*, Delbo presents the truckload of women passing a roll call on the way to the gas chamber after the emptying of Block 25 as wailing judges, a lamenting Greek chorus that responds to the gazing women in lines and their own demise (pp. 33–34). As Carolyn Dean argues in *Aversion and Erasure: The Fate of the Victim after the Holocaust*, 'Primo Levi's exemplarity [. . .] begs the question of why self-control should be not only admirable in those who have suffered grievously, but also characteristic of the ideal victim', who does not publicly lament or display anger.[13] Delbo's troubled witnesses do both and call attention to their own inadequacies, rather than hiding them, as a court of law would demand. Dean's work does not in any way demean what Gillian Rose has termed Levi's 'Olympian serenity': instead, it asks the question whether 'calm, sober language' provides the most effective form of testimony in the realms of the literary, rather than in the courtroom.[14]

Delbo seeks to make readers aware of the difficulty of testifying through a demand—as in many of the poems discussed in this book—for hyper-attentiveness. Hence the close readings in this chapter respond to her imperative that the reader should not blithely turn to the next passage of suffering, but instead ponder the experience that cannot—according to Felman and Laub—be fully 'assimilated'. Concerned that readers might respond to her prosaic prose with a disinterested 'look' akin to that of Doktor Pannwitz in *If This Is a Man* ('as if across the glass window of an aquarium between two beings who live in different worlds'), Delbo seeks, through poetry as testimony, the swiftest route to empathic unsettlement.[15] In contrast with Levi's testimony, *None of Us Will Return* 'shuns the narrative impulse' and consists primarily of prose poetry which is more poetic than the isolated, prosaic poems.[16] For example, the repeated synecdoche of the hand initiates the memorable poetic prose of 'the snow [blooming] like a discoloured sea anemone' (p. 19), and the 'faded mauve star upon the snow' (p. 25). Rosette C. Lamont's translation of the 'Stenia' section also succeeds in carrying over the assonance, alliteration (particularly the sibilance) and internal rhyme of the original French in the following passage: 'The wind blows and whistles and groans. It is a moan mounting from the marshes, a sob swelling, swelling and bursting, then subsiding into shivering silence, another sob swells, swells and bursts and dies down' (p. 42).[17] Delbo then juxtaposes this heightened rhetoric with the prosaic poetry of the isolated poem on the opposite page, which begins with 'A plain | covered with marshes | with tipcarts'.[18] These different forms of poetry point to the provisional nature of Delbo's testimony, as she works through varying perspectives to make the reader imagine scenarios that might in some way approximate to the original experience. In this chapter, I highlight the fact that not only the reader, but Delbo herself encounters such problems of 'seeing', due to the disassociations of trauma in the camp and the testimonial interventions of her civilian perspectives.

'SEEING' AND PROVISIONAL TESTIMONY

Delbo's work often reads against its own aesthetics: in his introduction to *Auschwitz and After*, Lawrence Langer notes her 'lyrical rendering of atrocity that is alarmingly beautiful'; in a resonant phrase, he describes this process as the 'aesthetics of agitation' (p. xvi). Langer argues that Delbo's poetics chafe against Theodor Adorno's claim about 'barbaric' post-Holocaust poetry (p. xvi). However, they comply with my reading of the 'barbaric' in *Holocaust Poetry* as awkward, self-referential attempts to engage with atrocity.[19] An explicit example of these aesthetics occurs in *None of Us Will Return*, when Delbo interrupts the narrative with the awkward poetics of metatestimony: as a 'female skeleton' begins to dance outside Block 25, the narrator interrupts and states that she is writing in a café, and that 'this story' is 'turning into a story' (p. 26). The repetition reflects Sarah Kofman's concerns about the 'idyllic law of the story' in testimony (which I discussed in the introduction) and a suspicion of narrative pleasure in the section's description of a dying woman.[20] Delbo attempts to undercut the '"idyllic" clarity of narrative' throughout *None of Us Will Return*—unlike the later sections of *Useless Knowledge*—with the unsettled chronology and lack of metatextual signs that frame the switches between prose poetry and isolated poems.[21] Her 'aesthetics of agitation' resist a clear story which might dupe the reader into thinking they (and the author) can 'see' the events, identify with stable characters (as in *If This Is a Man*), and thereby potentially colonize the victim's experience, as Pierre does with his wife Marie-Louise's testimony in *The Measure of Our Days* (pp. 286–88).[22] Similarly to Wilfred Owen, then, Delbo struggles against the reader's potential over-identification with the author and the ensuing misunderstandings and elisions of the victim's experience. This narrative agitation links with Robert Eaglestone's analysis of resistances to identification in testimony: even after 276 pages of the trilogy, a poem ends with the outburst that 'everything there is inexplicable'.[23] However, a dialectical desire to make the reader (partly) 'see' persists throughout *Auschwitz and After*. As in Keith Douglas's testimonial poetry (which I examined in the last chapter), Delbo insists that the reader 'Look. Look' (p. 17); at the same time, she impresses upon them the impossibility of 'seeing'. Hence she sometimes switches to a more inclusive, second-person narrative, as Seweryna Szmaglewska does (more often) in her testimony *Smoke over Birkenau*: in *None of Us Will Return*, the 'We' of the deportees includes the 'You' of the reader by the second paragraph of the 'Daytime' section.[24]

   In contrast, the first two isolated poems in *None of Us Will Return* are scathing attacks on readers who might think they can 'see' after only seven pages of the testimony. The second meta-testimonial poem begins 'O you who know': as with Levi's 'Shemà', the irony could be aimed at all non-survivors. Delbo might also be targeting the colonizing imagination of characters such as Pierre in particular (p. 11). Her 'aesthetics of agitation' prove to be more unsettling that Levi's 'Shemà', however. Whereas Levi isolates the poetry's invective from the serenity of the prose, Delbo's assault on the reader occurs within the main text after a few pages, rather than in the parenthetical form of an epigraph. John Jarmain (whose work I discussed in Chapter 3) and Levi's meta-testimonial poems also strive to make the reader appreciate the author's suffering, whereas Delbo's poetry grates against the possibility of identification. Nevertheless, even as she berates complacent readers (and non-readers), who, for example, do not know that 'hunger makes the eyes sparkle that thirst dims them', a para-doxical wish persists to force readers to at least conjure such images, even if they cannot understand the 'horror', which 'cannot be circumscribed'.[25] As Thomas Trezise puts it, when the 'you who know' is '"called into ques-tion,"' it does not mean that the invitation to listen has been rescinded, but instead that those presuming to know are accused of having already failed to respond to it' (p. 886). Sometimes the addressees of 'you' in *None of Us Will Return* encompass Delbo, as when she ruminates that 'you believed that only solemn words rise to the lips of the dying' (p. 108): 'O you who know' could also be read as prosopopoeia, as a poem spoken by a dead inmate, whose ire could be directed at survivors too. Similarly, the meta-testimonial poem 'Prayer to the Living to Forgive Them for Being Alive' suggests that Delbo could be included in the targets of prosopopoeiac nar-rators who attack the living for unthinkingly 'passing by | well dressed in all your muscles' (p. 229).

Rather than unsettle the reader at the beginning of the testimony, Delbo inserts this poem at the end of *Useless Knowledge*: she challenges the reader not to be seduced by the '"idyllic" clarity of narrative' that domi-nates the mid-section of the book, and not to think that the events have no relevance to post-war existence, as if they occurred 'across the glass win-dow of an aquarium'. Delbo's irony against those 'who [think] they know' partly arises out of her concern with the fascistic tendencies of post-war European society, and her sense in *The Measure of Our Days* that '[t]hose about whom I know from the very first glance that they would have helped me walk are so few' (p. 254). Trezise adds that the 'self-defensive deafness' of France towards 'the war itself was bound to be exacerbated by evidence of its complicity in the Holocaust' (p. 867). The poem 'Envoi' ends *The Measure of Our Days*, and accuses the Beggar in Giraudoux's *Electra* of a kind of 'self-defensive deafness' when the character ponders the rarity of '[a] man ready to die for another' (p. 354). In a post-Holocaust reading of *Electra*, Delbo retorts that there were thousands of political resisters who 'stepped forward for all the others'.

Utilizing Langer's model of 'deep memory' (which itself originated in Delbo's testimony), it might be tempting to conclude that—in contrast to the main addressees of 'O you who know'—the author has no problem in 'seeing' the events herself (p. xiii).[26] Yet Delbo fails to 'see' in one sense when she first enters the camp, since she interprets the conditions in terms of her civilian experience: corpses become the shop dummies she witnessed as a child in Montluçon (pp. 17–18). Even in the final paragraph of this section, when she presents herself as a seasoned inmate, corpses do not 'move' her, but they are still 'naked dummies'; the infantile diction ('I'm a big girl now') undercuts the overall assertion (p. 19). When the dummy motif reappears, Delbo compares the last movements of the dying woman to the death of her dog Flac (p. 27). As the narrative continues, the interventions of civilian time frames decrease: twenty pages after the Flac section, Delbo asserts that it was '[o]ne of those wintry days when people say: "It would be nice to take a walk." People. Somewhere else' (p. 49). Of course, there was no 'true' experience that denuded all memory in order to respond truthfully to the camps: in *Traumatic Realism*, Michael Rothberg notes that 'there is no pure language of testimony with which to respond to injustice' (p. 148). Delbo's attempt to represent her struggle to understand Birkenau reflects the reader's own difficulties in engaging with the testimony. This process continues throughout *None of Us Will Return*, since traumatic dissociation—and the fragmented narrative—conveys the sense that Delbo does not fully 'experience' the events she endures and witnesses. In 'Morning' she ruminates that—if she ever returned—she could lie and say she survived by consciously resisting day by day, but the truth would be that during roll call she 'thought of nothing' and 'could not account for what had taken place' (p. 64).

Moreover, in *Convoy to Auschwitz* Delbo records that 'March [1943] was the worst time: everyone was sick and so weak that their minds were dimmed, and their eyes did not *see*' (p. 189; my italics). In *None of Us Will Return* she suffers from typhus and admits that 'I can remember nothing about those weeks' (p. 73); she forgets eating tomatoes in Raisko and muses in *The Measure of Our Days* that '[t]here must have been many times like these, times when I was off my head' (p. 343).[27] (In contrast, Poupette claims that she deliberately 'succeeded in not seeing' in the camps (p. 273), as Delbo tries to in *None of Us Will Return* when she avoids looking at women being taken to the crematorium (p. 52).) *Useless Knowledge* also exposes the limitations of testimony when she admits that she has 'no memory of any odor. It's true that I can't recall my own smell when I lifted my dress' (p. 150). Delbo begins to fictionalize her imagined experience during this section, since she has 'no memory of it. I only recall the stream' (p. 153). Levi only fictionalizes his testimony to suit the novelistic narrative (as when he visits the old woman who wrote to Hitler in *The Truce* (*If This Is a Man*, p. 280)), whereas Delbo does so in order to focus on the limitations of witnessing. The epigraph to *Useless Knowledge* immediately exposes these inevitable shortcomings: she is not sure that the testimony is '*true*', but she is convinced that it is '*truthful*' (p. 1). As critics such as Nicole Thatcher and Trezise have pointed out, the original French ('*vrai* [. . .] *véridique*') suggests that the English terms should be reversed. Delbo is not sure that the testimony approximates to her original experience (in other words, that she herself can 'see' properly), but she is certain that it corresponds to the facts of the camps' existence.[28]

Hence, Felman and Laub's account of unassimilated knowledge fits with Delbo's implicit understanding of her own testimonial poetics. In *None of Us Will Return*, incremental repetition comprises part of an attempt to work through traumatic memory, as if Delbo is trying to come to terms with the experience as fact and its potential significance. For example, in 'The Same Day' the inmates 'were walking. Walking automatons. Walking ice statues. Exhausted women were walking' (p. 35): the narrator tries different metaphors in the non-sentences but then falls back on the positivistic simplicity of the final statement. In 'Sunday', the language as well as the referent becomes a 'maniacal run', as Delbo draws attention to the performativity of testimony: 'Run—schnell—the gate—schnell—the plank—empty out the earth—schnell [. . .] run run run schnell schnell schnell schnell schnell' (p. 94).[29] Repetition blends victim and perpetrator perspectives here and (unlike *If This Is a Man*) also challenges the reader to be bored, to adopt the disinterested stance of a Pannwitz, 'as if across the glass window of an aquarium'. Delbo's testimony is also provisional to the extent that she often undermines her potential effectiveness as a witness: after the 'race', she has 'no idea whether I reconstituted this whole scene after the fact or if I had an overall concept from the start. I always *thought* I was endowed with keen, attentive faculties so that I could *see* and grasp everything, as well as ward off the dangers. I ran' (p. 36; my italics). As with the section on the '[e]xhausted [walking] women', testimonial musing ends with empirical simplicity: 'I ran'. On the next page, Delbo admits the impossibility of objectivity: she had not 'seen' Yvonne B., even though '[s]he had never stopped being at my side'; she had 'run, run without seeing anything [. . .] without feeling the blows' (p. 38). This section turns into an allegory of testimony as the women later 'piece together' what happened during the race (p. 38).

'INFERNAL' MUSIC AND THE PARODY OF THE AESTHETIC

These meta-testimonial problems of 'seeing' result in a rigorous examination of the aesthetic throughout Delbo's work. Because of the conditions in Birkenau, the aesthetic often manifests itself as a form of parody.[30] Before the women enter the barracks, singing is an act of resistance: in *Convoy to Auschwitz*, they sing in the cattle trucks (p. 4); Raymonde Salez leads the Marseillaise when they arrive (p. 195). By 'The Orchestra' section of *None of Us Will Return*, however, music (in the form of waltzes) has become 'intolerable' (p. 106).[31] Whereas for Szmaglewska, Alma Rosé's orchestra momentarily makes the barracks float 'beyond the wires [. . .] the camp disappears' (p. 240), in *If This Is a Man*, Levi (along with Delbo) thinks that the camp music is merely 'infernal' (p. 56). In *None of Us Will Return*, music cannot be enjoyed outside of the context of Birkenau: the unnamed conductor (clearly Alma Rosé) '*parodies* the professional she used to be when she led an all-women's orchestra in a famous Vienna café' (p. 106).[32] (Given the execution of her husband, music as parody becomes particularly troubling for Delbo when the orchestra plays a piece from a Franz Lehár opera called 'The Merry Widow'.) For Delbo, Rosé can only parody her former life since she is forced to perform to 'naked men reduced to skeletons' (p. 107): the music thereby attains the status of a perpetrator aesthetic, rather than assuaging the victims' pain; as Shirli Gilbert comments in *Music in the Holocaust*, such aesthetics provided 'a framework within which the SS could maintain a self-image of refined German culture and personal "decency", not apart from but precisely in the context of the murderous activities in which they were involved' (p. 19).

Hence the next sentence in 'The Orchestra' section links the complicity of music with perpetrator rhetoric, since the men 'are going to delousing because there are decidedly too many lice in the barracks' (p. 107): Gilbert notes that the 'orchestras played a valuable role in the extermination process, helping the operation to run smoothly and assisting in the maintenance of discipline and order' (p. 145). In the final section of the testimony, the contamination of the aesthetic is sealed when the 'symphony' of spring appears as an intolerable parody; an 'injustice' (p. 111). Indeed, camp entities and rituals are often portrayed as parodies of civilian life throughout *None of Us Will Return*: the testimony opens with a station that is not a station (it is a 'roadside that was not a station' in *Convoy to Auschwitz* (p. 5)); the kapos' 'wedding' is placed in inverted commas because it is a 'masquerade' (p. 8); the anguished performance of Christmas teeters on the edge of being a parody in *Useless Knowledge* (pp. 162–66). Such concerns with the parody of the aesthetic affect the form of Delbo's work. Her fusion of poetry and prose resists the possibility that conventional Alexandrines about Auschwitz would—like Rosé's music—appear to be parodies of their pre-Holocaust forms.

As with this evaluation of the orchestra, the metatext contaminates the aesthetic throughout Delbo's testimony: as early as page 34 she introduces the conceit of the cries of the women taken to the gas chamber, which 'remain inscribed upon the blue of the sky'. By the end of *None of Us Will Return*, the tenacity of the aesthetic provokes exasperation: she experiences the memory of spring 'singing' alongside the blue sky and '[t]he stink of diarrhea and corpses' (p. 111). (Gilbert notes a comparable response in the revier during Christmas 1943, when musicians played and the inmates responded with 'Let us croak in peace!'; Szymon Laks—one of the players—concludes that 'I did not know that a carol could give so much pain' (p. 191).) Delbo's awkward aesthetics sometimes appear akin to Borowski's attack on the complicity of the aesthetic in *This Way for the Gas, Ladies and Gentlemen*. In Chapter 2, I argue that in 'Auschwitz, Our Home (A Letter)', Borowski satirizes such aesthetic moments: 'we marched to Auschwitz', he writes, 'along a very beautiful road, observing some *very interesting* scenery en route'.[33] Delbo similarly notes that the 'path leading to the crematorium' lies next to the Commandant's house, 'with a garden graced by a lawn, rose-bushes, and window boxes painted blue, full of multicolored begonias' (p. 100): the proximity of the gas chambers and beautiful flora are mirrored in the image of the Christmas tree erected next to the gallows in *Useless Knowledge* (p. 166).[34] Overall, Delbo's engagement with the aesthetic differs from Borowski's in that she does not completely condemn it as an agent of complicity or the 'accustomed', perhaps due to their different status as prisoners: Borowski is repulsed by his collaboration in the unloading of the cattle trucks, whereas Delbo only observes briefly that she orders soap from a Jewish transport (p. 97); she also remarks in *Useless Knowledge* that the Polish prisoners receive parcels much more regularly (p. 162). Instead of the savage irony that persists in *This Way for the Gas, Ladies and Gentlemen*, the aesthetic sometimes salves Delbo and her comrades' distress. In *Useless Knowledge*, theatre in Raisko is an act of resistance and allows Delbo to retain her memory (pp. 167–71); she later struggles to remember fifty-seven poems in Ravensbrück and learns the entirety of *Le Misanthrope* (p. 188).[35] The conceit of the cries inscribed on the sky in *None of Us Will Return* also functions as a memory sign, since the compromised aesthetic allows her to 'carry the word' of the silent (as she puts it in her play about Birkenau); in this case, the women taken from Block 25. Delbo's dialectic of non-/'seeing' is always echoed in her opposite desire to stress the endurance of the aesthetic in Birkenau. When Viva comments sardonically during roll call that she 'won't ever like winter sports again', Delbo muses that it is '[s]trange that snow might evoke something other than a mortal, hostile element, unnatural and until now unfamiliar', yet two paragraphs earlier she herself evokes the 'other' of the aesthetic in the description of the snow that 'sparkles in refracted light' (p. 32).

The persistence of the aesthetic in Delbo's work is also reflected in the enduring juxtaposition and fusion of poetry and prose, which continues into her final book, *Days and Memory*. Her concerns about 'seeing' and the utility of literature in relation to testimony remain in an unresolved dialectical tension, as she also attempts to engage—as Trezise puts it—'"an approachable you", a second person capable of understanding that knowledge itself is not the horizon of listening, that the tension between identification and estrangement is not a misfortune to be surmounted but a condition of community to be maintained' (p. 886). Poetry as testimony is central to this shuttling between identification and estrangement: it may be able to make people 'see and feel'—as Delbo claimed in interview—but readers are simultaneously encouraged to question exactly what they are 'seeing' when they read her disquieting testimony, which (unlike Levi's work) does not omit some of the more disturbing events in the camps. Hence Delbo's acute awareness of the gap between inmates and non-survivors results in hcr maintenance of provisional testimony, which—as Felman and Laub argue—never offers up a 'completed statement, a totalizable account [. . .] language is in process and in trial'. Her prose poetry is not only 'in trial' in relation to the reader, however, but also in the context of Delbo's own problems of 'seeing', of bearing witness to events that she initially framed through her pre-war experience and did not fully experience at the time due to traumatic dissociation and debilitating typhus. For Delbo as well as the reader, language in her poetic testimony remains tentative and cannot 'possess itself as a conclusion', as a true reflection of her own suffering.

5 Poetry as Metatestimony
Primo Levi's *Collected Poems*

I began this book with a challenge to the popular misconception that testimony is an 'unaesthetic' form of written or oral attestation to historical
suffering, opposed to more self-consciously literary forms such as poetry.
Some critics assume that 'the poetic and the testimonial [are] somehow
incompatible': as Sue Vice argues, 'it is not poetic testimony but prose testimony that is typical of Holocaust eye-witness, while Holocaust poetry is
considered a separate and self-contained genre'.[1] In this chapter, I illustrate
that Primo Levi's poems are sometimes positivistic, recounting historical
details in poetic form, but, more importantly, they also form metatestimonies, modulating Levi's famous prose narratives such as *If This Is a
Man* and *The Drowned and the Saved*. Whereas Wilfred Owen critiques
his own testimony within poems such as 'Insensibility' and 'Apologia pro
Poemate Meo', Levi juxtaposes his prose with the scathing rhetoric, and
demand for hyper-attentiveness, in texts such as 'Shemà'. In addition, these
metatestimonies often testify to the author's post-war experience, shedding
new critical perspectives on the 'grey zone' and Levi's ambivalent response
to the figure of the Musulmann, whom Jean Améry describes as a camp
inmate who was 'a staggering corpse, a bundle of physical functions in its
last convulsions'.[2] In *Remnants of Auschwitz* Giorgio Agamben discusses
the figure of the Musulmann as an aporia in Levi's prose testimony, but in
this chapter I argue that attention to the poetry reveals that Levi sometimes
figures *himself* as a Musulmann in both the poems and neglected sections
of *If This Is a Man*.

'BUNA' AND THE MUSULMÄNNER

The poem 'Buna' begins as testimony by recounting the experiences of
chemical kommando 98. Levi describes an '[e]mpty companion' in a strikingly similar way to the Null Achtzehn character in *If This Is a Man*, who
is similarly 'empty inside' and 'indifferent': hence in the following section
I read 'Buna' as an attempt to engage the 'other' of a musulmann.[3] Ending
with self-reflection on a troublesome aspect of the testimony, the narrator

ponders his abandonment of a musulmann who retrospectively becomes a 'sad friend'.[4] As with 'Shemà' and 'The Survivor' (as I illustrate later in this chapter), 'Buna' also functions as metatestimony in relation to Levi's prose texts: this poem comments as an intertext on the 'factory report' of *If This Is a Man*.[5] Whereas Levi's first prose work is content to explain the nature of the musulmann (ambiguously, as I go on to demonstrate), 'Buna' betrays the guilt and shame that the narrator suffers from in his prosopopoeiac address to a former, 'empty companion' (p. 5). This was this first poem that Levi wrote after his epic return from Auschwitz: it was completed on 28 December 1945, just a few weeks before the fourteen-page draft of the first section of *If This Is a Man* was completed in February 1946.[6] 'Buna' is evidence of what Ian Thomson terms his growing sense of shame, guilt, and 'survivor's sickness' (p. 223)—Levi calls it a post-war 'phase of anguish' in *The Drowned and the Saved*—the symptoms of which would be down-played in the realist prose, rather than the self-reflexive contemplation in the testimonial poems.[7] 'Buna' is an early, tentative exploration of survivor trauma in poetic testimony: it seems to be a traditional, elegiac address to a lost companion until the final line, where implicit guilt is registered in the question, 'With what kind of face would we confront each other?', if they saw each other again in the world denied to the inmate, who, like Alberto in *If This Is a Man* (p. 161), cannot return to tell his story.

The poem starts with a testimonial account of the chemical plant's clayey ground familiar to readers of *If This Is a Man*, where Levi writes of 'the greedy mud [. . .] this omni-present Polish mud whose monotonous horror fills our days' (p. 73). Just as 'Shemà' reads like the original version of a paragraph in *If This Is a Man* (p. 33), the positivistic details in 'Buna' are similar to another section: the plant is the 'negation of beauty [. . .] not a blade of grass grows, and the soil is impregnated with the poisonous saps of coal and petroleum, and the only things alive are machines and slaves—and the former are more alive than the latter' (p. 78). The 'monoto-nous horror', and robotic slaves, in these two quotations can be sourced in the first four lines of 'Buna', where the dehumanization of the prison-ers is registered in synecdoches of suffering. Repetitive labour—a 'day like every other day'—is refigured from the last poem Levi wrote before 'Buna' (nearly three years earlier) about factory life: 'Crescenzago', the first piece in the *Collected Poems*, has a sewing girl who 'never stops looking at the clock' (p. 3); men keep '[t]he grim black stonecrusher panting' (p. 4). As Jay Losey has pointed out, the 'multitudes with dead faces', the 'monotonous horror of the mud', and the 'day of suffering' also come from canto 7 of the *Inferno*, where the damned souls exclaim, 'Sluggish we were | in the sweet air made happy by the sun' (II. 121–24).[8] (Levi transfers the 'sweet air' to the 'sweet' world at the end of the poem.) The influence of T. S. Eliot also hovers behind the first eight lines (which effectively form a separate octet, as they do in the original Italian version): the 'multitudes with dead faces' also recall the hordes of workers pouring over London bridge in *The*

Waste Land; the narrator famously laments that 'I never thought death had undone so many'.[9] As in 'The Survivor' and 'Shemà', classic literature ('The Rime of the Ancient Mariner' and the Bible, respectively, in these cases) already mediates Levi's experience in the camp before its literary transformations in the poetry and prose.[10] Rather than lamenting the literary distortions of testimony, the poetry emphasizes that for Levi, many Holocaust experiences are inextricably bound up with the work of his favoured writers. Even in the first eight lines of 'Buna', poetry as testimony does not just recall positivistic details; rather, it indicates their mediation though other, sometimes literary, contexts.

After the synecdoches of dehumanization in the first few lines—images uncomfortably close to a perpetrator perspective at times—Levi shifts to an apostrophic address to a musulmann: the fraught nature of this encounter highlights that the figure is much more ambiguous in *If This Is a Man* than has previously been suggested. In 'Buna', the various ways in which the narrator addresses and describes the inmate illustrate the difficulties Levi experiences in writing about the musulmann—it is not even clear whether the poem is just about one person—and the slipperiness of the term itself: the 'tired companion', sad friend, '[c]olourless one', '[e]mpty companion', and '[f]orsaken man' is depicted as cold, hungry, empty, broken, loveless, nameless, unemotional, too poor to grieve, too tired to fear, and then, in a final, tautological, one-line sentence, a '[s]pent once-strong man'. The list of adjectives begin to appear as implicit self-accusation: this is clearer in the original Italian version, where the half rhymes begin to cluster at the end of the lines (*'più nome* [. . .] *più pianto* [. . .] *più male* [. . .] *più spavento'*).[11] 'Man', the final word of the isolated sentence in the English translation, hints that this musulmann, not the author, is the signified referent of 'This' in *If This Is a Man*. And the question behind the title of Levi's most famous book indicates the difficulty—that Agamben has dwelt on at length—of testifying about someone who by definition does not have control of their own story. Whereas Agamben focusses on the 'essential lacuna' of the musulmann's experience in survivors' testimony, however, the various approaches to the figure in 'Buna' indicate that *Musulmänner* are paradoxically both beyond representation and only encountered *in* representation.[12]

In *Remnants of Auschwitz*, Agamben argues that the witness chooses not to dwell on the musulmann if possible, yet Levi ruminates at length on one such particular figure in *If This Is a Man*. The musulmann Null Achtzehn gives the impression of being an empty shell—like (as quoted in the introduction) the 'slough of certain insects which one finds on the banks of the swamps' (p. 48)—and has a '*face*' with no thoughts written on it (p. 96; my italics), but Levi is aware that he can only assume (poetically, in the case of the simile) that he is providing truthful vicarious testimony for the forlorn inmate. Null Achtzehn is 'no longer a man' (p. 48) in the prose text, whereas in 'Buna' the narrator chooses to readdress the musulmann as a friend, companion, and 'once-strong man'. 'Man' is ambiguous in the sentence: it could mean the musulmann is still a man or that he used to be a man. This connects with the irony of *Mann* in 'musulmann' itself, since, according to Levi's logic in *If This Is a Man*, the *Musulmänner* cannot be men, since a man is defined (via Dante) as someone who can think with intelligence (p. 89).[13] Ethical uncertainty is endemic in the testimony, however, since all the 'personages in these pages are not men' (p. 127), but then three sentences later Lorenzo 'is a man' (p. 128). At times such judgements in *If This Is a Man* verge uncomfortably on a perpetrator perspective, particularly when the narrator becomes an older inmate who looks with derision on new arrivals, such as the Hungarian in the 'Kraus' chapter (p. 140). The ambiguities of the grey zone are also enacted in relation to Null Achtzehn, whom the inmates name—following a Nazi system—with the last three figures of his entry number (p. 48). As Levi notes in relation to this character, the term 'Musulmann' itself 'was used *by the old ones of the camp* to describe the weak, the inept, those doomed to selection' (p. 94; my italics).

Levi does not know where the phrase comes from. It was mainly used in Auschwitz-Birkenau: Wolfgang Sofsky notes that 'Kretiner' instead was deployed for emaciated inmates in Dachau, 'cripples' in Stutthof, 'swimmers' in Mauthausen, 'camels' in Neuengamme, and 'tired sheiks' in Buchenwald; Joram Warmund notes that they were 'goldstück' in Ravensbrück and 'gamel' in Majdaneck.[14] In *The Black Hole of Auschwitz*, Levi himself notes the use of 'Schmizstück' ('pieces of filth') for women at Ravensbrück.[15] Whatever its origin or synonyms, 'musulmann' was probably coined by the Nazis or 'the old ones of the camp'. The term necessarily betrays a derogatory perspective, as when François Wetterwald—a medical doctor deported to Mauthausen where he worked as a surgeon—addresses a musulmann thus in 'Poème Macabre': 'You walk aimlessly, hobbling, ridiculous [. . .] Hey, are you smiling? | Hey, are you dead?'[16] In *If This Is a Man*, 'if some Null Achtzehn vacillates, he will find no one to extend a helping hand', whereas 'Buna' testifies to Levi's remorse by imagining a contrary, literary space where the liminal status of the musulmann will not be mocked—as in the Wetterwald poem—and he can be addressed as a 'friend'. (In the original Italian, he is not an '*amico*', but only a '*compagno*', 'companion', as Null Achtzehn is when first introduced in *If This Is a Man* (p. 48): the translators' choice of word—as I shall demonstrate in relation to 'Shemà'—is crucial to the changed meaning of the poem.) The prose explores the reasons why a musulmann will be knocked aside, 'because it is in no one's interest that there will be one more "musselman" dragging himself to work', whereas poetry as testimony engages here with the guilt of the 'accustomed' inmate who can then reimagine a fraught re-encounter. This generic difference recalls Robert Antelme's argument in the introduction that prose testimony comprises 'the [factual] photograph which only makes you shudder', as opposed to the poetry of the camps, which comprises a 'poetry of truth' which is 'not merely discernable in the details of horror'.[17] The 'poetry of truth' in this poem encompasses an admitted complicity in an instance of the failure of homosociality in the camps.

The slipperiness and ambiguity of address in 'Buna' and *If This Is a Man* is mirrored in the spelling of the term 'musulmann' itself, which differs (musselmann/*Muselmann*) on a single page of the prose testimony in relation to Null Achtzehn (p. 94). It is also enacted in the possibility that the poem is a form of self-address, as at the end of Owen's 'Apologia pro Poemate Meo'. Poetry as testimony functions here through subtle ambiguity: the abstract 'I' and 'you' of the poem cannot be definitively separated. Little has been made of the fact that Levi himself is described as a musulmann on at least two occasions in *If This Is a Man*: when Alex calls him *'Was für ein Muselmann Zugang'*, which the author misleadingly translates as 'What a messy recruit!' (p. 110), and when he enters the hospital, Ka-Be (a nurse refers to him as 'ready for crematorium' [*sic*]) (p. 55). Perhaps the two instances are misleading, since some of the inmates use the concept of the musulmann as a survival strategy, marking out those who are doomed in order to perpetuate a potential illusion of personal survival, as when they reassure each other before the selections that they will not be chosen. Yet at the end of *Remnants of Auschwitz*, one of the former *Muselmänner* states that only other inmates or guards, rather than the subject him/herself, can recognize the musulmann:

> *I too was a* Muselmann, *from 1942 to the beginning of 1943. I wasn't conscious of being one. I think that many* Muselmänner *didn't realize they belonged to that category. But when the inmates were divided up, I was put in the group of* Muselmänner. *In many cases, whether or not an inmate was considered a* Muselmann *depended on his appearance.* (Jerzy Mostowsky)[18]

Mostowsky's testimony is resonant in the context of Levi's: in *If This Is a Man*, the two references to Levi as a musulmann appertain to comments from others on '*his appearance*'. Hence, when Levi asks how he would react to the other's face in a world outside the camp, the poem enacts a conventional form of prosopopoeia where the poet addresses—ostensibly through an 'other'—a former, lost self (as Tony Harrison does, for example, in the long poem *V*).[19]

The inextricability of the Levi-figure from the concept of the musulmann in the poem and prose testimony is also indicated in the ambiguity in *If This Is a Man* about who has reached 'the bottom'. The *Muselmänner* in Levi's first book have followed the metaphorical slope of the camp 'down to the bottom, like streams that run down to the sea' (p. 96), but after their initial shower the new inmates have also 'reached the bottom', where no human condition 'is more miserable [. . .] nor could it conceivably be so' (p. 32); on page 42 Levi is still 'on the bottom', and even in 'The Drowned and the Saved' chapter on Null Achtzehn he is still 'crushed against the bottom' (p. 93). In contrast, by the time of *The Drowned and the Saved*, Levi—and others who wrote about the camps—'never fathomed them to the bottom', unlike those who did not return (p. 6). However, even in Levi's last book, the former *Muselmänner* are also potential survivors, who cannot write the history of the camps because 'their capacity for observation was paralysed by suffering and incomprehension' (p. 6).

If the two instances in *If This Is a Man* when Levi is referred to as a musulmann are taken seriously, then Levi returns in 'Buna' as a former musulmann to testify about his former, emaciated condition; equally, the poem could be testifying to the survivor's guilt about an abandoned companion. The generic possibility of multiple—and co-existing—meanings in 'Buna' points to one of poetry's strengths as a form of testimony. Rather than function as Antelme's derided photograph which just makes the reader shudder, it can testify in two different ways at once, as both the testimony of a musulmann and testimony to the guilt about the absence of that testimony.

'SHEMÀ' AND HYPER-ATTENTIVENESS

Like 'Buna', 'Shemà' is poetic testimony in its own right: Levi invites the reader in stanza two to consider the description of a typical man and woman in Auschwitz. 'Shemà' also functions as metatestimony in relation to Levi's prose texts, more explicitly than 'Buna', since it was selected as an epigraph for *If This Is a Man*. This decision indicates that Levi was worried about the reception of the 'objective' prose testimony. His uncertainty about a potential readership is reflected in another instance of the ambiguity of address in the poetry (as in Owen's poems), since the '[y]ou who live secure' in the first line (p. 9) could refer to perpetrators, bystanders, civilian survivors, or future readers.[20] Rather than relying on an assumed, uncomplicated identification between the poet and reader, as in, for example, a poem which begins, 'The curfew tolls the knell of passing day', the first word of 'Shemà' ('you') accuses the reader of something before the testimony's narrative begins.[21] Levi was perhaps concerned that the prose testimony would be all *too* understandable: Antelme's criticism of prose as merely a photograph of horror appertains in the sense that images of atrocity might glide by in the reader's imagination without any pause for self-reflection or self-criticism. The fact that the poetic testimony is encountered before the main text also suggests that Levi was worried about a prurient response to the 'photograph which only makes you shudder'. In her essay on consuming trauma, Patricia Yaeger calls for a 'nervous' and 'stuttering' cultural criticism that 'refuses complacency and seeks the "jarring juxtaposition" of "places spattered with blood," with the heat of imperfect words'.[22] Levi's plea for hyper-attentiveness insists on a considered, 'nervous', and

'stuttering' response to *If This Is a Man*, rather than capitulating unreflec-
tively to the pleasures of the imagination.

The metatestimony as epigraph also suggests that testimony demands, as
Robert Eaglestone suggests in *The Holocaust and the Postmodern*, a different kind of reception to other literary genres: the reader should be hyper-
attentive to the text both during, and after, the reading process. Exploiting
the genre of poetry to give free reign to a bitter, ironic tone that is (for the
most part) exorcised from the prose, Levi gives the reader the task of con-
templating 'these words'—both the poem as testimony and the entirety of
If This Is a Man—when the reader resides in their house, walks, goes to
bed, and wakes up. In an appeal to the conventional poetic synecdoche for
the imagination, Levi asks the reader to engrave the poetic testimony and
metatestimony onto their hearts. The point of Levi's deliberate over-state-
ment is that it confronts the dialectic of im/possible secondary witnessing
in relation to testimony. Readers cannot possibly fulfil Levi's edict: it is the
traumatized survivor, perhaps, who thinks about 'these words' constantly,
rather than the distracted secondary witness who can consume testimony
and then butter a bagel, fold up the paper, and put their thoughts away.[23]

Yet Levi's appeal to future readers also confronts problems of witnessing
and identification in poetry as testimony, and the impossible necessity of
what Delbo terms 'seeing' the events of the Holocaust.[24] One survivor in
Auschwitz and After desires to address only 'a like' (p. 263), someone who
has witnessed atrocity at firsthand, whereas both Delbo and Levi's testimonies as a whole engage with the difficulties of making a non-survivor
'see' the events. Delbo laments the impossibility of a non-inmate 'seeing'
the event; however, Levi writes in *The Drowned and the Saved* about the
necessity of simplification through testimony as a possible route to understanding (p. 32). On the one hand, Delbo is right that 'seeing' is an impossibility: the secondary witness will always imagine signified referents, rather
than recall real referents, of any testimonial discourse. On the other hand,
the best that can be hoped for is an approximation, in which the reader,
rather than ignoring or misunderstanding the testimony—possibilities
which this poem as metatestimony directly addresses—begins to engage
with the other's suffering, rather than elide it with misapproximations of
his or her own experience.

In Kings and Deuteronomy, testimony is bound up with the word of
God; here, the Ten Commandments are replaced with the metatestimony
engraved in the readers' hearts and imaginations instead of in stone. Critics
have often noted that the poetic testimony's bitter overstatement is derived
from Deuteronomy. However, what is often overlooked is the subversion
of specific details from the morning prayer, and the conventional form of
the psalm. The psalms of lament usually begin with 'a cry of help to the
Lord', followed by a description of the distress of the psalmist, but with
a 'motif of trust [becoming] the heart of the prayer'.[25] Psalms which are
hymns, or songs of praise, begin 'on a joyful note in which the psalmist

summons [the] self or a community to praise the Lord' for reasons such as 'God's creative activity and saving intervention in Israel's history' (p. 627). Instead, in 'Shemà' (which was first called 'Psalm'), the 'description of distress' becomes the details of suffering, in which the Lord refused to intervene; the initial 'joyful note' turns into a criticism of an entire community of secondary witnesses.

Levi's subversion of the passages from Deuteronomy is even more conspicuously irreverent. This poem comprises a bitterly ironic parody, in which the Holocaust replaces God as the site of intense contemplation. The morning prayer demands *kavanat ha lev*, devotion from the heart, but in Levi's poem this concentration and single-mindedness is directed specifically towards testimony and metatestimony, rather than religious devotion. Demands in Deuteronomy (6:4–9 and 11:13–21) to 'love the Lord your God with all your heart', insert the words of the prayer 'in your heart', and serve God 'with all your heart' are replaced with the appeal to the readers to engrave testimony instead onto their 'hearts'. 'Shemà' becomes a metaphorical phylactery: the small leather box worn by men at morning prayer, containing Hebrew texts on vellum, signifies the poetic testimony that should, Levi intimates, be as all pervasive as the frontlets between the worshippers' eyes in Deuteronomy, and the sacred words (6:9) written on the doorposts and gates of the houses. The heart returns in Deuteronomy as a site of human weakness: if the worshippers' hearts are deceived (11:13–21), and they turn to other gods, then the Lord will 'blaze against you [. . .] close the heavens, and there will not be rain, and the earth will not give you its fullness, and you will perish quickly'. For Levi, turning to false gods is the equivalent of not paying enough attention to testimony. If the reader does not comply with the impossibility of thinking about 'Shemà' constantly, then an Old Testament–style curse awaits of destruction, disease, and ignorant offspring.

Levi famously stated that the existence of Auschwitz proved that there could be no God: the poem bitterly underwrites such sentiment, with its blasphemous erasure of sacred text with secular testimony.[26] In Deuteronomy, the narrator commands 'these words' to the listener (6:5), and promises succour for those who 'surely listen to the commandments that I command you today' (11:13). This diction is echoed in the Italian version of 'Shemà' in the line '*Vi comando queste parole*', which Feldman and Swann translate as: 'I commend these words to you'. As in 'Buna', the translation of a single word (*amico*, in that case) has the ability to change the entire meaning of a poem. *Comando* originates from *comandare*, 'to order, to give orders, to command', whereas 'to commend' in Italian is *commendare*. Feldman and Swann retain the switch from 'command' to 'commend' in the 1976 collection *Shema: Collected Poems of Primo Levi*, published by the Menard Press, and the Faber *Collected Poems*.[27] Critics often appear to misread the translation's 'commend' as 'command'. Thomson and Agamben, for example, quote the line 'I command these words to you'.[28] (They may, of course, be retranslating from the original Italian.) The two words have completely different resonances: 'to commend' means to entrust rather than to demand that someone do something (*OED*, 2nd edn). Rather than picking up directly on the resonances from Deuteronomy, 'commend' softens the Old Testament–style didacticism in favour of a bitterly ironic line which fits perfectly with the overall tone of the poem. To paraphrase, it ironically suggests that the reader might find some worth in the testimony if he or she chooses (rather than is forced) to be attentive.

Critics have often commented that Levi's poetry gives full reign to a subjective bitterness absent from the 'objective' prose testimony: this distinction is evidenced in the rewriting of 'Shemà' in *If This Is a Man*; the metatestimony's recriminations give way to a passage which contains a calm appeal to the reader to '[i]magine now a man [. . .] whose life or death can be lightly decided' (p. 33), echoing the man who dies 'at a yes or a no' in the poem. However, this opposition does not entirely hold true. The irony in the English translation of 'Shemà' connects with similar instances in *If This Is a Man* reminiscent of Tadeusz Borowski's work (which I discussed in Chapter 2), such as when Levi refers to the camp as 'the bosom of the Germanic social organism' (p. 89). Thomson argues that this ironic bitterness was symptomatic of Levi's writing when he returned from Auschwitz: there were days 'when his anger and hatred of what had been done to him exploded into unintelligible jottings' (p. 235). 'Shemà' is an example of an early text where Levi retains the 'anger and hatred' but channels it into a chillingly controlled, ironic declaration such as (according to the English translation), 'I commend these words to you'. Thomson goes on to state that such poems were originally not intended for publication; that they were part of a 'private ritual cleansing [. . .] the rage had first to be excised in poetry. Far from being an afterthought to the [. . .] prose to come, the verse was a vital part of the book' (p. 226). In the case of 'Shemà', it literally became part of the book, not as an exorcising warm-up, but as a form of metatestimony which warns the reader that if they choose to avert their faces from the subsequent text, then their offspring will in turn 'avert their faces from you'.[29]

'THE SURVIVOR' IN THE GREY ZONE

The narrator rails against uncomprehending secondary witnesses at the end of Owen's 'Apologia pro Poemate Meo' and Levi's 'Shemà', whereas 'The Survivor' directs all accusations against those who directly witnessed the events of the Holocaust. Like 'Buna', it functions as testimony partly by engaging with the metatext, and recalling positivistic details in the first eight lines, which (as in 'Buna') effectively form a separate octet. The next seven lines operate simultaneously as testimony and metatestimony, commenting self-consciously on the opening of the poem, but also testifying to the post-Holocaust guilt suffered by the generalized survivor(s) in the title. As I illustrated in the introduction, testimony does not end in 1945: once the genre is prised away from its historical and juridical contexts, it can be seen that the facts it describes are only one reason for its existence. In 'The Survivor', this post-war life includes wrestling with the ethical ambiguities of the grey zone.

Like 'Shemà' in relation to *If This Is a Man*, 'The Survivor' functions partly as metatestimony for Levi's prose work, in this instance, in relation to (the understudied) *Moments of Reprieve*. Whereas 'Shemà' as epigraph is enmeshed in the subsequent details of *If This Is a Man*, however, 'The Survivor' appears, at first, not to be the most suitable entry point for some of the 'stories' in *Moments of Reprieve* (p. 10). The latter is, in Levi's words, not about 'the anonymous, faceless, voiceless mass of the shipwrecked, but the few, the different, the ones in whom (if only for a moment) I had recognized the will and capacity to react, and hence a rudiment of virtue' (p. 10). 'The Survivor', with its concerns with guilt, shame, the grey zone, and 'the shipwrecked', would seem to have been a much more suitable epigraph for *The Drowned and the Saved*, which only retains the epigraph from Coleridge's 'The Rime of the Ancient Mariner', rather than the entire Levi poem. Suitability is not the only criteria for the deployment of an epigraph, however: 'The Survivor' works as a counterpoint to the prose about 'the different' inmates in *Moments of Reprieve*, reminding the reader that this poetic testimony engages with the different, 'anonymous [. . .] mass' surrounding the stories about the fitter inmates, such as the German political prisoner who strikes Levi when he finds him writing a letter home, but who then goes away to find him some more paper.

Metatestimony is immediately important to 'The Survivor' in a different way to 'Shemà' in that it forms an epigraph (with the Coleridge quotation) within the poem as epigraph (in the context of *Moments of Reprieve*). Levi instigates a post-Holocaust reading of 'The Rime of the Ancient Mariner' in a similar way to Geoffrey Hill's rereading of Keats and Hardy in 'September Song', where 'the decaying resplendence described by Keats [in 'To Autumn'] [. . .] is refurbished as a disturbing Holocaust metaphor', and Hardy's 'metonymic rose' in 'During Wind and Rain' is transformed 'into a terrible metaphor for the flaking skin of burnt victims'.[30] Levi reinterprets the mariner's constant 'agony' as a sign for recounting traumatic Holocaust experiences, and his seeking of an audience akin to Levi's demand for hyper-attentiveness in 'Shemà'. Urges to testify about trauma can, as in the Coleridge poem, happen *ad ora incerta*, at any time, a phrase which is repeated throughout Levi's work (and forms the title of one of his poetry collections). Hence the recounting of trauma forms a 'ceaseless struggle', as Cathy Caruth suggests, for both Levi and Coleridge's narrator. In the preface to *Moments of Reprieve*, Levi writes that the 'memory of the offence persists, as though carved in stone' (p. 10): this statement links with the function of the epigraph as metatestimony, since the poetic term also refers

to '[a]n inscription on a statue, stone or building'.[31] The fact that Levi is telling the 'ghastly tale' again in the 1984 poem, nearly forty years after writing *If This Is a Man*, emphasizes Coleridge's intimation that the mariner's
story will never be fully told. Nor will Levi's: thus *Moments of Reprieve*
fills in some of the narrative gaps in *If This Is a Man* as Levi remembers
extra details, and uncensors others; whereas the original testimony avoids
descriptions of violence—partly due to a fear of prurient responses—the
later work includes a passage where the character Elias nearly chokes Levi
to death. The 'struggles' of the mariner and Levi intertwine throughout
the poem: the repetition of 'mist' connects with the mist elsewhere in 'The
Rime of the Ancient Mariner', which represents the moment of artistic creation. (This inextricability is emphasized in the Italian original, in which—
unlike in the English translation—the Coleridge epigraph becomes part of
the main text.) For Levi, there exists a paradox in 'The Survivor' that the
'shipwrecked' might be turning into the aesthetic fodder of vicarious testimony, at the same time that—like the *Musulmänner* in 'Buna'—they can
only exist in his representation, in his 'mist'.

When Levi insists that the 'anonymous, faceless, voiceless mass' '[g]o
back into [their] mist' (which can only really be the writer's 'mist'), he concludes the testimony's engagement with the grey zone and the 'tainted luck'
of survival.[32] First discussed briefly in *If This Is a Man* (p. 43), the concept
describes a zone of ethical uncertainty that Terry Eagleton inadvertently
trivializes when he refers to the meaning of life as 'taking another's place
in the queue for the gas chambers'.[33] Feldman and Swann date the poem's
composition as 4 February 1984, when Levi was once again dwelling on
the potential culpability of complicity of various groups of inmates, but
in a more nuanced way than Borowski's claim that all those who survived
'bought places in the hospital, easy posts [. . .] shoved "Moslems" [. . .]
into the oven [. . .] [unloaded] the transports'.[34] Levi and Borowski were
both critical of survivors who pronounced about their virtue and 'chosen'
status: in conversation with Ferdinando Camon, the Italian writer rails
against someone who 'came to see me after my release to tell me I was
clearly one of the elect, since I'd been chosen to survive in order for me to
write *Survival in Auschwitz*' (p. 68). The dedication in 'The Survivor', 'to
B. V.', is also a thinly disguised criticism of Bruno Vasari's sense—in his
chronicle of his survival in Mauthausen, *Bivouac of Death*—that the 'ex-
deportees had survived the Nazi camps not by cunning or brutality but by
force of their virtue'.[35]

'The Survivor' thus comprises a brief testimonial account intimately
linked to the extended philosophy of the grey zone and 'Shame' chapters
in *The Drowned and the Saved*. The poem is a crystallization of their concerns, but focussing on Levi's own ambiguous status in relation to ethical uncertainty. In *The Drowned and the Saved*, Levi implores the reader
to suspend judgment on the *Sonderkommando*, the 'crematorium ravens'
(p. 43). 'The Survivor' redirects such ethical uncertainty at Levi and other

inmates in the Lager who were denied moral choices outside the camp, even if not in the extreme situation of the Special Squads. In *The Drowned and the Saved* he mentions that he did not steal anyone's bread (the sentence is repeated almost verbatim in the poem), yet the idea that someone else might have died in his place 'gnaws and rasps' (p. 62): this worry is repeated three times on the same page and becomes the central concern of the poem. The repetition of '[n]o one' (four times in the Italian original and twice in the English translation) betrays Levi's 'gnawing' worry that someone did indeed die in his place. Poetic testimony becomes here a paradoxical form of admitted denial and also a screening out of traumatic details already recounted in *If This Is a Man*: Levi claims at one point that he was mistakenly not selected (Alberto agrees) at someone else's expense. The outcome of another's death in this context is clearly not a sign of culpability in the sense of a moral choice, but it still results, for Levi, in 'guilt [. . .] unjustified [. . .] but I can't clear it from my conscience'.[36]

So far, my discussion of this testimony of guilt in 'The Survivor' has indicated that there are two distinct parties in the poem's addressivity: the accused, general survivor in the title (including Levi himself) and the 'shipwrecked'. However, this testimony as prosopopoeia—in which the silent 'anonymous [. . .] mass' cannot reply to the apostrophe in the last seven lines—demonstrates Cathy Caruth's 'impossibility of a story', never mind a 'comprehensible' story, from the companions in the poem, the *Musulmänner* in 'Buna' or Alberto in *If This Is a Man*. Unlike in most prose testimonies, the complexity of language in this poetic testimony begins to undo the apparent distinctions between the survivor and the 'submerged'. Linguistic intricacies function here similarly to the visual ambiguities in Alain Resnais's film *Night and Fog*: Emma Wilson argues that the director's 'wariness of images' leads to 'category disturbances'.[37] In the poem, it is often difficult to discern whether Levi (or the survivor figure), or the 'shipwrecked' are described, addressed, or speaking. It is unclear—until the reader reaches 'their' in line five—whether the author-persona or the companions are livid, grey, and nebulous. Even after the pronoun is revealed, lines two to four could still be parenthetical clauses appertaining to the narrator, before the inmates are uncovered as '[t]inged with death' in line five. The adjectives in the first few lines are also curiously ambiguous: 'livid' can mean both bright and dark (as it does in the opening to Hill's poem *The Triumph of Love*), as can 'nebulous'. (This ambiguity does not work in relation to 'nebulous' in the original Italian, where *Indistinti* means specifically faint or vague, as opposed to *nebuloso*.[38]) Such ambiguities are mirrored in the indeterminable location of the companions' faces: the clauses—like the different descriptions of the *Musulmänner* in 'Buna'—could refer to different places. Again, even after the pronoun, the ambiguous syntax makes it unclear whether the inmates are depicted dreaming or whether the narrator is burdened with their dreams. As in 'Buna', the ambiguities emphasize the difficulty, for Levi, of the guilty apostrophe. To put it bluntly, Levi is admitting that he does not know who he is talking about; 'The Survivor' enacts Agamben's concern that it is impossible to provide truthful vicarious witnessing on behalf of the 'shipwrecked', at the same time as the poem engages with the impossible necessity of trying to do so.

The abrupt switch to dialogue in line nine is also discomforting in this context: the presumption must be that this is Levi or the survivor-figure speaking, but the diction could also constitute the imagined speech of the prosopopoeiac sleepers, as they reflect on their *own* guilt as current survivors in the camp. The verbs in the final two lines can support this reading: the depiction of someone living but not surviving could appertain (paradoxically, given the title) to the narrator, but they could also refer to the pared-down existence of the inmates who merely '[e]at, drink, sleep and put on clothes'. The 'category disturbance' of the linguistic ambiguities indicates both the difficulty of representation for Levi in testifying about his companions (who—anonymous in the poem—may, or may not, have survived) and the moral slippages between the witness and the 'shipwrecked'. The testimonial poem may have been written, as the dedication suggests, against Vasari's concept of the inherently virtuous survivor, but it also warns against an opposition between the grey zone inhabited by the witness and the supposed moral virtuousness of those who died.

These ambiguities surrounding the narrator and meanings of 'The Survivor' are similarly encountered in the Levi poem 'Sunset at Fossoli'. The narrator appears to be Levi, who, close to the second anniversary of the deportations from Fossoli (21 February 1944), remembers 'what it means not to return' (p. 15). However, Carole Angier suggests that the poem might be a dramatic monologue spoken by Vanda Maestro, who accompanied Levi to Auschwitz and subsequently died there.[39] The meanings of the first line above are also ambiguous. Reading via the metatext, 'not to return' means not to go back to Turin from Fossoli, but it could also mean that the narrator felt *at the time* that he would not return home, as when the inmates 'took leave of their life in the manner which most suited them' in *If This Is a Man* (p. 21). The sentence could also mean that the narrator empathizes with those who did not return, or that he senses, psychologically, that some part of him did not return from the camps.

Such ambiguity highlights poetry's strength as a form of testimony. This compression of language allows the writer to testify in various ways simultaneously, as in 'Buna', where the ambiguous diction means that the poem testifies to the poet witnessing both as a musulmann and to the *Musulmänner*. Rather than lamenting its mimetic shortcomings, the critic should be aware of the poetic possibilities of 'throttled' testimony. Susan Gubar uses the same example as Sue Vice in her contention that poetry can only seem 'to conflate poetry with testimony': Miklos Radnóti's 'Picture Postcards' are not 'factual testimony' or 'mimetic representations of testimonies', since 'Razglednica 3' calls attention to its own 'constructedness' as poetry.[40] The argument is seductively clear and simple: poetry cannot be testimony because it is not prose, and it does not enmesh itself in the facts of traumatic experience. However, as I have shown in the introduction and throughout this chapter, poetry and prose testimonies do much more than simply recount historical details. Elsewhere in the same essay, Gubar makes a compelling case for lyrical Holocaust poetry as 'stymied testimony', which is a critical step closer to arguing—as I have done here—that poems themselves can perform a testimonial function. After all, poetry is particularly adept at expressing 'the phenomenological chaos of actual "experience"', as Levi does when he supplements his prose testimony with poems about differing responses to traumatic events.[41]

6 *Voices* Magazine
Working-Class Testimony and 'Everyday Suffering'

Having analysed poetry as testimony in relation to World War I, World War II, and the Holocaust, in the penultimate chapter I turn to the different, but related, context of testimonial working-class poems. Felman and Laub emphasize that their book is looking 'not so much for answers as for new *enabling questions*' in research about testimony: hence I discuss in the following sections whether Lauren Berlant and Laura S. Brown's reworking of previous models of trauma and testimony in terms of everyday suffering can be applied to working-class writing.[1] I argue that working-class poetry about everyday suffering can be read alongside this book's discussion about Holocaust and war poetry as testimony. Such a critical discussion involves not an overlap of disparate cultural memories (as in Michael Rothberg's *Multidirectional Memory*), but an engagement with different models of suffering and trauma. The chapter focusses on how the working-class magazine *Voices* forms a case study of how everyday suffering manifests itself in relation to working-class testimony, drawing on the work of Lauren Berlant, Laura S. Brown, Pierre Bourdieu, and Iain Wilkinson, who all explore—in various ways—the possibility of 'everyday', 'ongoing', or 'ordinary' trauma. Whilst being sensitive to the dangers of transplanting critical debates uncritically between disciplines (a position that Rothberg is careful to maintain in relation to Holocaust and Post-Colonial Studies), I ask whether the discourse of Trauma Studies might usefully engage with representations of everyday suffering in working-class culture. I shall begin with a brief cultural history of *Voices*, since it provides the context for the ensuing discussion of testimony in relation to working-class experience.

Ben Ainley, a former NUT-activist and Communist, founded the magazine in 1972. Ainley joined the Party in 1921, and—as revealed in his unpublished autobiography held in the Working Class Movement Library in Salford—used to meet fellow Communists in Higher Broughton to talk about the post-war crisis, the Revolution, and poetry.[2] He subsequently took part in the Ramblers' Movement in the 1930s and went on to teach at Chorlton High School, where he became head of English.[3] *Voices* developed out of the classes that Ainley ran in Manchester on literature and Marxism (funded by the Communist Party) in 1971–72. In a sense, the origin of

Voices also goes back to Resolution 42 at the Trade Union Congress in September 1960.[4] This 'extraordinary' proposal called for a union inquiry into the state of the arts in the UK and led to influential art movements of the 1960s, such as Centre 42.[5] The Unity of Arts was created after Resolution 42 and was temporarily located in Back George Street in the centre of Manchester: this UK-wide organization was associated with *Voices* throughout the early production of the magazine, which ran until 1984.[6] A leaflet entitled 'Unity of Arts' in the Working Class Movement Library names Ainley as the president of the organization, and lists quotations from a number of supporters, including Jack Jones, the general secretary of the Transport and General Workers Union, and the poet Adrian Mitchell.[7] Ainley's stated aim for the society was to 'bring the Labour, Trade Union and Co-operative movement to the point where they use the rich wealth of art and craft, drama and song from their own ranks for their own inspiration in struggle and their own enjoyment'; a quotation from Resolution 42 resides at the bottom of the statement, which commits the trade union movement to consider how 'it could promote and encourage the participation of its members in all cultural activities' (p. 3).[8] *Voices* was sponsored throughout by a 'long list of left luminaries' listed on the back of this leaflet, and on the Unity of Arts official letterhead, including the playwright Arnold Wesker, the folk singers Ewan MacColl and Peggy Seeger, and Adrian Mitchell.

Printed at the Communist Party's premises in Manchester, in twelve years the magazine published prose, poetry, and reviews; in total, 'almost half a million words by over 300 writers'.[9] It was distributed through the Party's Progress Bookshop and Grassroots Bookshop in Piccadilly. *Voices* readings and workshops were central to the magazine's ethos, such as the one that took place at New Cross Labour Club in Ancoats in July 1975.[10] Chaotic editorial meetings—one contributor called the board 'a bunch of f—ing amateurs'—were held at various locations, including the Black Lion pub in Salford and a damp cellar in a house in Stretford.[11] In 1976, Ainley announced at an editorial gathering that the new editor of the magazine would be 'a certain left-wing university lecturer', who then failed to turn up to the meeting.[12] The Arts Council once commented that the magazine contained no famous literary talents whatsoever, but they clearly missed the early work of writers such as John Cooper Clarke and Jimmy McGovern, the BAFTA-award winning scriptwriter who went on to work on *Brookside* in the 1980s and created the TV-show *Cracker* in 1993.[13]

TESTIMONY AND 'EVERYDAY SUFFERING'

Shoshana Felman and Dori Laub argue that testimony arises when there is a crisis of truth and representation: their book focusses on the traumatic events of World War II, but the 'figure' of testimony can be detected in many other contexts, such as the working-class writing in *Voices*.[14] In

1846, Friedrich Engels recognized a crisis of representation in relation to the working class, and what we would now term secondary witnessing and oral testimony: lambasting the 'utter ignorance on the part of the whole middle class of everything which concerns the workers', he promised to gain testimonial knowledge of the latter by 'obser[ving] you in your every-day life, to chat with you on your condition and grievances'.[15] Over a century later, this ignorance was still prevalent when Ainley started *Voices*, despite the augmentation of working-class literature after the publication of Robert Tressell's testimonial, working-class novel *The Ragged Trousered Philanthropists* in 1914.[16] In 1999, Pierre Bourdieu still deployed an Engelian discourse in relation to 'ordinary suffering'—or what he calls *la petite misère*—in working-class districts in Paris: 'Those who govern', he chided, 'often know almost nothing about the everyday lives of their fellow citizens and have no occasion to be reminded of their ignorance'.[17] Yet when journalists and politicians talk about 'the problem suburb', such districts are 'largely unknown [. . .] to the people who rush' to discuss them (p. 123). As for Tressell's Edwardian housepainters, the main worry for the Parisians nearly a century later was the spectre of 'the former worker whom the drop in employment dumps into the subproletariat, without any protection', who becomes 'impoverished, disorganized, worried about surviving from day to day, caught up with unpaid rent and unpayable debts' (p. 10). Despite Bourdieu's intervention—which resulted in passionate debate in France—Iain Wilkinson stressed the absence of wider reflections on *la petite misère* in the field of sociology in general in 2005.[18]

'Unspoken' truths in working-class literature will obviously differ from the 'unspeakable' truths of the historical atrocities Felman and Laub focus on in their study. However, *Voices* is still a conduit for working-class testimony in that it provided 'an opportunity for older people especially to record their memories of places which are fast being annihilated by the bulldozer. Stories long forgotten have been unearthed by dictation to a modern-day scribe, or by tape recording, particularly where the speaker lacks the confidence or ability to write it down'.[19] In this sense, *Voices* collected 'non-professional' testimony in a comparable way to Victor Selwyn's efforts for the Salamander Oasis archive, on behalf of 'ordinary' servicemen and women. Fanny Morgan's testimony in *Voices* 3 about the Manchester blitz is an instance of Bourdieu's 'unspoken' testimony. After the 'first big [. . .] blitz' she found herself 'settling down in this 140 year old hovel about 8 miles south of Manchester lacking gas and electricity'; she records how 'the word would go around that the Co-op had had a delivery of biscuits or oranges or suet'.[20]

The recordings by the Federation recall Felman and Laub's focus on the oral history archives at Yale, but *Voices* also published testimony such as Fanny Morgan's in the sense of writing specifically about everyday suffering. Testimony in a general sense—recalling its judicial origins—refers to the attestation and documentation of experience (which may be about to be bulldozed), but Felman and Laub deploy the term more specifically to refer to inscriptions of trauma. Rather than testimony being interwoven only with the specificity of traumatic events, however, the genre can also be detected in accounts of everyday suffering. Reacting against what she sees as the recent proliferation of testimony in the United States, and the subsequent competition to see who amongst subalterns is the most subjugated, Lauren Berlant argues that the judicial context is overrated as a step towards the amelioration of suffering. She suggests in contrast that the 'suffering of subordinated subjects *is an ordinary and ongoing thing* that is underdescribed by the traumatic identity form'.[21] In the specific context of capitalism, Slavoj Žižek refers to 'the *systemic* violence' that allows others to live in comfort, and the everyday, 'objective violence' that determines social reality.[22] The irreparability of violence and the discourse of ineffability are associated with Holocaust testimony, but Berlant and Žižek wish to discuss more mundane—but still extremely important—instances of suffering, such as domestic conflict and the Lacanian Real of the violent, 'spectral logic of capital' that creates poverty as if it were a natural occurrence[23]. These situations, 'ever so common, cruel but not unusual [are] an ordinary part of everyday citizenship for subordinate populations'; hence, Berlant advises 'replacing the model of trauma [she has] been describing critically as inadequate [. . .] with a model, say, of *suffering*, whose etymological articulation of pain and patience draws its subject less as an effect of an act of violence, and more as an effect of a general atmosphere of it' (p. 43). As Carolyn J. Dean argues, the danger in focussing on the figure of the victim in terms of catastrophe is that this 'risks normalizing the now invisible everyday violence against specific groups of people, whether the social and psychic suffering generated by poverty or other forms of structural oppression'.[24]

Berlant's quotation finishes with an account of the 'general atmosphere' of violence between heterosexual couples. In this chapter I focus instead on how Berlant's model of everyday suffering might account for textual inscriptions of *la petite misère* in working-class poetry. Laura S. Brown draws on Maria Root's work on trauma to emphasize—similarly to Berlant—that '[t]he private, secret, insidious traumas to which a feminist analysis draws attention are more often than not those events in which the dominant culture and its forms and institutions are expressed and perpetuated'.[25] Extrapolating on a case study of a working-class patient who was also subject to the 'insidious violence' of domestic brutality, Brown points to the inadequacy of the definition of trauma in the 1987 *Diagnostic and Statistical Manual* as 'an event outside the range of human experience' (pp.107, 100). Hegemonic discourse can accept atrocity as an affront to middle-class, white dignity, she argues (which underplays the working-class origins of many soldiers), as opposed to the 'constant presence and threat of trauma in the lives of [. . .] people in poverty', which has 'shaped our society, a continuing background noise rather than an unusual event' (pp. 102–03). Indeed,

Brown's patient is forced to undertake a number of manual jobs which entail exposure to 'sharp edges, toxic and caustic chemicals, hot grease, wet slippery floors' (p. 105). Such groundbreaking work in Trauma Studies as Root's and Brown's resulted, by 1995, in an alteration to Criteria A for post-traumatic stress disorder in the *Diagnostic and Statistical Manual*, which 'will no longer require that an event be infrequent, unusual, or outside of a mythical human norm of experience' (p. 111).

'Everyday suffering' and 'insidious violence' need to be applied to working-class literature with care, however. Berlant discusses primarily domestic violence, and Brown refers to 'insidious violence' in relation to physical abuse as well as working-class conditions. Bourdieu's notion of 'everyday suffering' pertains to working-class housing and employment conditions, and, like Berlant's work, does not transfer unproblematically to, for example, the specific context of working-class labour. For Brown's patient—and for many writers in *Voices*—*la petite misère* does indeed describe everyday working conditions, but for other writers in the Manchester magazine, repeated labour is described in terms of nostalgia, human dignity, or Stalinist eulogy rather than suffering. In the case of Tressell's *The Ragged Trousered Philanthropists*, *misère* would not describe the complex labour of the artisan protagonist, Owen, who works on Moorish ornamentation, and yet Berlant's notion of trauma as a 'general atmosphere of suffering' aptly describes the novel, in which, for example, Joseph Philpot, one of the housepainters, is killed whilst working with a faulty ladder attachment (p. 509). The sentence 'Only two more hours, but to these miserable, half-starved [. . .] wretches, standing here in the bitter wind that pierced their clothing and seemed to be tearing at their very hearts and lungs with icy fingers, it appeared like an eternity' could have been written by Charlotte Delbo, but it comes from Tressell's description of working conditions at 'The Cave' (p. 254). Tressell's novel also explores 'insidious violence' in terms of the poverty of Owen's—and other characters'—families, as well as the 'atmosphere' of domestic violence (inseparable from destitution) in relation to the female character Ruth.

ARTHUR ADLAM'S 'ODE TO WINTER'

I now wish to explore the ramifications, and conceptual problems, of this discussion of 'everyday suffering' and testimony alongside the work of (briefly) Carolyn Steedman, and then the *Voices* writer Arthur Adlam. It is not surprising that there is no discourse of trauma and testimony in relation to Working-Class Studies given that Felman and Laub's book was published in 1992, at the same time as John Kirk argues that a 'common-sense' view began to insist in the UK on 'the death of class, and in particular the demise of the working class'.[26] Such a view permeated British academia, so opportunities in the UK have been slight to expand Felman and Laub's engagement with testimony into the context of working-class literature. Carolyn Steedman's *Landscape for a Good Woman*, published six years before *Testimony*, does move towards a self-conscious discourse of testimony to describe the author's mother's plight. Similarly to Felman and Laub, she makes a distinction between a positivistic notion of the past and literary reinscription: she describes her book as not 'a search for a past, or for what really happened', but about 'how people use the past to tell stories of their life'.[27] In her footnote to this statement, Steedman makes the testimonial distinction between historical fact and lived experience, as in the famous case—discussed by Dori Laub—of the Birkenau inmate who heard four chimneys being destroyed in the camp, when there could only have been one.[28] Yet the term 'testimony' itself is never used, since it only entered common critical vocabulary in Trauma Studies after Felman and Laub's groundbreaking work in the late 1980s and early 1990s. Nevertheless, Steedman's work and *Voices* provide important attestations to ordinary suffering and open out the possibility of rereading working-class memoirs and autobiography as examples of testimony.

Literary inscriptions of everyday suffering in the context of fraught labour in *Voices* include Arthur Adlam's poem 'Ode to Winter'. Adlam was a pipe-fitter from Skelmersdale who attended the Federation workshops at the Red Star Social Club in Liverpool.[29] The critic John Davidson argued that working-class poetry should not aspire—as Ainley preferred—to an Arnoldian 'sweetness and light', but should instead focus on everyday suffering in the form of 'the actual sight of the misery in which so many millions live'.[30] Ostensibly, this is the case in Adlam's poem, since he avoids Davidson's critique of poems ascribing to the 'beauty of the moors, and the studious cloisters', and reinscribes a building site where smokers drink tea to stop choking. However, 'Ode to Winter' does not belong in the protest tradition of working-class writing: like Tony Harrison's work, it attempts to solve the 'crisis of [working-class] representation' by subverting a traditional genre from within its confines. The celebratory genre alluded to in the title is undercut in the poem's subsequently ironic depiction of the smokers and 'the wicked season workers hate':

Winter has arrived on site and turned in early
to catch us, trapped behind the yawning gate.
The change of wind has set our faces surly
against the wicked season workers hate.
The felt's blown off the cabin roof, the window's broken,
no fire to warm our boots and fingers by.
A cup of tea to stop the smokers choking,
then out into the world below the sky.

I waded yesterday through mud, now frozen dark and
jagged waves, the ice belies the depth of hidden ponds,

and on the walls where rain has dripped and hardened
hang icicles like summer's thickest fronds.
Here are men who summer like Olympian Greek gods
fallen to earth, victims of some elemental curse;
so now they scrape the hoar-frost from the handles of their hods
and pray the weather doesn't get much worse.

Yet in the midst of sorrow, cold and freezing,
there is still beyond the colours of the season,
reflected something I can find so pleasing
to echo Nature's dialectic reason.
White lime on bricks against the grey of mortar,
the scaffold that has browned to deeper rust,
a block of wood green in a pool's iced water,
and working hands as red as robin's breast.

Tea-time's still no nearer, and I'm sinking
more into my mood, pensive on the beauty and the pain;
but some-one bellows louder than I'm thinking;
'C'mon yer scabby get, gerrout the rain.'

Adlam's poem 'Before the Rape' in *Voices* 17 may seem a more obviously testimonial piece in its allusion to a previous trauma, but the temporal scope of 'Ode to Winter' allows for an ironic ode to ordinary suffering in its contrast between workers on a building site who enjoy labouring like 'Olympian Greek gods' in the summer, but who suffer the everyday indignities of a felt-less roof, rain icicles, and frozen mud in inclement weather.[31] Luckily, Michael Rowe guest-edited *Voices* 19 rather than Gwilt, otherwise the poem may never have been published, given Gwilt's aversion to the supposedly bourgeois mythologies that Adlam manipulates. (Gwilt would have approved, however, of Adlam's use of a northern dialect work for useless individual, when the witness-poet becomes a mistreated 'get' in the rain.[32]) What the writer sees as the seasons' dialectical tension is mirrored in his dialectical attempt to celebrate the aesthetics of winter amongst general depravities. Imagistic images follow of such contrasts as the white lime of bricks against grey mortar, and (emphasized with a metrical break) a green block of wood in iced water. Such examples grate with a model of specific trauma which would stress the vexations of coming to terms with the 'unspoken' event, but provide one answer to the everyday difficulties of confronting a job where the worker feels 'trapped behind the yawning [site] gate'. As Jane Kilby has argued, representations of trauma can be 'light': here Adlam attempts to 'make light' of everyday suffering by stressing its aesthetic potential.[33] Of course, this logic can be turned on its head: as Theodor Adorno argued (rather histrionically), 'even the blossoming tree lies the moment its bloom is seen without the shadow of terror'.[34]

Yet for Adlam, the very possibility of testimony means making 'light' of his suffering through aesthetics, which begins with the breathless poetics of enjambment and elision in the first three lines of the second stanza. The imagistic moments in stanza three mirror the potentially redemptive initiation of the poem itself in a reminder of Arnoldian 'sweetness and light'. It is no accident that the aesthetic spell is broken as soon as a workmate intervenes and dispels the reflective testimony with the final line, 'C'mon yer scabby get, gerrout the rain'. The brief period of aesthetic reflection is also subtly indicated to be momentarily anti-capitalist: as Marx pointed out—quoting from a factory report in 1860—'Moments are the elements of profit'.[35] This pondering ultimately connects with the tenderness behind the dialect, since a fellow workman tells him to avoid the rain—and, by implication, working—in the final line.

This close reading of 'Ode to Winter' illustrates the possibility of providing testimony to everyday suffering, but such a methodological approach has an instrumentalist tendency to plunder complex 'gems' (such as Adlam's poem) from the many issues of *Voices* in order to support a specific thesis, at the expense of a wider appraisal of the magazine's cultural history, and other issues, such as literary-critical value. As I outlined in the introduction, in *The Singularity of Literature*, Derek Attridge outlines the dangers of instrumentalist approaches to literary texts: rather than relying on a 'pragmatic utilization' of texts to further (with critical blinkers) an existing project, he argues that the critic should come to the work ready to respond openly to its 'distinctive utterance'.[36] An instrumentalist approach to working-class testimony might occlude the poor quality of much of the writing. When I referred earlier to the dialectical tension between the seasons and aesthetic paradigms in Adlam's poem, it could be pointed out that there are aesthetic deficiencies, with clumsy full rhymes 'freezing | season | pleasing | reason', elisions, inversions, archaisms, and Hopkinesque alliteration ('hoar-frost from the handles of their hods'). Indeed, in 1980 the magazine as a whole failed in its bid to attract Arts Council funding due to Blake Morrison's controversial (and unpublished) report in which he lambasted the (instrumentalist) tendency of the editors to print 'bad poems' because they express '"good", i.e. politically acceptable, opinions: shallow and overt propagandising has been more common than work of literary merit'.[37] Morrison correctly points to the polemicist work that dominates *Voices* and echoes the opinion of some reviewers of the magazine. Jim Burns notes that 'too often their work tends to suffer from the assumption that kind thoughts make good poems'.[38] Plundering the poem 'Ode to Winter' from the creative morass has the effect of suppressing a debate about the (poor) quality of much of the poetic writing from the protest tradition, including *Voices*'s 'Hello You Walrus Faced Bastard', which begins, 'What crime did they commit | but stand up for their rights?'[39] However, to ignore the magazine entirely due to a judgement about aesthetics would be to occlude the process of testimonial poetics unfolding in the magazine.

Morrison's report still offers a methodological challenge to the study of testimony in general. It is no accident that Felman and Laub focus on the canonical testimonies of Celan, Camus, and Mallarmé, amongst others, whereas recently critics such as Margaret-Anne Hutton have moved beyond the canon to look at the testimonies of non-professional writers where issues of aesthetic competency are more fraught.[40] After the Federation complained to the Arts Council about rejected funding in 1990, the new director, Alastair Niven, wrote a letter back stating that the writing was 'less developed, less polished and technically achieved than in our well-known national writers. But it may, through that very lack of sophistication have something that is fresher and truer'.[41] Niven's missive is uncannily similar to Jacqueline Simms's appraisal of Victor West's poetry for Oxford University Press: although the World War II poet has '[w]eaknesses in much of the writing', she feels 'ungracious to say this when there is more vivid and lived experience in any one or two of your poems than in most people's whole books'. Future methodological challenges for the study of testimony are contained in the letters' (potentially patronizing) reference to something 'fresher and truer' in non-professional writing.

Niven's comment responds to the crisis of representation in working-class literature by arguing that it covers 'fresh' subjects unbeknownst to the middle-class reader. On the other hand, it risks the danger of turning the working-class writer into a kind of noble savage, who, as Gwilt put it in an editorial, can call a spade a spade rather than embellish it as a long-handled rod.[42] Yet the Arts Council letter also reminds us that whereas critics used to consider testimony to be an unaesthetic form of writing, we now, after the work of writers such as James Young, stress its literariness. Rather than just concentrate on canonical, testimonial aesthetics that, to echo Adorno, 'desecrate each other' in their attempts at aesthetic supremacy, might it also be possible to devise a critical vocabulary for non-professional testimony in its 'very lack of sophistication'?[43] The concept of awkward poetics that I have outlined elsewhere might begin to account for such writing.[44] In Adlam's poem, the awkwardness of elisions, archaisms, and grammar are evident, but these allow the singularity of lines such as 'I waded yesterday through mud, now frozen dark and | jagged waves, the ice belies the depth of hidden ponds' to resonate in contrast to—and in tandem with—the aesthetic deficiencies. Singularity can be difficult to separate from metatextual concerns, such as the death of Wordsworth's daughter that lies behind the 'emotional force' that Attridge detects in the opening lines of 'Surprised by Joy'.[45] In 'Ode to Winter', the 'emotional force' of singular lines are inextricable from working-class labour, but also the metatextual concerns of *Voices*, which allow for the testimonial poetics of working-class writers such as Adlam.

Creative writing workshops in university and community environments are often regarded as only a relatively recent phenomenon in the UK (as opposed to their longevity in the United States). It is worth remembering that *Voices* and the Federation workshops were providing creative outlets for working-class experience thirty years before the rise of 'community-engaged' projects currently issuing from British universities. With testimony to *la petite misère* and 'insidious violence' of diurnal labour and poor living conditions—amongst a variety of working-class experiences—the magazine illustrates how testimonial poems can flourish outside of the 'overtly violent [and] threatening' contexts of the poetry discussed in the other chapters in this book.[46] Texts such as Adlam's are less concerned with dialectics of in/articulacy and problems of witnessing than the work of Owen, Levi, Delbo, and Borowski, but they share a focus on the representational possibilities of poetry as testimony, a form of writing that always seeks to redress violence in the form of singular events or insidious and continuing suffering.

7 A 'Map of Trauma Whose Borders Are Still Missing'
Poetry and 9/11

The paradox that aspects of witnessing cannot be articulated—at the same time as the supposedly inexpressible is discussed in literature—is central to Shoshana Felman and Dori Laub's study of testimony, as well as many of the works discussed in this book, such as Charlotte Delbo's *None of Us Will Return*.[1] Critical responses to 9/11 iterate this apparent contradiction: despite the wealth of literature on the subject published since 2001, Judith Butler describes the 'enormous trauma that undermines narrative capacity'; Richard Gray similarly asserts that if 'there was one thing that writers agreed about in response to 9/11, it was the failure of language'.[2] Kristiaan Versluys draws too on this diction of incommensurability within Trauma Studies when he offers 9/11 as an example of a 'limit event that shatters the symbolic resources of the culture and defeats the normal processes of meaning making and semiosis'.[3] At the same time, he concedes that the 'inevitability of discourse' remains (p. 3). Laura Frost explains this paradox in familiar psychoanalytic terms: writing does not inevitably mean engagement; indeed, she goes so far as to frame 9/11 as a 'Holocaust subject, hallowed ground to be approached with awe, trepidation, and utmost caution'.[4] Such rhetoric does not primarily imply that the Holocaust and 9/11 are comparable events, but indicates instead that cultural commentators are reiterating discourses of in/articulacy in order to approach 9/11 with critical vigilance. Frost's evocation of the Holocaust does not even suggest the comparative singularity of the events—or, as Galway Kinnell puts it in his poem 'When the Towers Fell', a 'corollary'—but, rather, continuities and discontinuities in discussions about the possibility of representation and witnessing.[5]

Despite this critical and artistic caution, narrative capacity has clearly not been undermined in relation to the perpetrator. Novels such as John Updike's *Terrorist* (2006) and Mohsin Hamid's *The Reluctant Fundamentalist* (2007) have engaged in the fraught act of imagining perpetrators.[6] In contrast, 9/11 poetry focusses primarily on the victim; or, more exactly, on experiences of those living in New York at the time, and, in addition, the wider impact on poets across the world living in the aftermath of the attacks.[7] Yet the way in which these two parties witness the event is often discussed as if these experiences were indistinct. One reason for this lies in the contention that there were no survivors of the event, and so 'the closest we have to something like a firsthand account' is only possible—as Versluys argues—in telephone messages sent from the towers (p. 5). Such delineations of 9/11 testimonies transpose Primo Levi's sense that the 'true' witnesses of the Holocaust were those who perished onto the events in the towers, resulting in the near impossibility of testimony.[8] If there are no survivors of 9/11, then secondary witnesses across the globe can be of equal import. However, in the political rush to nationalize the events of 9/11 as an American tragedy, victim testimony written and recorded by survivors of the twin towers, bystanders, rescue workers, and inhabitants of Manhattan has been forgotten or never even sought; excerpts from Columbia University's Oral History Narrative and Memory Project, published in 2011, form one of the few notable exceptions.[9] Hence this chapter will focus on the slippages between discussions of primary and secondary witnessing in relation to 9/11, and argue that, as a result, 9/11 testimony has been obscured in a supposedly global process of witnessing.

Suheir Hammad—as I shall examine later in this chapter—reiterates Holocaust dialectics of in/articulacy when she claims, at the beginning of her oft-discussed poem 'first writing since', that there is 'no poetry in the ashes south of canal street'.[10] Hammad registers Frost's conception of 9/11 as a 'Holocaust subject' with the reference to Theodor Adorno's claim that '[t]o write poetry after Auschwitz is barbaric [. . .] it has become impossible to write poetry today', which, as I argue in *Holocaust Poetry*, opens up the possibility of awkward poetics in poems that self-consciously discuss the possibility of representation and witnessing.[11] Felman and Laub's paradox finds its origin here in Adorno's polemic: testimony is impossible and yet also in abundance, even if this proliferation finds us no closer to understanding traumatic events. Despite Hammad's openly self-defeating sense that there can be 'no poetry' in 9/11 (whilst writing a poem), it has almost become a cliché to note the increased visibility of poetry after the event. Liedeke Plate describes this phenomenon as follows:

> For in the days following the events of 9/11, poetry was everywhere. On the Internet and through e-mail, on radio and television, in newspapers and magazines, poems home grown and famous were shared with friends and family, with colleagues and with total strangers. In the streets of New York, poems were stuck on lamp posts and phone booths, on the walls of bus shelters and subway stations. Across the United States, poetry readings were organized; most notably, the benefit reading for the American Red Cross on October 22 at New York's Cooper Union College [in the East Village].[12]

Karen Alkalay-Gut adds that poems appeared 'on the sidewalks of southern Manhattan, on pages tacked to trees near the site of the twin towers, and on bulletin boards across the country'.[13] Following my argument in the introduction about Levi and Delbo's recourse to poetry, it is clear that the prosaic accounts of newspaper reports, magazine articles, and TV bulletins were not felt to be commensurate with the advent of 9/11. After recounting how people 'scrawled poems in the ash that covered everything' in their introduction to *Poetry after 9/11*, Dennis Loy Johnson and Valerie Merians note, 'Prose wasn't enough. There was something more to be said that only poetry could say. Everybody, apparently, knew this' (p. ix). As a form of heightened rhetoric and memorable speech, as well as signalling cultural continuity, poetry—unlike prosaic prose—assuaged what Butler termed the new 'precariousness' of U.S. life.[14] Many commentators, including Art Spiegelman and Homi Bhabha, stress the importance of W. H. Auden's 'September 1, 1939' to New Yorkers as a confirmation of, and antidote for, precarious living in the first few months after 9/11. As part of Freud's process of 'true' mourning, the Auden poem—as Bhabha argues—elucidated a 'threshold moment' and then 'restored' New York to its inhabitants, with, for example, its reference to the poet's busy club on Fifty-Second Street.[15] This glut of poetry readings and poetic production was not without its detractors, however. Johnson and Merian note that poems were so dispersed in downtown Manhattan behind 'mountains of flowers' and photographs of the dead, that a fire chief issued a statement: 'Thank you for the food and the blankets and the flowers but please—no more poetry'.[16] The fire chief's echo of a draconian reading of Adorno's polemic was clearly unheeded, given Gut and Plate's comments on the proliferation of poems. However, within this sense that poetry was everywhere after 9/11, what exactly constituted poetry as testimony?

One of the problems encountered in answering this question lies in the oft-repeated claim for a democracy of mourning in the wake of the event. Gut notes that poems by survivors at Ground Zero appeared on the Internet alongside those of TV witnesses, and concludes that the web's 'intrinsic democratic character was utilized [. . .] every testimony of emotion or witness was accepted as equally privileged, so a television witness had as much right to feel and express this emotion as an actual witness' (p. 257). This chapter focusses on the issue of whether we should accept this conflation of primary and secondary witnesses. Equally problematic are the overlapping but ultimately incommensurate models of witnessing played out in relation to the event, inflected by judicial contexts, conceptions of primary and secondary trauma, a psychoanalytic sense of the 'wound', and—as in Gut's article—reactions to 9/11 across the world. As opposed to the specificities of legal compensation, some psychoanalytical versions of witnessing have accounted for grief based on a broader masculine, primarily American (but also potentially Western), sense of emasculation after 9/11: Butler writes of the 'enormous narcissistic wound opened up by the public display of our physical vulnerability' (p. 7). A national, and potentially international, sense of a 'narcissistic wound' grates, or, at least overlaps, with the particularities of survivors in Lower Manhattan applying for emergency aid, dealing with insurance claims, and working with the Federal Emergency Management Agency. Hence Nancy K. Miller refers to 'a map of trauma whose borders are still missing' in relation to accounts of the aftermath of 9/11.[17] Against the a priori assertion that everyone witnessed the event, this chapter will focus on New York writers figuring themselves (sometimes problematically) as survivors in *Poetry after 9/11: An Anthology of New York Poets*.[18] Their localized conception of witnessing connects with the recent testimony published as part of the Oral History Narrative and Memory Project in *After the Fall: New Yorkers Remember September 2001 and the Years That Followed*. These testimonies illustrate that we do not know what happened during 9/11. The looped footage of the collapsing Twin Towers functions—as Kristeva argues in relation to photographs of atrocity—as a site of 'compassionate melancholy', which screens out the actual testimonies from survivors from the World Trade Center, rescue workers, bystanders, and temporary refugees.[19]

POETRY AND INCOMPATIBLE WITNESSING

In the following section I ask the deceptively simple question: who actually witnessed the event? Since there are so many incompatible modes of witnessing expressed in relation to 9/11, Who are the equivalent of the primary witnesses discussed elsewhere in this book? If we argue that there are no survivors, then we are left with Versluys's sense of 9/11 as 'limit event', in which the possibility of primary testimony is virtually negated.[20] If, however, the term 'survivor' can encompass, for example, evacuees from the towers and rescue workers at Ground Zero, can testimonial literature only be written by someone who was present at the site of the event, or does it encompass the work—as Gut contends—of someone watching it on television thousands of miles away?[21] (And does the 'site' of the attacks denote only Lower Manhattan, or nearby districts and boroughs such as Brooklyn?) If the writing of European poets about 9/11 counts as testimony, have the categories of primary and secondary witnessing—with their origins in a judicial context—somehow become blurred in the context of the mass media reporting of twenty-first-century events? Has this potentially radical change in the process of witnessing gone relatively unremarked, so that now—as Versluys argues—'In a time of globalised witnessing and shared vicarious experience, an event like 9/11 is a *rupture for everybody*', since '[m]odern communication technology makes us part of the tragedy, live and in real time'?[22]

This chapter argues that we need to critique this concept of global witnessing, and refocus attention on the testimony of, for example, the Oral History Narrative and Memory Project and anthologies of writing such as *Poetry after 9/11*, in which New York writers engage, in a variety of ways and

poetic forms, with the aftermath of the event. The apparent democratiza-
tion of suffering through footage actually elides the testimony of primary
witnesses in New York. Emphasis on the metatext in the poetry anthology—
through the detailed biographical notes—includes geographical specificities
as an implicit response to the occlusions of global witnessing: the poet Anna
Rabinowitz 'is a life-long New Yorker'; Andrea Carter Brown was 'displaced
from her home in Battery Park City by the events of September 11'; George
Murray, who works 'at the corner of Washington and Rector Streets', just
escaped 'the rain of debris' (pp. 108, 104, 107). It would not be possible for
the poems to authenticate proximity in the poetry itself, of course: hence the
framing of the texts through the biographical sketches, or what Susan Suleiman terms the 'conventional' relationship between the author and reader,
which, as I argued in the introduction, is central to the way in which we read
testimonial poetry differently from other kinds of poems.[23]

Inhabitants of New York more widely often respond to 9/11 in terms of
this localized witnessing outlined in the anthology. As Anne Whitehead
points out, Art Spiegelman 'insists on the surprisingly local nature of the
trauma, so that the "intensity of response" lasted longer in Lower Manhattan than in uptown New York, while "all New Yorkers were out of
their mind compared to those for whom the attack was an abstraction"'.[24]
Spiegelman's *In the Shadow of No Towers* posits a centrifugal 'map' of
trauma, which moves from Lower Manhattan to 'abstract' versions of the
attacks for all those living outside New York City. For Spiegelman, 'zip
codes seemed to have *something* to do with the intensity of response', but
that 'something' denotes the vagueness of geographical specificities within
his continuum of trauma.[25] Judith Greenberg's *Trauma at Home: After
9/11* illustrates that the relationship between trauma and space cannot
be clearly defined. In 'Wounded New York', Greenberg refers to the 'secondary trauma' of New Yorkers with children living on the Upper West
Side (approximately five miles from Ground Zero) in the days following
9/11 (p. 21). Two pages later, however, the circumspection of quotation
marks has disappeared: 'Most New Yorkers I've encountered do not consider themselves victims and frequently explain: "no one close to me died"
[. . .] these disclaimers also perform a kind of distancing from the grief of
secondary trauma' (p. 230). In *After the Fall*, the psychologist Ghislaine
Boulanger speaks tentatively about the 'vicarious traumatisation' of volunteers, such as the young girls on Rudy Giuliani's staff who handed out little
urns of ashes taken from Ground Zero (p. 259).[26]

Nevertheless, as with Greenberg, the scare quotes soon disappear, but
she still wishes to maintain:

> a distinction between those who were right there—who saw it, who
> experienced it, who ran from it, or may have lost someone, or first
> responders who went in and started seeing these awful things—and
> those who watched it on television. I don't believe the TV constitutes

massive traumatization. You may well have repetitive thoughts and what I call vicarious traumatization. But it hasn't got the same impact. (pp. 260–61)

This account of secondary witnessing is insightful, but 'those who watched it on television' could still include Greenberg's inhabitants of the Upper West Side, whom Spiegelman wishes to distinguish from people living outside New York City. Like Spiegelman and Boulanger, Greenberg makes a distinction between witnesses in Lower Manhattan and a 'secondary' phenomenon that she cannot describe accurately (hence the quotation marks): 'location affected a sense of vulnerability [. . .] people uptown were less affected than were those downtown' (p. 23). Yet she still refers to the aftermath of 9/11 on the Upper West Side that 'could be felt viscerally [. . .] I could see a huge gray cloud hovering over the southern end of the city, and when the winds shifted and blew uptown I inhaled the death-infused air [. . .] New York felt newly "unhomey"' (p. 22). Spiegelman mirrors Greenberg's attempt to distinguish between primary and secondary witnesses when he concedes that '[t]hose crumbling towers burned their way into every brain, but I live on the outskirts of Ground Zero and first saw it all live—unmediated'.[27] Boulanger's emphasis on mediated images leading only to vicarious trauma connects with Spiegelman's oft-discussed description of the North Tower glowing just before it collapsed: this embodies the 'pivotal image from [his] 9/11 morning—one that didn't get photographed or videotaped into public memory'. The unique moment of primary witnessing can then only be represented via a pixellated image in the book, which is still, Spiegelman points out, only an approximation. In contrast to this claim for the primary witness, however, Spiegelman is nevertheless 'haunted now by the images he *didn't* witness [. . .] images of people tumbling to the streets below' (p. 6; my italics). This disturbance of what Greenberg terms New Yorkers' 'psychic homes' (p. 23) illustrates the difficulties of separating primary and secondary witnessing even for those, like Spiegelman, who 'saw it all [. . .] unmediated', a conundrum which—as I outlined in the introduction—has led historians to distrust testimony's access to historical truth. It is significant in this context that Spiegelman's diction describing primary and secondary witnessing is strikingly similar, since the iconic images of the collapsing towers '*burned* their way into every brain', just as the glowing tower 'remains *burned* onto the inside of [his] eyelids several years later' (my italics).

These illuminating commentaries, and their fraught diction, illustrate the difficulty, but also the importance, of distinguishing between primary and secondary witnesses in this 'map of trauma whose borders are still missing'.[28] However, in contrast to the localized notion of witnessing outlined in the anthology and the examples above, for Gut, 'the entire world was literally witness to the event' (p. 261). In one sense, her adverb registers the common misuse of 'literally', but, more importantly, it registers the tangible (if potentially indescribable) effect of television footage; as Versluys notes, viewers outside New York were somehow 'part of the tragedy' (p. 7).[29] Gut invokes the example of George Lakoff, who, in an essay entitled 'Metaphors of Terror', recalls a process of traumatization 'even three thousand miles away' from Ground Zero (p. 261): he deploys a similar diction to Spiegelman when he describes how the television images 'got into [his] brain', resulting in 'nightmares keeping [him] awake' (p. 262). Gut concludes that, following such instances of Boulanger's vicarious traumatization, '[E]veryone was [. . .] transformed as [a] victim' (p. 265).

The critic might be tempted to detect here the problems of 'trauma culture' and the universalization of the victim that detract from primary witnesses such as Spiegelman who saw the events at Ground Zero 'live—unmediated' (p. 1). As Butler points out in *Precarious Life*, 'The "victim" is a quickly transposable term' (p. 103). However, attention to the potentially traumatic effects of the footage (and Gut and Versluys's thesis) deserves further analysis, given that vicarious traumatization is—as Boulanger stresses—such a recognized (if not explained) phenomenon after 9/11. In *Trauma at Home*, Jill Bennett argues that 'the impact was felt as profoundly in London as in parts of the United States'.[30] Michael Rothberg concurs in the same volume that the event was traumatic '*potentially* for [. . .] even witnesses at a remove'. (Rothberg's adverb is the equivalent of Spiegelman's abstract noun 'something'.)

However, the ensuing problem for this complex 'map of trauma' is, as Bennett asserts: 'if attributes of identity such as [. . .] city of residence are understood to qualify one as, in some sense, a victim or traumatised subject [in relation to 9/11], how might we acknowledge the range and specificities of experience within this grouping' (p. 132)? Despite Bennett's laudable attempt to account for imagined communities of victims, Butler's analysis of 'ungrievable' lives underlines that not *everyone* suffered vicarious traumatization. The invisibility, to Western audiences, of non-military lives lost in Afghanistan points to the impossibility of a globalized community of vicarious trauma victims. Charles Bernstein's poem 'Some of These Daze'—quoted extensively in Gut's article—actually subverts the text's assertions about global witnessing and the universal victim, since a distinction is made between 'the many who watched the events unfold, how to put it?, live and in person', and those glued to 'live' television: 'Those who saw the towers collapse, who saw the people jumping, were seared in a way the rest of us have been spared' (Gut, p. 271). Spiegelman's assertion of primary witnessing, live and unmediated, grates against the embarrassment and awkwardness of Bernstein's 'how to put it?'[31]

Perhaps my attempts to distinguish between different modes of witnessing in relation to 9/11 could be criticized as insensitive to those that suffered secondary trauma, with an unseemly concern with fine categorical distinctions, and ultimately irrelevant in an era of global witnesses. My point, however, is that these gradations are intimately linked to the politics of testimony. Gut writes of a 'universal "entitlement"' to grieve after 9/11 (p. 267), but this should not obscure, for example, the specific testimonies of the Oral History Narrative and Memory Project, about rescue workers who had to abandon people in order to survive the towers' collapse, a priest who blessed body parts from the wreckage, and those evacuated below Fourteenth Street, who, for a few weeks, effectively became refugees. The untimely switch after 9/11 to talk of retaliation, without a consideration of the 'cycles of violence' that Butler critiques in *Precarious Life* (p. xii), subsumed the local effects of 9/11 into a national narrative of victimization and armed response. The Oral History Narrative and Memory Project, and other attempts to engage with the subsequent effects of 9/11 on, for example, the inhabitants of Lower Manhattan, thus counteracts this testimonial 'forgetting' in the face of national politics and foreign policy. The archive at Columbia University has lead to exhibitions such as 'Ground One: Voices from Post-9/11 Chinatown', which illustrated how, for eight days after the event, Chinatown (ten blocks from Ground Zero) was a 'frozen zone'.[32] Traffic was prohibited, and inhabitants lost their telephone service for nearly two months: such details resist the collapse of 'the experiences and suffering of thousands of individuals into the symbolic realm of the nation'.[33] 'Ground One' thus aimed to 'provide an in-depth portrait of the ways in which the identity of a community, largely neglected by national media following 9/11, has been indelibly shaped by that day'.[34] Through the testimony of local residents such as the politician Margaret Chin, 'you see 9/11 not so much as an international catastrophe as a catastrophe for neighbourhood people, of jobs lost, homes destroyed, lives disrupted'.

'WE SEE NOTHING CLEARLY': GEOFFREY O'BRIEN 'AUBADE 2'

Geoffrey O'Brien's poem 'Aubade 2' responds to the testimonial specificities of Lower Manhattan by engaging with his experience of evacuation. In *Poetry after 9/11*, his biographical note explains that he 'was displaced from his home in Battery Park City for four months by the events of September 11' (p. 107). In *After the Fall*, the editors note that twenty-five thousand people were evacuated from Lower Manhattan (p. x). An interview with Donna Jensen in this compendium reveals how she endured 'a seven-week odyssey when [she] stayed with a friend and in hotels, applying for emergency aid, dealing with insurance claims and FEMA [the Federal Emergency Management Agency], researching the health consequences of living near Ground Zero, and finally moving back into her apartment in Lower Manhattan' (p. 58; original in italics). Brian Conley recalls being held in a police cordon during 9/11 and eventually being let out 'into the Hoboken terminal. At that point, we went into the terminal like refugees' (p. 107).[35] Jaron Lanier, a Tribeca resident like Conley, employs Holocaust discourse in order to try and make sense of the evacuation: 'my family has survived concentration camps [. . .] what I've gone through wasn't nearly as bad [. . .] by any stretch of the imagination, but I have a little more of a sense of what it's like to be a refugee and to experience real uncertainty and real fear' (p. 166).[36] Some writers in *Poetry after 9/11* respond to this refugee status through positivistic testimony that recounts their former routines in Lower Manhattan. Andrea Carter Brown, for example, mourns the disappearance of the diverse food stalls close to Ground Zero in 'The Old Neighborhood'. Evacuated, like O'Brien, from her home in Battery Park City, she wonders where the fruit sellers have gone, as well as the purveyors of doughnuts, franks, roti, falafel, nuts, and sweets. Their vanishing mirrors her evacuation, but also hints at post-9/11 racism (more bluntly addressed in Hammad's poem) with the departure of the 'dark brown man with dreadlocks' and the 'small-boned Egyptian in white robe and crocheted skullcap' (p. 7).

Instead of focussing on such positivistic details, O'Brien produces a poem which engages with his displacement at a tangent, through an evocation of a fantasy world that is clearly linked—through the diction and biographical note—to the aftermath of 9/11:

> Hysteria of morning. A clearing, the half-gnawed
> bones of last night's feast, a cry in the ravine.
> There is too much smoke in the jungle, or not enough.
> Nothings fits, nothing is quite right. Pieces of cloud-cover
> litter the overgrown path. It's as if no one
> had ever lived here, yet we still have to get up
> to find wood. Neurasthenia of morning. The clearing
> breaks down into bands of colors, the violent greens
> soothed by outbursts of red. It's patched itself
> together once again, even if the sky
> is still partly ripped. The cracks in the burnt bones
> seem almost pictures of roads. The roads
> are so much like burnt bones I regret that the day
> even at this early hour is no longer black. (p. 99)

The lack of recognizable 9/11 iconography might seem to position this poem uneasily as testimony, yet the metatextual details of O'Brien's displacement clearly frame the text as a 9/11 poem. Such appeals to Suleiman's notion of the 'conventional' are common in the anthology, as in relation to Paul Violi's 'House of Xerxes' and O'Brien's 'The Bed in the Wilderness' and 'Techniques of Mass Persuasion', which, on the surface, appear to have little to do with the event. In 'Aubade 2', hints in the diction—with the smoke, 'ripped' sky, 'violent' landscape, and burnt bones—evoke the metatext without pinpointing the events of September 11. As I have argued throughout this book—following Felman and Laub's study—this is not testimony in terms of a chronicle of historical events, but as an inscribed response to suffering and, in this instance, a specific 'apprehension of the precarious-ness of life' after 9/11.[37] 'Aubade 2' switches between different states of psychological disorientation: the pathetic fallacy of the morning (with a pun on 'mourning') is at first hysterical, but then, by the mid-point of the poem, it reflects the traumatic listlessness of neurasthenia. Precarious life is embodied in the inversions: green—rather than red—denotes violence, and 'cloud-cover' (with its hint of military discourse) litters the ground, not the sky. Metre and form mirror the sense that 'nothing is quite right': the metri-cal break in the first line (on 'gnawed') gives way to dissonant half-rhyme ('day | black'), as well as the awkward enjambment of lines such as 'half-gnawed | bones' and '[i]t's patched itself | together once again'.[38]

The hypercatalectic metre of the last line emphasizes the poem's engage-ment with vision, and the lack of it, throughout the text: 'the day | even at this hour is no longer black'. Perhaps surprisingly for poetry as testi-mony, the speaker has misgivings about his ability to see the detritus of the event, regretting—ironically, given the title—that dawn has come. Line three anticipates this spurning of the visual with the claim that there is 'too much smoke [. . .] or not enough'. The smouldering connotes the aftermath of the traumatic event, but also registers the narrator's desire to turn away from the wreckage. Rather than encapsulating denial or trau-matic disassociation, the regret can be read as a response to Jean Baudril-lard's oft-quoted claim that, in relation to 9/11, 'the image consumes the event'.[39] A refusal to see resists the perpetrators' exploitation of 'worldwide transmission', as photographs and footage of the towers 'exalt' the event, and 'take it hostage' (p. 27). Instead of thinking about 9/11 as purely an 'image-event', the testimony draws the reader into the contemplation of an individual's psychological response. 'We see nothing clearly', as Robert Sheppard puts it in his remarkable poem sequence written in the days after September 11: O'Brien concurs that there is 'too much smoke', too many images, to take stock of the event.[40] 'Aubade 2' edges towards positivism in its account, at the closure, of 'roads [. . .] like burnt bones', which recalls the footage of streets covered in ash, and famous *National Geographic* photographs such as Jason Florio's 'Street in Ruins'.[41] However, the poem turns away from the image in its plea for a blackout, rather than further representation of what Simon Armitage terms 'the blitz of that awful snow' in his 9/11 film-poem *Out of the Blue*.[42] In *Trauma at Home: After 9/11*, Marianne Hirsch argues that 'still photography is the visual genre that best captures the trauma and loss associated with 9/11' (p. 71): in contrast, O'Brien is attentive to Butler's sense in *Precarious Life* that the 'reality is not conveyed by what is represented within the image, but through the challenge to representation that reality delivers' (p. 146). For O'Brien, this contest results in a poem that depicts a fractured landscape in which—despite (ironically) the repetition of the word 'clearing'—a desire for the non-visual ultimately reigns.

'THE RULES HAVE CHANGED': NIKKI MOUSTAKI'S 'HOW TO WRITE A POEM AFTER SEPTEMBER 11TH'

As with 'Aubade 2', Nikki Moustaki's poem in *Poetry after 9/11* responds to Felman and Laub's conception of the testimonial difficulties (and paradox) of representation outlined at the beginning of this chapter. Rather than end with a plea for 'non-seeing', however, 'How to Write a Poem after September 11th' subverts the title's confidence throughout the text:

> First: Don't use the word *souls*. Don't use the word *fire*.
> You can use the word *tragic* if you end it with a k.
> The rules have changed. The word *building* may precede
> The word *fall*, but only in the context of the buildings falling
> Before the fall, the season we didn't have in Manhattan
> Because the weather refused, the air refused . . .
> Don't say the air smelled like smoldering desks and drywall,
> Ground gypsum, and something terribly organic,
> Don't make a metaphor about the smell, because it wasn't
> A smell at all, but the air washed with working souls,
> Piling bricks, one by one, spreading mortar.
> Don't compare the planes to birds. Please.
> Don't call the windows eyes. We know they saw it coming.
> We know they didn't blink. Don't say they were sentinels.
> Say: we hated them then we loved them then they were gone.
> Say: we miss them. Say: there's a gape. Then, say something
> About love. It's always good in a poem to mention love.
> Say: If a man walks down stairs, somewhere
> Another man is walking up. Say: He sits at his desk
> And the other stands. He answers the phone and the other
> Ends a call with a kiss. So, on a rainy dusk in some other
> City of Commerce and Art, a mayor cuts a ribbon
> With giant silver scissors. Are you writing this down?
> Make the executives parade through the concourse,
> Up the elevators, to the top, where the restaurant,
> Open now for the first time, sets out a dinner buffet.
> Press hard. Remember, you're writing with ashes.
>
> Say: the phone didn't work. Say: the bakery was out of cake,
> The dogs in the pound howled. Say: the world hadn't
> Asked your permission to change. But you were asleep.
> If you had only written more poems. If only you had written
> More poems about love, about peace, about how abstractions
> Become important outside the poem, outside. Then, then,
> You could have squinted into the sky on September 11th
> And said: thank you, thank you, nothing was broken today. (pp. 95–96)

Moustaki's biographical note records that she is the author of *The Complete Idiot's Guide to Writing Poetry*: the poem deliberately undercuts the diction of such textbooks and engages with the difficulty, not the rules, of 'How to Write a Poem after September 11th'. The text forms a seriously playful version of Felman and Laub's sense of the radical inexpressibility of the traumatic event. On the surface, the poem warns against cliché: in Frédéric Beigbeder's novel *Windows on the World*, the narrator recounts the second plane as 'A silver flash of lightning coming from the south, a Paleolithic bird, a spear point, a scimitar glittering in the morning sunshine'; Moustaki reacts to such mixed metaphors with the simple plea, 'Don't compare the planes to birds. Please'.[43] In the poetry anthology, skyscrapers are 'mute gongs in an infinite forest' (p. 17), and the towers have been compared to 'Mammon, Goliath, Lucifer, Polyphemus, the Mayan pyramids of Chichen Itza': in contrast, Moustaki's narrator just states, 'Don't say they were sentinels' (p. 95).[44] However, as the poem as a whole indicates, the post-9/11 poet cannot avoid metaphor and cliché as easily as the imperatives might suggest. Hugh Seidman's 'New York' in *Poetry after 9/11* puns on 'souls' and 'sole' in relation to those killed in the towers (p. 41), whereas Moustaki's poem opens with 'First: Don't use the word *souls*' (p. 95). However, 'How to Write a Poem after September 11th' then challenges its own imperative nine lines later, as the 'air is washed with working souls'. In the antecedent line, the narrator implores writers not to 'make a metaphor about the smell', but this comes after the simile of the air like smouldering desks and drywall and leads to the (already banned) trope of the 'working souls'.

As well as subverting its own title, the poem can be read as a rejoinder to the concept of global witnessing. Invocations not to 'use', 'say', 'make' metaphors, or 'compare' are in this sense a warning to writers who were not present in New York during, and after, the attacks. Moustaki makes a reference to the specificities of localized witnessing as early as the fifth line: 'falling' buildings link to the 'fall', the season *we* 'didn't have in Manhattan'. The imagined community of New York inhabitants then recurs in the repetition of 'we' throughout the poem. Moustaki's details about the smell near to Ground Zero, the smouldering 'desks and drywall | Ground gypsum, and something terribly organic', also mark the narrator out as a witness: as Bhabha points out, numerous New Yorkers (including Greenberg) remarked on the odour of 'dioxins, asbestos, shattered glass, mercury and metal dust', making Auden's reference to the 'unmentionable odour of death' in 'September 1, 1939' appear prescient for some.[45] For the New York speaker here, the important thing is not the smell, but the 'working souls' in the aftermath: the phrase connotes the deaths of those trapped in the towers, but primarily denotes the potentially redemptive process of workers rebuilding the city, 'Piling bricks, one by one, spreading mortar'. The imperatives throughout the first half of the poem are in this way a means of articulating what the Manhattan inhabitants actually witnessed during, and soon after, 9/11, as well as warding off potentially insensitive secondary witnesses.

Textbooks such as *The Complete Idiot's Guide to Writing Poetry* usually suggest that abstractions should be distrusted in poetry: for the narrator at the beginning of the poem, this indictment is particularly pertinent, since they could obscure testimonial specificities: hence the ironic demand to 'say something | About love. It's always good in a poem to mention love'. ('Abstractions' also recalls Spiegelman's claim that the event was 'abstract' for anyone not living in New York City.) Yet the poem also gestures towards the impossibility of recounting what the 'true' witnesses of the event, in Levi's and Versluys's sense, experienced. Whereas writers such as Frédéric Beigbeder and Simon Armitage attempt verisimilitude (up to a point) in order to represent the events unfolding in the Twin Towers, Moustaki switches from the commands reminiscent of Henry Reed's 'Naming of Parts' to the disconcerting lines about the 'rainy dusk' in another city and the executives parading through the concourse to a restaurant.[46] Moustaki indicates here the inexpressibility of the event in an alternative way to the imperatives: ending a call 'with a kiss' evokes the messages sent from the towers, but this is as close as we get to a representation of the event. The poem immediately evades this temptation and mirrors Reed's turn to increasingly surreal juxtapositions in 'Naming of Parts' with its reference to the obscure mayor with scissors and the teasing question 'Are you writing this down?'. 'Executives', 'concourse', and 'elevators' suggest that the next three lines recall the opening of the Windows of the World restaurant in 1976: whereas Beigbeder imagines at length the tribulations of a family trapped in this part of the North Tower, Moustaki turns away from the brief imaginative reconstitution and asks the 9/11 writer to 'Remember, you're writing with ashes'.[47] This line comes at the end of a page in *Poetry after 9/11* and would seem to be a suitably cautionary ending to the poem.

However, on the next page, abstractions return as potential, but necessarily fraught, sites of redemption. Whereas writing guides, and creative writing classes, normally warn against the abstract, the narrator concedes how important abstractions such as 'love' and 'peace' are to the world 'outside the poem'. The unlikely conclusion—given the ironic rejection of the amorous earlier in the text—is that, if only the narrator had written more poems about love and peace, they could have 'squinted into the sky on September 11th', and said that 'nothing was broken'. If the line is to be read at face value, we are left with an emotive closure similar to many early 9/11 poems, as in Wendy Cope's 'Spared' (published in October 2001), which ends, 'how well I understand | That love is all, is all there is'.[48] (For Martin Randall, the poem displays a 'mawkish banality'.[49]) Colette Inez's poem 'The Skeptic' in *Poetry after 9/11* similarly ends with a plea for abstractions, including 'love [. . .] reason and beauty' (p. 36). Cope, Inez, and Moustaki's salvaging of the embarrassment of the amorous should certainly be taken seriously, but given the tone that pervades 'How to Write a

Poem after September 11th', it is difficult to read Moustaki's ending (unlike Cope's) without a trace of irony. The closure should be read instead as a continuation of the theme of inexpressibility introduced at the start of the poem. Just as 9/11 poetry cannot be reduced to the rules of an instruction manual, the succour of concepts such as 'love' remains, even if it is difficult to articulate convincingly.

'THERE IS NO POETRY IN THIS': SUHEIR HAMMAD'S 'FIRST WRITING SINCE'

Hammad's performance poem reacts in a more politicized and less playful way to Felman and Laub's paradox of representation than Moustaki's 'How to Write a Poem after September 11th'.[50] Like Moustaki, Hammad stresses the importance of localized witnessing: she has 'never felt less American and more new yorker, particularly brooklyn, than these past days'. 'Less' American because she does not support U.S.-sponsored 'bullying', she is still aware, during the vitriolic attacks on 'u.s. transgressions', that 'it could have been [her] in those buildings'. National narratives of retaliation obscure the local testimonies of bereaved families and 'lovers', so that 'the stars and stripes on all these cars and apartment windows' represent the dead primarily as abstract citizens, not family members. Rather than an 'abstract' representation—as Spiegelman terms it—of someone living outside New York City, Hammad views a localized 'abstract reality' straight outside her kitchen window: 'sky where once was steel | smoke where once was flesh'. Later in the poem, 'across the river [to Brooklyn], the smell of burning rubber and limbs floats through': localized witnessing is also stressed through the juxtaposition of the 'advertisers [. . .] back on the air' with the 'rescue workers [who] are traumatized'. Hammad defines her identity partly through a New York borough, but at the same time she confronts, throughout the poem, Butler's sense of the 'amorphous racism' that followed 9/11: 'as a palestinian', she is asked 'if [she] knew the hijackers', and in 'what navy' her Muslim brother serves. Hence 'first writing since' functions as an important testimony akin to those in the Oral History Narrative and Memory Project: Hammad also reflects 'about what it means to be a member of a community, to be a New Yorker, a Muslim in New York [. . .] after 9/11', and what it meant to 'reenter the everyday routines'.[51]

Despite this localized witnessing, however, the poem begins with the nod to Adorno's concept of 'impossible' literature:

> there have been no words.
> i have not written one word.
> no poetry in the ashes south of canal street.
> no prose in the refrigerated trucks driving debris and dna.
> not one word.

As mentioned in the introduction to this chapter, the text evinces the Beckettian paradox of not writing anything whilst writing words. There is no poetry in the ashes south of Soho, Little Italy, and the Lower East Side, at the same time as the piece goes on to describe the experiences of a primary witness, already announced in the title 'first writing since'. The repetition and emphasis of 'not one word' at the end of the first stanza indicates the self-consciousness of the paradox. In one sense, the poem responds to Adorno's potentially draconian statement by warning against cursory engagements with the attacks, whilst leaving open the possibility of an awkward, 'barbaric' response that registers the difficulty of articulation.

In another way, however, the poem reacts, with its plea for linguistic caution, against the subsuming of a local narrative of trauma under the national flag of retaliation. Ann Keniston and Jeanne Follansbee indicate, in their introduction to *Literature after 9/11*, that Hammad's performance poem follows a convention of 9/11 poetry that begins 'with a sense of the dangers of identification and speech' (p. 4). Composed in the days following the attacks, 'first writing since' is, in this way, primarily a rebuff to President Bush's words on the evening of 11 September 2001, when he referred to emergency response plans, and emphasized the possibility of a 'powerful' military retaliation before mentioning the emergency teams in New York City and Washington, D.C.[52] In contrast, Hammad mentions the local efforts in the first stanza: professionals 'driv[e] debris and dna', without the frame of a national narrative. For Hammad, there were too many words uttered too quickly in the public sphere about 9/11, without the necessary space for reflection on the attacks outlined in Butler's *Precarious Life*. In 'first writing since', Hammad figures national rhetoric throughout as obfuscation, the 'exhaust' of the fourth section, in which Butler's 'cycles of violence' lead to a desire for happiness through bombs dropped vaguely 'over there', and a passion to 'burn' an unspecified 'them'. Significantly, 'word' reappears—as a retort to the opening stanza—after the single moment of empathy in the poem: a woman embraces the narrator, who explains that she has a brother in the navy; 'wow, you got double trouble', responds the anonymous interlocutor. 'Word' then follows this statement in the slang sense of 'indeed', but also to stress that this conversation signifies an openness to personal and political understanding, rather than cycles of violence.

Hammad seeks briefly to engage with (if not understand) the perpetrators in the first section of the poem, as an alternative to the perpetuation of violent conflict. To counteract Bush's binary response to the proposed U.S. military intervention ('Either you're with us or you're with the terrorists'), and concurrently endorse Butler's sense of America's ignorance of 'ungrievable' lives, the stanza attempts to think about human interdependence, and 'how bad a life has to break in order to kill'.[53] Ultimately, however, the poem recognizes the limits of recognition and ability to 'know' the other: the section ends with the simple statement that the narrator has never been 'this broken'. In contrast with this stanza's mulling over how angry a terrorist has to get 'to want to control a gun', the ending of the poem deliberately forgets the perpetrator. Butler points out that Bush's binary precludes a retort, since his language 'makes it untenable to hold a position in which one opposes both and queries the terms in which the opposition is framed' (p. 2): Hammad responds to this quandary by trying to reinvigorate the binary with the humanist statement that 'you are either with life, or against it.' The poem attempts to break through the smokescreen of national rhetoric following 9/11, but the text cannot completely free itself from ideology. Unlike Butler, who understands how different 'lives' are conceived in American terms, Hammad's binary risks a liberal platitude: which of her American readers, or members of the audience during the Brooklyn reading of 'first writing since', would disagree with such a stark opposition? Yet the perpetrators who do not conceive of life in such terms are precisely those people that Hammad engages with at the start of the poem. Her seemingly liberating reinvention of Bush's binary actually obscures those who are 'broken' enough to kill in the first section: her opposition would not be applicable to perpetrators in the context, for example, of the Israeli–Palestinian conflict. Rather than ruminating at length on the terrorists, as in Amis's, Updike's, and Hamid's 9/11 fiction, 'first writing since' concentrates instead on the local effects of 9/11 on Brooklyn and Manhattan, and what Randall terms the 'racism, cultural paranoia [. . .] and global political tensions' that followed the attacks (p. 36). Indeed, there is more emphasis on these concerns at the local level in the revised version of her poem performed in Brooklyn, since Hammad cuts the details about families looking for dead relatives after the attack on the World Trade Center, and focusses on, for example, the problems for one brother, as an 'arab', serving in the American navy.[54]

After considering the emphasis on localized witnessing in the three poems discussed above, the argument that everyone has a right to testify about 9/11 should appear untenable. Personal testimony arising from the event not only allows us access to forgotten narratives, such as the effect of the attacks on districts such as Chinatown and families such as Hammad's in 'first writing since'. At the same time, the politics of such testimonies offers redress to national narratives and the 'cycles of violence' that have arisen out of 9/11. The poems in the New York anthology, and the Oral History Narrative and Memory Project, should not be overshadowed by appeals to 'democratic' and 'global' witnessing. Unintentionally, such claims align themselves with post-9/11 foreign policy in terms of their occlusion of local politics. The stories behind, and an integral part of, such poetry and the Project testimonies illustrate that—as Anne Whitehead argues in relation to Spiegelman's *In the Shadow of No Towers*—'we do not yet know or understand the events of 9/11' (p. 234). If we propose that the advent of global witnessing means that we have all 'seen' 9/11, and can thus begin to work through its traumatic scenes and impact together, then we are merely adding to the process of forgetting the event.

Conclusion

Thinking about testimony as a 'figure of reading or of understanding', and as a cross-generic genre, opens up the possibility of a variety of testimonial forms beyond realist prose.[1] This book has been resistant throughout to a simplistic opposition between the supposedly non-representational character of poetry, and the representational nature of realism.[2] Yet compared to testimony written in prosaic prose, many testimonial poems in this book can indeed be evaluated as errant, rather than ignorant, in their responses to historical facts. According to Shoshana Felman and Dori Laub's focus on professional, literary testimony, however, the deviancy of literature in no way detracts from its testimonial power. In this book, I demonstrated that Tadeusz Borowski's love poems set in Auschwitz are forms of testimony—despite their elision of meta-testimonial facts—just as his journalistic pieces more obviously are, written after his release into Munich. Indeed, the literary complexity of Borowski's earlier Auschwitz poems means that they are—following Jorge Semprun's logic about 'transparent density'—the more effective (and affective) forms of testimony.[3] In contrast, for Semprun, 'rough' testimony offers only '[a] jumble of images, an avalanche of facts, impressions, pointless commentary', comparable to contemporaneous newsreels which 'said nothing precise about the reality they showed, because they delivered only confused scraps of meaning'.[4] When Charlotte Delbo recounts an episode of her washing in a stream which she cannot remember, she adheres to Semprun's sense that 'reality often needs some make-believe, to become real' (p. 262).[5] In Delbo's own terms, testimony might be 'true' in the sense that it draws on historical events, but it might not be 'truthful' in that it records accurately the subject's every sensation. A literature of the latter would, of course, constitute an impossibility: as Semprun states bluntly in *Literature or Life*, 'I'm not going to tell you the story of our lives, as I haven't the time' (p. 8).

Throughout this book I have noted the important characteristics of this errant poetry as testimony, such as the importance of the metatext, the demand—exemplified in Levi's 'Shemà'—for the reader's hyper-attentiveness, dialectics of in/articulacy, and the problems of identification, in which the author draws the reader into the narrative, but also resists any attempt at the colonization of the victim's experience. These characteristics demand a shift in the way we read testimonial poetry, just as prose testimony requires a different response to fiction. I am not arguing for a completely new way of reading poetry, as Derek Attridge does when he presents a way of reacting to the performative unfolding of singular poems in *The Singularity of Literature*, which nevertheless still draw on the tested proclivities of close reading. Yet Susan Suleiman's consideration of the 'conventional', the way in which we read and respond to books based on knowledge of the author's biography, its marketing through genre (etc.), illustrates that poetry as testimony (and all testimony and autobiography) immediately engages with the metatext in a way that other literatures do not when the 'figure' of autobiography is not so important to understanding the text.

Testimonial poetry is particularly adept—as opposed to prosaic prose—at resisting mediation, superficial affect, integration, and, potentially, the neo-liberal demand for testimony, anticipated by Robert Tressell in *The Ragged Trousered Philanthropists* when an Edwardian unemployment committee asks so many intrusive, and humiliating, questions that it successfully repels applicants' requests for charity.[6] Poetry as testimony stands firm against, but not does not completely alienate, the reader; it does, however, oppose any conception of testimony as a mimetic vehicle for the transmission of experience unproblematically into the public sphere. Hence my argument resists Karen Alkalay-Gut's conclusion that studies of testimony are symptomatic of 'a growing trend in literature and literary criticism away from the convoluted, academic and remote and back to the immediate, popular and direct'.[7] This book has engaged with 'non-professional' testimony—as in the chapters on the Oasis poets and *Voices*—but it primarily draws attention to examples of autonomous, testimonial art, such as Borowski's 'October Sky', Owen's verse, Geoffrey O'Brien's 9/11 poems, and Delbo's trilogy. The latter examples draw on, but also chafe against, the metanarrative and any sense that their stories can be simply told. As Theodor Adorno argues in 'Commitment', the most engaged works of art sometimes fail by very dint of their faithfulness to the metatext. Only equally committed art that grates against its origins can achieve singularity: in 'On Lyric Poetry and Society', Adorno uses the example of Eduard Mörike's nature poetry composed during the Industrial Revolution.[8] Borowski's ironic poems about 'homecoming' after his liberation from Dachau are thus found wanting, aesthetically, because they recount, rather than resist, what he evocatively termed the 'fishtank of blurred events' in post-war Europe.[9] In contrast, the incremental repetition in *The Voice in the Closet*, Raymond Federman's linguistically-innovative poem about his family's deportation, is both singular and terrifying.[10]

Poetry as testimony thus paradoxically resists history, and reflects on events—as in Levi's poems—at a micro-level, rather than just 'telling the story'. Historians (and Marxists) might baulk at this emphasis on the subjective and epiphanic, but to turn the dialectic round—and to return to

General Sir John Hackett's comment on the Oasis poems—such texts are 'part of the structure within which the "history" was made [. . .] without which all the factual chronicles of events and all the hardware on display have little meaning'.[11] 'Objective' history obscures its meaning without the presence of testimony and threatens to replicate a perpetrator perspective in its eradication of the singular. Robert Antelme was attuned to this process in his analysis of the potential tyranny of the 'objective', evidential photograph that teaches nothing.[12] The chilling objectivity of prosaic prose, and the overarching historical narrative complicit with the victim's fate, is obviated through the aesthetics of the autonomous, testimonial lyric.

Notes

NOTES TO THE INTRODUCTION

1. Critical suspicion towards the overlap of autobiography and artifice continues, despite Paul de Man's upbraiding of critics, nearly forty years ago, who
   deny that autobiography can be written in verse, so that 'it becomes irrelevant to consider Wordsworth's *The Prelude* within the context of a study
   of autobiography, an exclusion that anyone working in the English tradition
   will find hard to condone' ('Autobiography as De-Facement', *MLN (Modern
   Language Notes)*, 94.5 (December 1979), 919–30 (p. 920)). In contrast with
   de Man's evaluation of autobiography studies in the late 1970s, Anthony
   Rudolf argues in 'Rescue Work: Memory and Text' that 'the foundational
   text of modern autobiography [. . .] is surely Wordsworth's *The Prelude*, in
   its second version' (*Stand*, 5.3 (2004), 80–112 (p. 85)).
2. Shoshana Felman and Dori Laub, *Testimony: Crises of Witnessing in Literature, Psychoanalysis, and History* (New York: Routledge, 1992), pp.
   1–56.
3. The quotation comes from de Man, p. 921. Felman uses this quotation in
   'The Alignment of Witnesses', a response to Cathy Caruth's paper at the
   Future of Testimony conference (University of Salford, 2011). Felman's essay
   appears in *The Future of Testimony*, ed. by Jane Kilby and Antony Rowland
   (New York: Routledge, 2014).
4. As I argue in Chapter 4, this precociousness does not mean—following Felman and Laub's conception of trauma—that the witness's articulation of
   their experience will ever settle into understanding. The vicarious, 'breathless gasps' of poems (p. 21) are not much use in a courtroom, where prosaic
   testimony must lead to the certainty of the verdict.
5. Gary D. Mole, *Beyond the Limit-Experience: French Poetry of the Deportation, 1940–45* (New York: Peter Lang, 2002), pp. 18–19; Sue Vice, 'Holocaust Poetry and Testimony', *Critical Survey*, 20.2 (2008), 7–17 (p. 7).
6. One reason for the critical reluctance to regard poetry as testimony may be
   the Heideggerian view that poems function as revelations of the transcen-
   dent, or Adorno's sense that such texts are 'self-enclosed beautiful object[s]',
   'an organic unity made of words' (quoted in J. Hillis Miller, *The Conflagration of Community: Fiction before and after Auschwitz* (Chicago: University
   of Chicago Press, 2011), p. x). Miller opens out the possibility of testimonial
   poetry in his claim that 'Auschwitz imposes something like Celan's almost
   impenetrable complexity of poetic language' (p. 206), but he does not pursue
   this point.
7. Sara Guyer, 'Before *The Human Race*: Robert Antelme's Anthropomorphic
   Poetry', *Critical Survey*, 20.2 (2008), 31–42 (p.32).

8. Samuel Hynes's excellent book *The Soldier's Tale: Bearing Witness to Modern War* (London: Pimlico, 1998) similarly looks at witness literature across the twentieth century—focussing mainly on soldiers' accounts of warfare—but Hynes primarily studies prose narratives, and uses the terms 'personal narrative' (p. xiv), 'the Literature of Atrocity', and 'Sufferers' Tale' (p. 223) rather than testimony specifically. Hynes's informative analysis of witnesses' stories is—unlike this study—not informed by the work of Felman and Laub or other theoretical engagements with the concept of testimony. Hynes focusses on commonalities in the writing, such as 'Battlefield Gothic' (p. 26), but does not pinpoint generic characteristics of testimony highlighted in more recent criticism, such as in Robert Eaglestone's *The Holocaust and the Postmodern* (Oxford: Oxford University Press, 2004). In contrast, this book applies Eaglestone's (and others') insightful work on prose testimony—with his focus on the process of identification, the hyper-attentiveness of the reader, and the pressures of the metatext, amongst others—to the genre of poetry specifically. Susan Gubar's groundbreaking *Poetry after Auschwitz: Remembering What One Never Knew* (Bloomington: Indiana University Press, 2003) focusses on the same kind of literature as this book, but, as the subtitle suggests, the emphasis is on post-Holocaust, rather than testimonial, poetry. As with Hynes, Gubar's analysis of witness literature nevertheless does not focus on the generic characteristics of testimonial poetry. Unlike Hynes—and again, as the title suggests—Gubar's emphasis is on Holocaust poetry, whereas this study engages with witness poetry across the twentieth century. This book also engages with the work of Holocaust poets not covered in *Poetry after Auschwitz*, such as Tadeusz Borowski and Primo Levi. Andrés Nader's *Traumatic Verses: On Poetry in German from the Concentration Camps, 1933–45* (Rochester, NY: Camden House, 2007) provides an extensive, and laudable, account of testimonial poems in a specific context, but does not analyse the 'genre' of camp poetry (p. 32) as an instance of testimony.

9. I also argue for an extension of the limits of witness poetry: rather than thinking about testimonial poetry as merely a commentary on historical events, I discuss, for example, Tadeusz Borowski's pastoral and love poetry written in Auschwitz as a form of testimony, as well as Primo Levi's post-war poems about trauma.

10. More work needs to be done—beyond the scope of this book—on the relationship between twentieth-century poetry as testimony and the writing of 'confessional' poets in the 1950s and 1960s. It would be tempting to insist on a link, for example, between Holocaust poets and the late work of Sylvia Plath, but—as I illustrated in *Holocaust Poetry* (Edinburgh: Edinburgh University Press, 2005)—the effect of writers such as Celan on Plath is purely speculative, since his work had only recently been translated into readily available anthologies in English at the time of her death (p. 48). The 'confessional' style of poets such as Plath owes more to Robert Lowell's *Life Studies* (London: Faber, 1959) and Anne Sexton's influence than any intense reading of testimonial poetry. The influence on Holocaust testimony and reportage in general on the 'confessional poets' is clear, however, as in the case of John Berryman's engagement with the 'Black books' in his sequence of post-Holocaust poetry.

11. In the United States, the Civil War poets could be argued to be the precursors for twentieth-century U.S. poetry as testimony. In *War No More: The Anti-War Impulse in American Literature 1861–1914* (Baton Rouge: Louisiana State University Press, 2010), Cynthia Wachtell notes that, after the Battle of Chickamauga in 1863, 'an assortment of men and women, northerners and

southerners, crafted poems, short stories, and other literary works about the battle' (p. 16). Even though this war encompassed widespread conscription for the first time in the United States, not all these poets were writing from firsthand experience: Herman Melville was a 'distant onlooker' (p. 80), who nevertheless travelled to the battlefront and 'ate cold rations, took part in a charge (albeit a thoroughly uneventful one), and passed two near sleepless nights on the hard and unwelcoming ground' (p. 44). Walt Whitman was a civilian volunteer in military hospitals in New York, Virginia, and Washington: his diaries are more explicit about the fighting than the published poems in *Drum-Taps* (London: Chatto & Windus, 1915 [1865]) (p. 88).

12. This flourishing of testimony after conscription distinguishes modern testimony from, for example, medieval accounts of the War of the Roses. A medieval soldier would be unlikely, of course, to produce testimony, since literature was the preserve mainly of clergymen during this period. *Pearl*, on the other hand, might be regarded as an early form of poetic testimony in another sense, since it refers to the trauma of a lost child. The allegory functions as an inability to confront the traumatic loss of the spotless 'spot' of the child, as well as a contemporaneous literary convention (*Sir Gawain and the Green Knight, Pearl and Sir Orfeo*, trans. J.R.R. Tolkien (London: Unwin Hyman, 1979), p. 82). The possibility (ultimately illusory) of redemptive 'wonderment' in heaven's iconography (p. 83) persists, but only love of Christ finally redresses the speaker's melancholic grief (p. 104).

13. Dan Todman, *The Great War: Myth and Memory* (London: Continuum, 2005), p. 7.

14. Recent examples include Miller's *The Conflagration of Community*, which discusses novels as 'acts of testimony' (p. xiii), and Geoffrey Hartman's excellent article on video testimony in his special edition of *Poetics Today*: 'The Humanities of Testimony: An Introduction', *Poetics Today*, 27.2 (2006), 249–60 (p. 249). In the field of poetry and poetics, testimony is often conflated with autobiographical representations. The blurb to Carol Ann Duffy's collection *Rapture* (London: Picador, 2005) records that she provides 'a moving act of personal testimony' to 'the contradictions of love'. Testimony here is deployed in the sense of a heightened, autobiographical experience, which, it must be noted, does not preclude the possibility of finite suffering (as depicted in the last three poems 'Art' (p. 60), 'Unloving' (p. 61), and 'Over' (p. 62)). Poetry nevertheless in this way becomes testimony to all kinds of subjective experience, rather than—as in most psychoanalytical engagements with testimonial literature—referring to the specificities of trauma. Locating itself in a continuum of discourses about testimony, this book argues that the use of testimony in the first (Duffy) instance is too broad, and in the second instance too specific. Testimony refers to artistic reflection on traumatic events, but—as distinct from Felman and Laub's detection of diagnostic categories—the resultant texts might not display literary or visual signs of trauma. The chapter on working-class poetry in this book also argues that a wider model of everyday suffering might be more pertinent to discussions of testimony in such contexts than the specificity of trauma.

15. In addition to popular tastes, Carolyn J. Dean discusses the emphasis on minimalist writing in *Aversion and Erasure: The Fate of the Victim after the Holocaust* (Ithaca, NY: Cornell University Press, 2010). *If This Is a Man* arguably constitutes Levi—in Dean's terms—as the ideal victim for a postwar audience, who, without anger or (seemingly) embellishment, calmly outlines the victim's experience.

16. Hynes, p. 25.

17. Roland Barthes, *The Rustle of Language*, trans. by Richard Howard (Oxford: Basil Blackwell, 1986); Hayden White, *Tropics of Discourse: Essays in Cultural Criticism* (Baltimore, MD: Johns Hopkins University Press, 1978). Their critiques of realism do not suggest that realism is an unreflective form of writing, as can be evidenced in the self-reflexive, realist novels of Victorian authors such as George Eliot.

18. Primo Levi, *If This Is A Man/The Truce*, trans. by S. Woolf (London: Abacus, 1987), p. 35.

19. Tadeusz Borowski, *Selected Poems*, trans. by Tadeusz Pióro with Larry Rafferty and Meryl Natchez (Walnut Creek, CA: Hit & Run Press, 1990), p. 17.

20. Theodor Adorno, 'On Lyric Poetry and Society', in *Notes to Literature*, trans. by Shierry Weber Nicholsen (New York: Columbia University Press, 1991), pp. 37–54 (p. 37).

21. Derek Attridge, *The Singularity of Literature* (London: Routledge, 2004), p. 71.

22. Susan Gubar, 'The Long and Short of Holocaust Verse', *New Literary History*, 35.3 (2004), 443–69 (also available online at http://lion.chadwyck.co.uk).

23. James Young, 'Interpreting Literary Testimony. A Preface to Rereading Holocaust Diaries and Memoirs', *New Literary History*, 18.2 (1987), 403–23 (p. 404).

24. This book is not critical of the complexities of realist prose; rather, the sometimes unreflective *reception* of realism in Holocaust Studies. The consideration that such prose is 'closer' to the reality of events than other artistic genres betrays a flawed assumption that aesthetic choices have, necessarily, mimetic consequences. I do not wish to suggest either here that modernist and postmodernist writing is somehow inherently 'closer' to the events than realism, since this too would suggest an uncomplicated mimesis.

25. Slavoj Žižek, *Violence* (London: Profile Books, 2008), p. 4.

26. Felman and Laub, p. 12.

27. Vice, p. 8.

28. Levi, *If This Is A Man*, pp. 48, 96.

29. *OED*, 2nd edn.

30. In *Against Forgetting: Twentieth-Century Poetry of Witness* (New York: W. W. Norton, 1993), Carolyn Forché stresses that witness poetry presents the 'poem as evidence', a traumatic event which nevertheless belongs 'to a different order of being from the trauma that marked its language in the first place' (p. 31).

31. Elie Wiesel, 'The Holocaust as Literary Inspiration', in *Dimensions of the Holocaust* (Evanston, IL: Northwestern University Press, 1990), p. 7.

32. Before the publication of Felman and Laub's groundbreaking work, many critics responded to testimony as an act of impossibility in its desire to convey historical truths. For example, Ulrike Kistner argues in 'Writing "After Auschwitz": On the Impossibility of a Postscript' (written in 1991) that 'The desperate act of making these [truth] claims heard can [. . .] only be a negative one' (*Acta Germanica*, 21 (1992), 171–83 (p. 171)). After Felman and Laub's book, the prerogatives of testimony can be re-evaluated as not ostensibly revolving around such claims, but as a form of life writing in which historical truth may be less important than the traumatic 'truths' of witnesses to atrocity. Laub famously discusses the case of a female witness who miscounted the number of chimneys exploded in the Auschwitz uprising. Instead of incurring the censure of historians, the testimony should be regarded as engaging with the 'reality of an unimaginable occurrence' (p. 60).

33. General Sir John Hackett, 'Forward', in *From Oasis into Italy: War Poems and Diaries from Africa and Italy 1940–1946*, ed. by Victor Selwyn, Dan Davin, Erik de Mauny, and Ian Fletcher (London: Shepheard-Walwyn, 1983), p. xvii.

34. Donald Bloxham and Tony Kushner, *The Holocaust: Critical Historical Approaches* (Manchester: Manchester University Press, 2005), p. 45.

35. Giorgio Agamben, *Remnants of Auschwitz*, trans. by Daniel Heller-Roazen (New York: Zone Books, 2002), p. 12.

36. Even *within* the genre of poetry, there are mimetic distinctions made between allegedly transparent, realist verse, and more hermetic modernist and post-modernist writing. In relation to war poetry, for example, anthologies and critical studies of the genre have privileged realist poems, which are 'discussed as "truly" reflecting war experience, perhaps because the conventions and tropes of poetic realism bear a resemblance to prosaic representations of war in history, memoir and journalism' (*Twentieth-Century War Poetry*, ed. by Philippa Lyon (Basingstoke: Palgrave Macmillan, 2005), p. 12).

37. Robert Antelme, 'Poetry and the Testimony of the Camps', in *On Robert Antelme's 'The Human Race': Essays and Commentary*, ed. by Daniel Dobbels (Evanston, IL: Northwestern University Press, 2003), pp. 31–37 (p. 34). In *Sovereignties in Question* (New York: Fordham University Press, 2005), Jacques Derrida argues similarly to Antelme that 'all responsible witnessing engages a poetic experience of language' (p. 66).

38. Julia Kristeva, 'For Shoshana Felman: Truth and Art', in *The Claims of Literature: A Shoshana Felman Reader*, ed. by Emily Sun, Eyal Peretz, and Ulrich Baer (New York: Fordham University Press, 2007), pp. 315–21 (pp. 316–17).

39. In *Descent into Barbarism: A History of the 20th Century 1933–1951* (London: HarperCollins, 1999), for example, Gilbert deploys briefly a range of personal testimonies within the historical narratives, including Roy Fuller's poem 'October 1940' (p. 346). Gilbert's use of testimony is noteworthy beyond these brief expositions: in *The Holocaust* (London: HarperCollins, 1986), almost an entire chapter (Chapter 16, 'Eye-Witness to Mass Murder') is given over to the testimony of Yakov Grojanowski about Chelmno, without any ensuing comment by the historian; as if—at such moments—personal testimony 'speaks' for itself and supersedes the requirement for professional intervention (pp. 252–79).

40. Quoted in Mole, pp. 11–12.

41. Janina Struk, 'The Death Pit', *The Guardian*, 27 January 2004, 12–13.

42. I refer here to the opposition Levi constructs between his subjective, outraged poems and the serenity of his 'objective' prose. By 'self-reflexive', I mean that poetry often reminds us that we are reading poetry in a way that conventional photographs and realist prose can only do to a lesser extent. Indeed, the illusion of mimesis in the latter genres often results in the realist author or photographer's drive to oust such reflexivity in order to sustain the illusion.

43. James Hatley, *Suffering Witness: the Quandary of Responsibility after the Irreparable* (Albany: State University of New York Press, 2000), p.109.

44. Antelme presumably means that an abstract lyric in Alexandrines, say, about Buchenwald forms a 'melodic counterpoint' to the metanarrative. I would disagree with Antelme on this point, since I evaluate Borowski's love and nature poems set in Auschwitz as examples of testimony in Chapter 2.

45. Žižek discusses the failure of prose in relation to rape reports and Holocaust testimony: 'the very factual deficiencies of the traumatised subject's report on her experience bear witness to the truthfulness of her report, since they

signal that the reported content "contaminated" the manner of reporting it [. . .] the witness able to offer a clear narrative of his camp experience would disqualify himself by virtue of that clarity' (pp. 3–4). Testimonies in general are not equivalent to the specificity of crime reports, however: 'factual deficiencies' may be present in reports of rape, but are more scarce in relation to considered, literary narratives. The serenity of Levi's prose in *If This Is a Man* and Borowski's seemingly untroubled accounts of his incarceration do not square with Žižek's (and Felman and Laub's) causal sense that diagnostic criteria are embedded in traumatic texts.

46. Theodor Adorno, 'Rede über Lyrik und Gesellschaft', in *Gesammelte Schriften II: Noten Zur Literatur* (Frankfurt: Suhrkamp, 1974), pp. 49–68 (p. 49); 'On Lyric Poetry and Society', in *Notes to Literature*, pp. 37–54 (*Noten Zur Literatur*, p. 53; 'On Lyric Poetry and Society', p. 41).
47. Primo Levi, *Moments of Reprieve*, trans. by Ruth Feldman (London: Abacus, 1987), pp. 99–100.
48. On the back cover of *Ad Ora Incerta*, Levi comments that '[t]here have been times when poetry has seemed to me more suitable than prose for transmitting an idea or an image' (translated and quoted in Giovanni Tesio, *'At an Uncertain Hour*: Preliminary Observations on the Poetry of Primo Levi', in *Primo Levi: The Austere Humanist*, ed. by Joseph Farrell (New York: Peter Lang, 2005), pp. 160–70 (p. 163)).
49. Sarah Kofman, *Smothered Words*, trans. by Madaleine Dobie (Evanston: Northwestern University Press, 1998), p. xv.
50. Susan Gubar, 'The Long and Short of Holocaust Verse', New Literary History, 35.3 (2004), 443–69 (also available online at http://lion.chadwyck. co.uk). Here I am discussing a certain kind of poem as testimony in relation to Gubar's notion of the 'broken' lyric. Her description fits the aporetic poetry of Celan much better than the prosaic ruminations of Tadeusz Borowski. Jack Bevan's verbal energy in 'Ubique'—which I discuss in Chapter 3—forms a different example of Felman and Laub's concept of 'precocious' testimony.
51. Bloxham and Kushner, p. 42.
52. Borowski, p.89.
53. Felman and Laub, p.21.
54. The variety of inscriptions does not ensure an ensuing notoriety in terms of the literary canon, however. Poetry comprises a neglected genre in both the literary marketplace and academic studies: all the texts discussed herein are in this sense paradoxically voiceless. Poetry as testimony may—as in Levi's case—give vent to anger expunged from the prosaic record, or—as in the case of World War II poets—express reactions released from masculine banter and the censor's ink, but it often remains voiceless in the context of the literary canon. Whereas Levi and Delbo are familiar names in Holocaust Studies in terms of their prose work, their poetry has received much less attention. The study will also explore a connection between the various contexts in terms of the ways in which professional and non-professional writers engage with the genre of testimony. Levi, primarily a chemist, only became a writer after his traumatic experiences in Auschwitz. Whereas Oasis writers such as Vernon Scannell and Kingsley Amis were fledgling writers at the beginning of World War II, others were driven to poetic testimony by the events they witnessed.
55. Some historians (and historicists) will deplore such critical connections between such diverse traumatic events. The singularity of, and links between, the various historical events will be stressed, but rather than deploy a psychoanalytic paradigm to connect them all, the focus will be on the generic characteristics displayed in different types of testimony. However, the study

does not blithely reject the groundbreaking work of psychoanalysists such as Felman and Laub. Trauma Studies has been unfairly attacked in recent times as pathologizing texts rather than people, and as flattening out patent dissimilarities between historical phenomena. Cathy Caruth had already anticipated such criticism in *Trauma: Explorations in Memory*: the 'irreducible specificity of traumatic stories' creates the difficulty of 'responding to traumatic stories in a way that does not [. . .] turn them all into versions of the same story' (*Trauma: Explorations in Memory*, ed. by Cathy Caruth (London: Johns Hopkins University Press, 1995), pp. ix, v, vii). Nevertheless, the singularity of trauma outlined here then contrasts with its ubiquity at the end of the introduction: Caruth writes of our 'catastrophic age' and the 'departures we have all taken from ourselves' (p. 11). In contrast, the critical focus in this study will be on genre rather than trauma. The book locates testimony both within and beyond trauma: generic characteristics link testimonies of Holocaust survivors with working-class writers pointing out the drudgery of repetitive labour, without cancelling out the obvious differences in the authors' experiences. Testimony in the latter case responds to particularized 'everyday suffering' and a crisis in representation rather than trauma *per se.*

56. Attridge, p. 47.
57. Keith Douglas, letter to J. C. Hall (10 August 1943), in *Keith Douglas: The Letters*, ed. by Desmond Graham (Manchester: Carcanet Press, 2000), pp. 294–95 (p. 294).
58. Such diverse traces might be criticized as an instance of what Attridge terms critical instrumentalism, in which the pragmatic utilization of literary texts results in the valorization of an (already decided) ideological approach. In other words, Sassoon's satires might only look like testimony because the author has decided a priori to seek out instances of testimony in literature. Yet the study's central argument was initiated primarily not by trauma theory, previous discussions in Holocaust Studies, or Attridge's book itself, but by rereading the poetry of Borowski and allowing for 'an openness that allows for a range of possible outcomes—including a challenge to the very project they are supposed to be serving' (p. 8). It seemed, initially, that Borowski's modernist poems written in Auschwitz should be contrasted with the post-liberation pieces, which are more prosaic and journalistic—and, therefore, more obviously potential instances of testimony. However, it became clear that both forms of writing can be considered forms of testimony, even though they are written in very different registers, tones, and levels of linguistic complexity. Modernist poetry is not usually considered to be testimony precisely because of its linguistic density, and yet the apparent accessibility of Borowski's journalistic pieces should not dupe the writer or reader into constructing a binary between these poems (as non-literary testimony) and the (non-testimonial) allusiveness of complex poetic forms. Eaglestone points out that an important effect of testimony is its paradox of non-/identification: readers are often told that they cannot understand the enormity of the traumatic experiences, at the same time as 'we expect identification to happen when we read prose narratives' (p. 23). The defamiliarizing strategies of modernist and postmodernist poetry immediately assuage this paradox for much prose writing, since in such poems we can often not rely on simple structures of identification, such as knowing who is speaking to whom (as, famously, in Sylvia Plath's post-Holocaust poem 'Daddy'), and coherent narratives.
59. *Witness and Memory: The Discourse of Trauma*, ed. by Ana Douglas and Thomas A. Vogler (London: Routledge, 2003), pp. 173–206 (p. 191).

60. Morris Grossman, 'The Holocaust, or, Once More with Feeling', *Centennial Review*, 35.3 (Fall 1991), 625–60 (p. 625).
61. Young, 'Interpreting Literary Testimony', pp. 23, 24.
62. Susan Rubin Suleiman, 'Problems of Memory and Factuality in Recent Holocaust Memoirs: Wilkomirski/Wiesel', *Poetics Today*, 21.3 (Fall 2000), 543–59 (p. 546).
63. In *More Poems of the Second World War*, ed. by Victor Selwyn, Erik de Mauny, Ian Fletcher, and Robin Ivy (London: J. M. Dent & Sons, 1989), Selwyn argues that war poems should be regarded as a different kind of art to the poetry of civilians. '[T]he poems' in the anthology, he stresses, 'have to be judged not just as poems—but as *war* poetry, a genre on its own' (p. xv).
64. I discuss this poem briefly in Chapter 3. In a letter in the Salamander Oasis archive to Ivan Henson (3 August 1988), Victor Selwyn complains, 'We really are tired of having this bogus poem sent to us by so many. It was not written by an unknown soldier, but from the comfort of a Guards Mess a long way away' (SOTA Box 18 H, folder HE (p. 1)).
65. Derrida, *Sovereignties in Question*, p.77.
66. In *Literature or Life* (trans. by Linda Coverdale), Semprun writes, 'Only the artifice of a masterly narrative will prove capable of conveying some of the truth of such testimony', and create 'transparent density' in the writing (New York: Penguin, 1997), p. 13. He adds: 'there's nothing exceptional about this: it's the same with all great historical experience' (ibid.).
67. *Poems from Italy: Verses Written by Members of the Eighth Army in Sicily and Italy July 1943–March 1944* (London: George G. Harrap, 1945), pp. 62–63. *From Oasis into Italy*, pp.167–69. I discuss the advent of the Salamander Society further in the chapter on the 'Oasis' poets. In this section, I refer to the version of the poem in *From Oasis into Italy*.
68. 'The Second World War Papers of NT Morris' (short biography).
69. P116 Folder NTM/1. Letter to Mrs Morris (August 1942), p. 1.
70. SOTA Box 26 M. Note to 'On Guard' (undated), pp. 1–2.
71. 'The Second World War Papers of NT Morris' (short biography).
72. There *is* a circular—not triangular—painting by Pietro Perugino in the Louvre of the Virgin and Child enthroned between saints, but the potential referent here is less important that the 'truth' of memory, remembering war through the aesthetics of an elusive picture. 'Triangular' may refer to the composition of the picture as opposed to the shape of the frame, but this description does not fit this particular Perugino picture either.
73. Henry Reed, *Collected Poems*, ed. by Jon Stallworthy (Manchester: Carcanet, 2007), pp. 49–60.
74. The 'common touch' of the robin is less 'common' (in the sense of appertaining to mere humans) than it first might seem, given that the robin—with its distinctive red breast—stands for the crucifixion of Christ in many Renaissance paintings.

NOTES TO CHAPTER 1

1. Todman, p. 7.
2. Episode four ('Private Plane') of the final series of *Blackadder* (quoted in Todman, p. 153).
3. James Campbell, 'Combat Gnosticism: The Ideology of First World War Poetry Criticism', *New Literary History: A Journal of Theory and Interpretation*, 30.1 (1999), 203–15 (p. 203). John Purkis, for example, in *A Preface to Wilfred Owen* (London: Longman, 1999), argues that survivors'

'experiences were, in all senses of the word, "indescribable"' (p. x). In *An Adequate Response: The War Poetry of Wilfred Owen and Siegfried Sassoon* (Detroit, MI: Wayne State University Press, 1972), Arthur E. Lane similarly asserts, 'There is no way for the reader, even a sympathetic one, to share, and thereby comprehend, the nightmare world of the soldier [. . .] the war has created a gulf between soldiers and civilians that no verbal communication could properly bridge' (p. 158). Desmond Graham notes that 'virtually every-one who has written about that war, whether as participant, historian or literary critic, has spoken of the gulf between the experience of the soldiers at the Front and everyone else' (*The Truth of War: Owen, Blunden, Rosenberg* (Manchester: Carcanet, 1984), p.12). In his account of his war experiences in *Journey to the End of the Night*, trans. by Ralph Manheim (London: John Calder, 1988), Louis-Ferdinand Céline states the matter plainly when the narrator asserts that 'things happened and then a lot more things that it's not easy to tell about now, because people nowadays wouldn't understand them any more' (p. 48). As Todman argues, this 'gulf' was a tangible sense that 'returning veterans truly did not feel that they could make those who had stayed at home understand them' (p. 10); Campbell's attack on gnosti-cism risks insensitivity in this context. Yet his critique of the inarticulacy of conflict survivors inadvertently makes a wider point about the limitations of language and the process of reading. The elusive referent will always evade the reader's engagement with an author's signifiers; a process which is focal-ized in response to war and atrocity.
4. John Silkin opens his account of World War I poetry with a critique of an aspect of memory transmission when he attacks potentially compassionate responses. 'At best [. . .] compassion walks behind the system' that pro-duced war (*The Penguin Book of First World War Poetry* (Harmondsworth: Penguin, 1981), p. 15). This politicized opening about the affective is, inter-estingly, not carried through the rest of the introduction.
5. These quotations are taken from Adrian Caesar's *Taking It Like a Man: Suffering, Sexuality and the War Poets* (Manchester: Manchester Univer-sity Press, 1993), p. 158. Campbell also, and rightly, attacks the equation of war with combat (p. 204), a conflation that impacted on the collection of material for the Salamander Oasis archive and World War II poetry (as I discuss in Chapter 3). 'Exposure' questions the concept of 'action', since very little happens during this 'front line' poem; as the opening conjunc-tion in the fourth stanza of 'Spring Exposure' indicates, the poem devotes more lines to the inaction of soldiers resting than the subsequent assault. And as Todman notes, by July 1918, almost a third of the army were non-combatants, 'far removed from the popular conception of trenches and relentless mud and guts' (p. 4). Without noting Campbell's contribu-tion to the field, Todman illustrates that 'post-war culture came to focus on the soldier in the trench as the iconic experience of the real war' (p. 26). However, critics before the publication of Campbell's essay in 1999 had begun to be troubled by the prevalence of gnosis, as when Desmond Graham—as early as 1984—writes in *The Truth of War: Owen, Blunden, Rosenberg* of Owen's 'relish for being the one who knows better' (p. 19). Nor is 'trench lyric' as homogenous as Campbell suggests (p. 204): Owen—as Dominic Hibberd points out in *Wilfred Owen: A New Biog-raphy* (London: Weidenfeld and Nicolson, 2002)—'endured very little of what is thought of as the standard Western Front experience, the ghastly monotony of routine trench duty' (p. xvii). Campbell also complies with the ideology (as he puts it) of trench lyricism by refusing to think outside the dangers of solipsism, where 'it remains impossible to tell others of

one's own experiences unless these others have also undergone identical experiences' (p. 209). He makes the same methodological conflation that he accuses previous war critics of at the beginning of his essay—writing criticism that complies with the thinking and writing of the authors in question—since he does not explain how writers might overcome a gulf in communication. Rather than being caught in a solipsistic, 'epistemological trap' (p. 210), testimonial poets actually confront—to borrow Delbo's terminology—an im/possible process of 'seeing': readers can engage with some of their experiences, but they will never 'see' them entirely. This process is deemed more fraught by the fact that the writers often cannot articulate to themselves the 'gnosis' of what they have experienced, as illustrated in 'Insensibility', when Owen frets over his poetic diction at the start of the poem.

6. Antony Rowland, 'The Future of Testimony', in *The Future of Memory*, ed. by Rick Crownshaw, Jane Kilby and Antony Rowland (New York: Berghahn Books, 2010), pp. 113–22.

7. In *Afterlife of Holocaust Memory in Contemporary Literature and Culture* (Basingstoke: Palgrave Macmillan, 2010), Rick Crownshaw points out that 'such practices [of over-identification] prevail in current cultures of memory [. . .] in which authors are the subjects of over-identification and their texts colonised' (p. xiii).

8. Charlotte Delbo, *Auschwitz and After*, trans. by Rosette C. Lamont (New Haven, CT: Yale University Press, 1995), pp. 286–88.

9. Antelme, p. 34. I discuss Antelme's defence of the poetry of truth in my introduction. The first quotation is from Tim Kendall's 'Wilfred Owen's Concern', in *Modern English War Poetry* (Oxford: Oxford University Press, 2006), p. 49. The letter comes from Owen's *Collected Letters*, ed. by Harold Owen and James Bell (Oxford: Oxford University Press, 1967), p. 489 (quoted in Kendall, p. 49).

10. This phrase comes from 'Introduction by Lawrence L. Langer' in Delbo's *Auschwitz and After*, pp. ix–xviii, p. xvi.

11. Campbell, p. 211.

12. *The Penguin Book of First World War Poetry*, p. 189. The metaphor of the trenches 'cobbled' with corpses is used in Owen's letter to Mary Owen ([25(?)] March 1918), where he notes that soldiers 'are dying again at Beaumont Hamel, which already in 1916 was cobbled with skulls' (p. 542). The repetition of 'cobbled' may suggest that 'Insensibility' was composed around this time.

13. '[F]leers' ('mocks') is the only word that requires a dictionary in the first stanza.

14. Hynes, *The Soldier's Tale*, p. 25.

15. In 'Break of Day in the Trenches', Rosenberg fuses flowers and soldiers with the '[p]oppies whose roots are in man's veins', that '[d]rop, and are ever dropping' (*The Penguin Book of First World War Poetry*, p. 209). Seven out of eleven lines are hypercatalectic in the first stanza of 'Insensibility': lines one, five to nine, and eleven:

Happy are men who yet before they are killed
Can let their veins run cold.
Whom no compassion fleers
Or makes their feet
Sore on the alleys cobbled with their brothers.
The front line withers.
But they are troops who fade, not flowers,
For poets' tearful fooling:

Men, gaps for filling:
Losses, who might have fought
Longer; but no one bothers.

16. General Sir John Hackett, 'Forward', in *From Oasis Into Italy*, p. xvii.
17. Felman and Laub, p. 12.
18. *The Penguin Book of First World War Poetry*, p.191. The opening 'But' in the final stanza avoids, of course, a confusion between the civilian and conscripted dullards.
19. Letter to Susan Owen (4 January 1917) (Owen, *Collected Letters*, p. 422).
20. These are quotations from letters to Susan Owen (14 March 1916) (p. 385), (19 June 1916) (p. 395), and (19 June 1916), respectively. Sassoon is privy to this class distaste, too, when he writes of '[t]he dilemma of an ignorant private' in his notes to 'Christ and the Soldier' (*Sassoon: The War Poems*, ed. by Rupert Hart-Davis (London: Faber and Faber, 1983), p. 47).
21. Letter to Nick Gammage (15 March 1991). Box 61, folder 16, in the Emory archive; reprinted in *Letters of Ted Hughes*, ed. by Christopher Reid (London: Faber, 2007), pp. 592–94 (p. 594).
22. The quotation here comes from Caesar. Caesar similarly argues that 'it is difficult to avoid the massive condescension he displays towards the private soldiers' (p. 159).
23. These attacks on army staff contrast with the national mourning for General Hague in 1928 but comply with the modern view of Haig and his generals (as in *Blackadder*) as 'the villains of the war, the enemies most likely to account for the unfortunate private soldier with idiotic plans based on their incomprehension of modern warfare' (Todman, p. 73).
24. *Wilfred Owen: The Complete Poems and Fragments*, 2 vols, ed. by John Stallworthy (London: Oxford University Press, 1983), II, p. 301.
25. *Owen: The War Poems*, ed. by Jon Stallworthy (London: Chatto and Windus, 1994), p. 42.
26. *Sassoon: The War Poems*, p. 93.
27. *Owen: The War Poems*, p. 85.
28. *The Penguin Book of First World War Poetry*, p. 89.
29. Primo Levi, *Collected Poems*, trans. by Ruth Feldman and Brian Swann (London: Faber, 1988), p. 9; *From Oasis into Italy*, p. vi.
30. I discuss this aspect of Delbo's work further in Chapter 4.
31. *Wilfred Owen*, II, p. 48.
32. *Philip Larkin: Letters to Monica*, ed. Anthony Thwaite (London: Faber, 2010), p. 319.
33. Letter to Owen, c.22 December 1917 (*Collected Letters*, p. 596).
34. Theodor Adorno, 'Cultural Criticism and Society', in *Prisms*, trans. by S. and S. Weber (London: Neville Spearman, 1967), pp. 17–35 (p. 34).
35. Letter to Owen c.17 October 1917, in *Collected Letters*, p. 595.
36. Tim Kendall, 'Gurney and Fritz', *Essays in Criticism*, 59.2 (2009), 142–56 (p. 152). 'Strange Meeting' has been read as the archetypal pacifist text of World War I, but, as Kendall notes (p. 152), it also comprises one of the few texts in which the 'business of killing' is represented, when the narrator is revealed to be the frowning killer of the strange friend.
37. In contrast, officer Max Plowman—who had been wounded on the western front—resigned his commission on 14 January 1918, protesting his conviction that 'organised warfare of any kind is always organised murder', and that '[s]o wholly do I believe in the doctrine of Incarnation (that God indeed lives in every human body) that I believe that killing men is always killing God' (quoted in Martin Gilbert, *First World War* (London: HarperCollins, 1995), p. 395).

38. Kendall discusses Raine's evaluation of Owen as the most overrated poet of the twentieth century ('Wilfred Owen's Concern', p. 46). The metrical complexity of 'Spring Offensive' is evident in the first stanza, with the metrical breaks emphasizing the uneasiness introduced into the poem in the first line: is the 'last hill' the final one in a range, or the last hill that some unlucky soldiers will come across? Metrical breaks then occur on 'hill', 'load', 'blank', 'hung', 'end', 'sharp', and 'pains'.
39. I discuss Levi's concept of the 'grey zone' further in Chapter 5.
40. Quoted in Caesar, p. 147. Syntactically, the phrase could refer to the 'fiends and flames' in the previous line, but, given the overall tenor of the stanza, it most likely refers to the attackers.
41. Paul Fussell, *The Great War and Modern Memory* (Oxford: Oxford University Press, 1977), p. 169.
42. I discuss the latter two poems in detail in Chapter 3.
43. Ironically, in this context, Todman at one point notes the 'prurient interest in second-hand gore which had encouraged the war books boom' (p. 28).
44. *The Penguin Book of First World War Poetry*, p. 115.

NOTES TO CHAPTER 2

1. Tadeusz Borowski, letter to Zofia Świdwińska (5 February 1946) in *The Correspondence of Tadeusz Borowski*, ed. by Tadeusz Drewnowski, trans. by Alicia Nitecki (Evanston, IL: Northwestern University Press, 2007), p. 60.
2. Tadeusz Borowski, *This Way for the Gas, Ladies and Gentlemen*, trans. by Barbara Vedder (New York: Penguin, 1967).
3. Antony Rowland, 'Interview with Tadeusz Pióro (re Tadeusz Borowski's *Selected Poems*)', in *Holocaust Poetry*, ed. by Robert Eaglestone and Antony Rowland (*Critical Survey*, 20.2 (2008)), pp. 43–52.
4. Levi, *Collected Poems*; *Holocaust Poetry*, ed. by Hilda Schiff (London: HarperCollins, 1995), pp. 55, 119, 120.
5. *The Auschwitz Poems*, ed. and trans. Adam A. Zych (Oświęcim: Auschwitz-Birkenau State Museum, 1999), pp. 43–52.
6. Borowski, *Selected Poems*.
7. *Holocaust Poetry*, pp. 39–40, 67, 205.
8. Felman and Laub, p. 21.
9. Adorno, 'Cultural Criticism and Society', pp. 17–35 (p. 34). In a sense, Borowski was one of the few post-war poets to take Adorno at his word (without having read his work), since he stopped writing poetry in the summer of 1946. In a letter to Maria Rundo which is undated—but was sent around July 1946—he states that he has 'given up poetry. It's the wisest step I've taken in life. So-called prose is very easy, and depends on remembering things one's observed and putting them together into a whole—the longer, the more entertaining' (*The Correspondence of Tadeusz Borowski*, p. 130). The anticipatory nature of Borowski's poetics connects with recent interest in pre-1960s Holocaust literature, when the critical paradigms which now dominate Holocaust Studies had not been established. As Michael Rothberg states in *Multidirectional Memory: Remembering the Holocaust in an Age of Decolonization*, 'the early postwar period is richer and more complex than earlier studies, with their stress on a period of silence and repression that lasts until around the time of the Eichmann trial in 1961, have allowed' (Stanford, CA: Stanford University Press, 2009), p. 22. More research needs to be done

on post-Holocaust European poetry between 1945 and the early 1960s, when Adorno's comments on 'barbaric' poetry had not yet been widely translated and the aesthetic agenda of self-critical poetics—which still predominates in studies of contemporary post-Holocaust poetry—had not yet been established.

10. Keith Douglas, letter to J. C. Hall (10 August 1943), in *Keith Douglas*, pp. 294–95 (p. 294). I discuss this quotation from Douglas's letter further in Chapter 3 (on the Oasis poets).
11. Theodor Adorno, *Minima Moralia: Reflections from Damaged Life*, trans. by E. F. N. Jephcott (London: Verso, 1978), p. 52.
12. See my interpretation of the original German in *Tony Harrison and the Holocaust* (Liverpool: Liverpool University Press, 2001), p. 13.
13. Rowland, *Tony Harrison and the Holocaust*, p. 14.
14. In a letter to Zosia Świdwińska (6 October 1945), Borowski points out that, ironically, the Munich camp 'was closely guarded (ostensibly on account of typhus and theft')' (p. 39).
15. Rowland, *Holocaust Poetry* and *Tony Harrison*.
16. Borowski, *Selected Poems*, p. 17.
17. The poem does appear in the Zych anthology (pp. 45–46).
18. Borowski, *Selected Poems*, pp. 16, 17; *This Way for the Gas*, p. 127.
19. *Keith Douglas*, p. 294.
20. Frieda W. Aaron, *Bearing the Unbearable: Yiddish and Polish Poetry in the Ghettos and Concentration Camps* (New York: State University of New York Press, 1990), p. 8; Borowski, *Selected Poems*, p. 7. Questions arise out of this assertion that 'October Sky' and 'Night over Birkenau' were written in Auschwitz-Birkenau. Did Borowski carry versions of these poems on the forced march to Dachau from Auschwitz? What did he use for writing material in the camp? Or did he compose the poems in his head (as he did early on in Pawiak prison) and then write them down later? In a letter to Tadeusz Sołtan (22 February 1946), Borowski suggests he did not have writing materials in Auschwitz: 'I survived the camp with parcels and luck. Summer of '43 I was ill and thought about poems that I would write if I'd had paper and pencil and—wasn't in the camp' (*The Correspondence of Tadeusz Borowski*, p. 69). In private correspondence, Pióro has confirmed that he cannot be certain that the poem was written in Auschwitz, but that critics in Poland generally assume this to be the case. Writing materials were hidden in some of the camps: in *Beyond the Limit Experience*, Mole records that Eugène Malzac's poem 'Le Convoi du 2 juillet 1944' was 'written on a piece of wrapping paper [in Dachau] with a stub of pencil' the day after his arrival (p. 88). In *The Drowned and the Saved*, trans. by R. Rosenthal (London: Abacus, 1986), Primo Levi points out that the idea of Jewish prisoners, as opposed to political prisoners, writing and preserving notes in Auschwitz was 'unthinkable' (p. 7).
21. The implied reader may be Maria Berta Rundo in particular. Maria was captured by the Gestapo in Warsaw (which led to Borowski's own arrest); she was then sent to the women's camp in Birkenau. Tadeusz used to see her occasionally across the wire, and he managed to see her more in summer 1944 after becoming a nurse in the camp hospital. In a letter to Stanisław Kazimierz Marczak (7 November 1945), Borowski describes her illnesses as 'angina, flu, lungs, malaria, typhus [. . .] and the most painful of all—scabies, incessant scabies' (*The Correspondence of Tadeusz Borowski*, p. 45). After the liberation, Maria found herself in Sweden, but was then reunited with Tadeusz in Poland, where they were later married. Borowski registers his desperation to find Maria (Tuśka) after the war in a letter to Zosia Świdwińska

(16 October 1945): 'Find Tuśka for me. In August 1944, she went to Bergen-Belsen or Ravensbrück. If she's alive and is in Poland, tell her that I still exist. If she got married, it would be best for her to divorce right away, and if she didn't, okay, I'm writing very romantic poems about her' (*The Correspondence of Tadeusz Borowski*, p. 42). Maria had just given birth to Borowski's first child when he committed suicide in 1951 (see Stanisław Barańczak's introduction to the *Selected Poems*, pp. 1–8). She remarried in 1954 and published her camp memoirs in 1995—in the style of Borowski—as 'Farewell to Tuśka' (*The Correspondence of Tadeusz Borowski*, p. 341).

22. A similar process is afoot in 'Idyll', which is printed after 'October Sky' in the *Selected Poems*. Naturalistic poetics are undercut when Borowski reflects on the moment of liberation:

    The people came out, cheerful, free,
    into a free world, into the green summer.
    They forgot to look for ashes in the fields—
    they gathered handfuls of wildflowers. (p. 19)

    Unreflective 'freedom' (the repetition of 'free' emphasizes the irony) is a charade, according to this poem, when not considered in the context of Auschwitz. The final lines become emblematic of the inseparability of aesthetics and atrocity for many Holocaust poets.

23. Antelme, p. 33. Borowski's concerns about his lyrical poem reflect Robert Antelme's worries in the 1945 article that camp poems could 'risk fleeing the reality of the camps, letting that reality be glimpsed only through a melodic counterpoint, through themes of nostalgia that surround but never penetrate this reality of fog and words—the sun, laughter, color, and so on' (p. 33). (Antelme also had reservations about prose testimony—as I point out in the introduction—arguing that it was a kind of 'photograph which only makes you shudder.')

24. Nader refers to the 'restorative impulse' in poetry from the camps in Germany in *Traumatic Verses*, p. 22. This reading of the last few lines connects them with the opening sentence ('October was beautiful'). Another way to read the final metaphor would be to argue that by the end of the poem, the October sky itself stands for radical uncertainty. Whereas it represents an uncomplicated lyricism at the beginning, its subsequent 'contamination' in Auschwitz means it can never return to its previously idealistic, pastoral state. As opposed to the more monologic testimonial poems written in Munich, the dialectical ending of 'October Sky' is able to sustain its lyrical ambivalence.

25. *Keith Douglas*, p. 294.

26. The phrase 'partnership in evil' comes from the *OED* definition of 'complicity' (second edition). In his memoir *Beyond Lost Dreams* (Edinburgh: Pentland Press, 1994), J. N. Siedlecki describes complicity in Auschwitz in terms of everyday violence: 'tie everything into a compact bundle and hit hard if an anonymous hand gropes for it in the darkness [. . .] Find your place [at roll call] and stand quietly for the roll-call and kick any blunderer disrupting the ranks. At work secure the tool with a smooth handle, hang on to it and don't argue but hit first anybody trying to take it off you' (p. 153). Siedlecki—who co-authored *We Were in Auschwitz* with Borowski and Krystyn Olszewski—notes that his time as a hospital auxiliary saved him from 'mussulman' status (p. 157). The first reference to Borowski is on page 226: in the Munich barracks Siedlecki meets 'a poet whom I christened "Puppy" as he was not only very young but behaved like an unruly whelp'. Tadeusz 'worried and needled everybody with his leftish views and merciless exposure of people's hidden weaknesses which he spotted unerringly' (p. 226). During their time

in Munich, Siedlecki argues that 'Puppy got "stoned" at every opportunity and grew viciously sarcastic about the West' (p. 234).

27. Borowski, *Selected Poems*, p. 13. The 'lead foot' may, of course, refer only to another prisoner, sleeping top-to-toe in the bunk. However, Borowski emphasizes the metaphoric weight of the 'lead' foot: my reading of this line as an epiphanic moment surrounding complicity links with the whole stanza, which stands out as the only one to focus on the unnamed narrator exclusively, rather than the classical metaphors about the camp as a whole (the moon, for example, is like Cerberus, 'a crouching beast over the camp').

28. Borowski, *This Way for the Gas*, p. 22.

29. Siedlecki, p. 180.

30. Matthew Boswell, *Holocaust Impiety* (Basingstoke: Palgrave Macmillan, 2011), *passim*; *The Correspondence of Tadeusz Borowski*, pp. x–xi (from the preface to *Twórczość*). In a letter to Zofia Świdwińska (5 February 1946), Borowski wrote that he produced the camp stories 'so as to show (though in a few fragments) everyday camp life and to strip man of so-called martyrdom; and finally, because evil was not the work of one side' (*The Correspondence of Tadeusz Borowski*, pp. 57–58).

31. Borowski, *This Way for the Gas*, p. 30. In a letter to Tadeusz Sołtan (22 February 1946), Borowski writes that he 'survived the camp with parcels and luck' (*The Correspondence of Tadeusz Borowski*, p.69).

32. Janusz Nel Siedlecki, Krystyn Olszewski, and Tadeusz Borowski, *We Were in Auschwitz*, trans. by Alicia Nitecki (New York: Welcome Rain Publishers, 2000), p. 83. In contrast, Levi famously refers to the 'foul link of imposed complicity' in *The Drowned and the Saved* (p. 38). In his memoir, Siedlecki discusses the origins of *We Were in Auschwitz* in a similar way to Borowski: 'The survivors carried forth their banners of "martyrdom" and sowed the seeds of future legends. They wanted glory—I wanted to bear witness for the tortured, gassed, burnt; for all the unknown, unnamed, already forgotten dead. So I coaxed Puppy and argued with Krystyn and Tol, till we sat down and wrote a book about Auschwitz. We swore to write only the truth, and agreed that nothing would be printed until endorsed by all of us' (p. 232).

33. Levi, *If This Is A Man*, pp. 92, 43. Levi is slightly evasive: he only writes that 'if' he saw a spoon, he would take it without compunction. The supposition is, perhaps, attempting to hide Levi's regret, and 'guilt'.

34. Borowski, *This Way for the Gas*, p. 32. Complicity is measured in various other ways in the prose narratives. The narrator internalizes Nazi ideology by referring to other prisoners as animals and insects: the Greeks are pigs (p. 41) and the inmates 'swarm' in yards without the 'diversion' of an arriving transport (p. 30). The guards are envied, and even desired for their 'dreamy blue eyes' (p. 34); the narrator quotes with approval their instructions that there should be 'no trace left of the *Schweinerei*' from the transport (p. 42). A corpse becomes a 'mound of meat' (p. 45), and there are instances of anti-Semitism (p. 43). Paradoxes of complicity are evident in that 'Muslims' ('Muzulmen' in the 1946 edition) have 'neither the strength nor the will to go on living' yet '*scurry*' (my italics) to their bunks (p. 32). The internalization of camp hierarchies is clear in the footnote in the 1967 edition which describes the 'Muslims' as 'ripe for the gas chamber' (p. 32).

35. In a letter to Maria Rundo (21 January 1946), Borowski includes a slightly different version of this poem (untitled in the letter) (*The Correspondence of Tadeusz Borowski*, pp. 97–98).

36. Borowski, *Selected Poems*, p. 15.

37. Borowski, *Selected Poems*, pp. 15, 14. It turns out that 'lightly' in the second line refers to the 'green of the distant meadows', which is 'lightly | lifted

to the clouds by birds' (p. 15). 'The Sun of Auschwitz' comprises a rare, undialectical love lyric set in Auschwitz (it certainly does not wrestle with the potential inefficacy of the aesthetic in the camps), but 'Farewell to Maria' does form its palinode. In the latter poem, the romantic moments in 'The Sun of Auschwitz' are now regarded as 'hollow theatrics' (p. 111). Left, after his camp experiences, with only 'bitterness', the narrator implores the lover not to come back to him: 'My love I burned away in the flames of the crematorium', he explains. 'Love' could refer here to Maria, in particular, or amorous desire in a more abstract sense.

38. Borowski, *This Way for the Gas*, p. 113.
39. *The Correspondence of Tadeusz Borowski*, pp. 54–55. Borowski's attitude towards the countryside may well have been influenced by his reading of the work of Louis-Ferdinand Céline. In *Journey to the End of the Night*, the narrator comments: 'One thing I'd better tell you right away, I'd never been able to stomach the country, I'd always found it dreary, those endless fields of mud, those houses where nobody's ever home, those roads that don't go anywhere. And if to all that you add a war, it's completely unbearable' (p. 18). This scathingly ironic tone dominates Borowski's prose. Residues of humanist thought endure in both writers' work, however, as when the same narrator comments that his ideas 'were like faint, flickering little candles, trembling throughout a lifetime in the middle of a ghostly, abominable universe' (p. 437).
40. Tadeusz Borowski, letter to Zofia Świdwińska (5 February 1946) in *The Correspondence of Tadeusz Borowski*, p. 60.
41. In *Landscape after Battle* (1970), the film's director, Andrzej Wajda, provides an insightful reading of Borowski's short stories when he focusses on these issues of aesthetic culpability and inappropriateness. This film is based on Borowski's post-liberation short stories (many of which, including 'The Grunwald Battle', have not yet been translated into English). In an early scene, an adaptation of the story 'Silence' (printed in *This Way to the Gas*), Wajda adds the detail of the 'accustomed' Borowski character reading a book, whilst a Dachau guard is trampled to death. The classical score is already ironic by this early point in the film: whereas it celebrated liberation in the first few minutes, it now signifies that the former violence of the camp continues in a post-war context. Indeed, the whole film illustrates the inmates' frustration that life in Dachau, and then the former SS barracks in Munich, continues much as normal: the prisoners are still subjected to food rationing and can still be shot by the Americans if they attempt to escape. In another early scene, a violinist visits Dachau and plays Beethoven to the inmates while they are effectively on roll call: as they shiver in the snow, it is difficult to discern whether the prisoners are swaying to the music or the intense cold. The violinist—at the head of the assembled group—effectively takes the place of an SS guard or kapo, playing (possibly) the same music that the inmates used to hear on their way to work before the camp's liberation.
42. No commonly recognized adjective arises from 'testimony', which testifies in itself to a supposedly self-contained and self-defining form. 'Testimonial' primarily comprises a noun meaning a gift of money (as in a testimonial football match) to mark outstanding service (*OED*, 2nd edn).
43. Eaglestone, p. 38.
44. Felman and Laub, p. 8.
45. I am referring specifically here, of course, to written, rather than oral, testimonies.
46. These survivor poems also illustrate that Holocaust testimony paradoxically does not end with the moment of liberation: Borowski's bitter ruminations

on the displaced persons' camp form the poetic equivalents of Levi's prose narrative *The Truce*, which outlines the Italian writer's convoluted return to Italy via Russia.

47. *The Correspondence of Tadeusz Borowski*, p. 55.
48. Borowski, *Selected Poems*, pp. 57, 91, 93. Henri Frenay (not 'Fresnay', as Borowski has it) was the French minister des prisonniers et déportés in 1945: he escaped from a POW camp in 1940, and was the founder of the Resistance network Combat. According to *le Monde*, on 20 and 21 May 1945 there was a ceremony at Bourget for the 'cent millième' French prisoner repatriated by airplane (*le Monde, index Analytique 1944–45* (Paris, 1969)). William I. Hitchcock, in his book *Liberation: The Bitter Road to Freedom, Europe 1944–1945* (London: Faber, 2008) records the celebrations on 3 June 1945 when the millionth returnee—a tall blond POW named Jules Caron (not 'Garron', as Borowski spells it)—'was received with huge acclamation and driven home to his village in southeastern France in a limousine' (p. 264). Many French POWs still did not feel their homecoming reception was sufficient: the French Communist Party staged a series of protest marches and public denunciations of Frenay. Some stood under his ministry window shouting 'Food! Clothing! Shoes! Down with the black market! Out with Frenay!' (p. 266).
49. Borowski may have felt the same urgency during his internment but could not record extensively due to the difficulties in obtaining writing materials and the limitations of memory. The second quotation is taken from Hitchcock's book (p. 367).
50. In a letter to Zofia Świdwińska (5 February 1946), Borowski argues for the interdependence of these poetics and his experiences in Auschwitz: 'If I don't write as well now as I used to, it's not my fault. The camp has an effect, one has to learn the simplest things afresh, even writing' (*The Correspondence of Tadeusz Borowski*, p. 57). His letters testify to bouts of ill-health for himself and Maria in the early post-war years: 'It turns out that Tuśka has a heart condition, and I have rather low blood pressure and am also on medication, getting strychnine injections from Tuśka in the evenings and huge doses of lecithin and some kind of powder of which I'm to consume ten bottles' (letter to Wanda Leopold (22 October 1946), *The Correspondence of Tadeusz Borowski*, p. 184).
51. Levi, *If This Is A Man*, p. 140.
52. Borowski, *Selected Poems*, pp. 91, 97.
53. Felman and Laub, p. 39.
54. See, for example, 'Night from across the Ocean', where the French are depicted as mindlessly patriotic, gluttonous, sexually rapacious and generally insensitive (p. 29). Mole argues that 'the profound disdain with which the Poles and Czechs held the French in Dachau was due to what they saw as the betrayal at Munich in 1938 and the unforgivable defeat of 1940 followed by the official collaboration of Vichy' (p. 37). In 'Homecomings', Poland is described as the graveyard of Europe, compared to a relatively (according to Borowski) untainted France (*Selected Poems*, p. 57). 'To ***' illustrates how the poet feels his homeland has been contaminated: the German language has pervaded Polish culture to the extent that Borowski refers to the deportation 'Umschlagplatz' (p. 35). 'Homecomings' also argues that it would senseless to return home (as Borowski did in 1946), since the 'KGB' awaits all returnees (p. 59).
55. In a letter to Zosia Świdwińska (6 October 1945), Borowski explains that 'I went from near Stuttgart [Dautmergen] to Dachau in a transport of sick people destined—according both to those of us who went and those who

remained behind—for the gas. They didn't gas us. They wanted to shoot us wholesale the day of liberation, but the Americans came a few hours too soon' (*The Correspondence of Tadeusz Borowski*, p. 39). The journey to Dachau-Allach took six days, and in a letter to Tadeusz Sołtan (22 February 1946), Borowski describes the transport more specifically as one of *muzulmen* rather than the less specific 'sick people' (p. 69).

56. In 'I Have Learned to Waste My Time', Borowski blames his lack of development as a poet on his camp experiences; his need to think 'like the dumbest man in my quarters' and 'live for the day', treating hunger 'with disgust' (p. 55). In 'Return to Life', the first two lines promise poetic self-recovery, but they are subverted with the comparison between poems locked in a drawer and a woman burning leaves (p. 61). The two stanzas may have independent meanings, but the implication is that the lyric fails to satisfy the poet's demands in a post-war context. Paradoxically, this sentiment is conveyed—as with 'October Sky'—in a lyrical epiphany.

57. *The Correspondence of Tadeusz Borowski*, p. 40.

58. Czesław Miłosz, *The Captive Mind* (London: Penguin, 2001), p. 129. In this book, Miłosz famously portrays Borowski as 'Beta', a romantic poet who gives in to the Communist regime in Poland all too easily in the late 1940s. In my interview with Pióro, the Polish translator argues that the portrayal is 'unfair and silly', primarily because Miłosz did not share Borowski's experience in the camps and also because of the latter's youth. Drewnowski notes, 'At the Szczecin meeting of the Polish Writers' Association promoting socialist realism in January 1949, his writings became the main object of attack in official lectures. Borowski attempted to go to the United States, but was not allowed. From among the realistic possibilities, he chose to work as cultural editor at the Polish Press Information Office in East Berlin' between June 1949 and March 1950 (*The Correspondence of Tadeusz Borowski*, p. 324). The writer Aleksander Wat has a different take to Miłosz on Borowski's turn to political journalism:

> After [Borowski's] famous attack on non-Communist writers [in *Rozmowy*] he justified himself to me saying that the arguments and even the sentences in the article were dictated to him over the telephone to Berlin. He had become completely disillusioned with communism in East Berlin. It was painful to watch Communist scribblers using this excellent writer as an errand boy. During the period when he was writing the most aggressive columns for *Nowa Kultura*, he'd come to me from time to time for a 'soulful confession'. When I warned him that he was in danger of becoming clinically schizophrenic, he maintained that, in fact, after Auschwitz, he couldn't go on living; he immersed himself in communism which, for him, was a kind of 'ersatz suicide'. (p. 342)

59. Borowski, *This Way for the Gas*, p. 18. In a letter to Zofia Świdwińska (24 April 1946), Borowski depicts a more ambivalent response to Paris: 'For the past few days I've been wandering around Paris with the nonchalant mien of a parvenue [*sic*] [. . .] A mad jealousy grabs me when I look at the buildings by the Seine drowning in verdure, at the Etoilles with the unharmed Arc de Triomph, at Napoleon's grave, massive and cheerful. The norms of war were different here than at home [. . .] Bitterness and envy apart, however, it's a wonderful country' (*The Correspondence of Tadeusz Borowski*, pp. 79, 80). Paramour should perhaps be added to 'parvenu', since in a letter four days later to Stanisław Marczak-Oborski, Borowski is 'living at a pork butcher's and his daughter's. What a wonderful thing—the bourgeoisie! And the wine! It's a pity I have a weak head—for wine, and for the daughter' (p. 82).

60. *Literary Chapters of Ezra Pound*, ed. by T. S. Eliot (London: Faber, 1960), p. 12.
61. Felman and Laub, p. 21.
62. *The Correspondence of Tadeusz Borowski*, p. 41.
63. Alan Ross, *Poems* (London: Harvill Press, 2005). In the dust jacket blurb for Ross's book, it is claimed that he 'invented a poetic genre [. . .] poetry as a brief, intense form of journalism, easy to read, quick to stir response'. The comment is neglectful of the context of 1930s writing across Europe, as well as the testimonial poetics developing in the 1940s. These poetics arose partly out of the documentary writing of 1930s Europe: Samuel Hynes argues in *The Auden Generation: Literature and Politics in England in the 1930s* (London: Faber, 1979) that Gollancz's publication of *The Brown Book of Hitler Terror* (London: Victor Gollancz, 1933) resulted in an increase in documentary poetics (p. 131); the most influential examples are W. H. Auden's recording of *Night Mail* and Louis MacNiece's *Autumn Journals* (London: Faber, 1996 (1939)). Hynes contends that the First Soviet Writers' Congress in 1936 also influenced the increase in documentary writing in Europe, where, he argues, the 'recording of events was a moral act, and one that took priority over merely aesthetic issues' (p. 216). Documentary writing in the 1930s put pressure on the lyric to prove its worth in a time of constant emergency.
64. The phrase 'naked' poetry is taken from Miłosz's introduction to Różewicz's work in *Post-War Polish Poetry* (Harmondsworth: Penguin, 1970), p. 69. Różewicz's anti-metaphorical minimalism is similar to Borowski's testimonial poetics in the Munich poems. However, it is inherently more *poetic*, whereas Borowski mimics the characteristics of prose testimony (he describes himself as like a 'reporter | from some third-rate paper' in 'New Deal' (*Selected Poems*, p. 79)). In contrast, Różewicz deals with symbolist and allegorical abstractions in poems such as 'In the Middle of Life', which begins, 'After the end of the world | after my death' (*Post-War Polish Poetry*, p. 70). Similarly, Miłosz's anti-rhetoric could be compared to Borowski's journalistic style, but the allegorical tendencies remain in the former's 'A Poor Christian Looks at the Ghetto', with its population of abstract bees, ants, and 'guardian mole' 'like a Patriarch' (pp. 59, 60).
65. Marzena Sokołowska-Paryż, *The Myth of War in British and Polish Poetry 1939–1945* (New York: Peter Lang, 2002), p. 182.

NOTES TO CHAPTER 3

1. Dylan Thomas, quoted in Daniel Swift, *Bomber County: The Lost Airmen of World War Two* (London: Penguin, 2010), p. xix.
2. Wiesel, p. 7.
3. James Young, *Writing and Rewriting the Holocaust* (Bloomington: Indiana University Press, 1988), p. 21.
4. Levi, *The Drowned and the Saved*, p. 33.
5. Borowski, *This Way for the Gas*, p. 22.
6. *The Norton Anthology of English Literature (8th Edition)*, II, ed. by Stephen Greenblatt (New York/London: W.W. Norton & Co., 2006), p.2426. George Orwell criticized some of the lines in 'Spain', and Auden revised the 'necessary murder' to 'the fact of murder'.
7. *OED*, 2nd edn.
8. Of course, there are specific instances in which Allied soldiers *have* been described as perpetrators. Swift discusses the condemnation of Bomber Command, including Eric Markusen and David Kopf's *The Holocaust and*

Strategic Bombing (Oxford: Westview Press, 1995), which 'presents the Allied bombing as "genocidal"' (p. 180). Swift's book presents the author as coming to terms, partly, with the grandfather as a killer, a successful bomber of devastated German towns such as Münster.

9. The appeal letters and newspapers are mentioned in *Return to Oasis: War Poems and Recollections from the Middle East 1940–1946*, ed. by Victor Selwyn, Erik de Mauny, Ian Fletcher, G. S. Fraser, and John Waller (London: Shepheard-Walwyn, 1980), p. xxi. The figure of 'some 20,000' manuscripts is taken from the Salamander Oasis Trust website (www.salamanderoasis.org). The 'Catalogue to the Archive held at the Imperial War Museum' estimates that there are 17,000 manuscripts (p. ii), but this document (dated December 1997) predates the inauguration—and updating—of the website.

10. SOTA Box 43 W Separates. Mrs Whitfield replied (14 May 1996) and sent the original copy of her husband's Mention in Despatches (4 April 1946). The original letter to 'The Executors' states, 'It is with reluctance that I write to you at what is very clearly an inappropriate time. This Museum, however, has been concerned for many years with the collection of personal papers of men and women who have served this country in the great conflicts in which it has been involved during this century. These are all too quickly lost to posterity if prompt action is not taken to secure their permanent retention in a suitable repository. I hope therefore that his family will pardon this intrusion' (p. 1). The letter goes on to state that any further papers will be held with Whitfield's Oasis poems.

11. *From Oasis into Italy*, p. vi.

12. 'Catalogue to the Archive held at the Imperial War Museum', p. iii.

13. *Oasis: The Middle East Anthology of Poetry from the Forces*, ed. by David Burk, Denis Saunders, and Victor Selwyn (Cairo: Salamander Society, 1943). A copy of the anthology is held in the British Library. *Return to Oasis* recounts the story of its compilation, from its beginnings in Lady Russell Pasha's 'Music for All' service club in Cairo, where 'there [was] a sitting room where Poetry-Reading, etc., [was] held' (pp. 3, 244). The editors advertised for submissions in Middle East newspapers and periodicals and via Egyptian State Broadcasting (p. 3). Rachel Haugh's Ph.D. dissertation, 'Versed in War: The Preservation and Publication of Second World War Poetry by the Salamander Oasis Trust' (Rutgers University, 2009), constitutes one of the few extended critical accounts of 'Oasis' poetry.

14. *Poems of the Second World War: The Oasis Selection*, ed. by Victor Selwyn, Erik de Mauny, Ian Fletcher, and Norman Morris (London: J. M. Dent & Sons, 1985); *More Poems of the Second World War*; *Schools Oasis: Poems of the Second World War*, ed. by Dennis Butts and Victor Selwyn (Cheltenham: Nelson Thornes, 1992); *The Voice of War: Poems of the Second World War*, ed. by Victor Selwyn (London: Penguin, 1996).

15. SOTA Box 15 F.

16. *From Oasis into Italy*, pp. 232–34.

17. SOTA Box 16 G, folder GA (p. 1), and Box 7 CA-CO. The Cooney letter is addressed to 'Dear Sirs', and was sent on 15 November 1983 (p. 1).

18. *More Poems of the Second World War*, pp. 249–50.

19. *More Poems of the Second World War*, p. xii.

20. Victor West, letter to M. Suddaby at the Imperial War Museum (no date) (SOTA Box 44 V. West). Selwyn notes that 'all ranks were forbidden to keep a diary on active service' (*From Oasis into Italy*, p. xix).

21. The reference to handcuffs is from an undated biographical note in SOTA Box 44 V. West. One of West's memoirs about his internment and escape,

'The Second World War Memoirs of V West', is held separately on microfilm in the IWM archives (PP/MCR/239).

22. The acknowledgements section in *More Poems of the Second World War* notes that some manuscripts were destroyed on 16 October 1987 when 'the most severe storm in two hundred years hit the south of England' (pp. 352–54). The 'debris' quotation originates in *From Oasis into Italy* (p. xxv).

23. For the inextricability of testimony and the Holocaust, see Wiesel, p. 7; Eaglestone, pp. 1–2.

24. The policy is relaxed slightly in *From Oasis into Italy*, 'so as to be able to include material written later but based on letters, diaries and other recollections of the wartime period' (p. xix), but returns to stringency in *Poems of the Second World War*, where the poets are allegedly 'writing *during* [. . .] War, for such poetry enjoys an immediacy, a quality, that cannot be recreated in later years' (p. xxiv). The policy is the same in *More Poems of the Second World War* (p. x), but in *The Voice of War*, '[t]here are one or two exceptions where the poem must go in' (p. ii).

25. Philip Reed, letter to G. W. Canham (1 November 1982), Box 7 CA-CO (p. 1).

26. C. W. Canham, letter to Philip Reed (undated), Box 7 CA-CO (p. 1).

27. Keith Bosley, 'The Khaki Muse', *Times Literary Supplement*, 6 July 1984, p. 760b.

28. SOTA Box 16 G, folder GE-GID. The date of the submission is 2 June 1990.

29. Mary Harrison's letter to Selwyn (2 September 1988) indicates that she worked at the Allied Central Interpretation Unit (Photographic Intelligence) at RAF Medmenham (p. 1) (Box 18 H, folder HARR-HART). *Poems of the Second World War* also contains a 'civilian' poem by Elsie Cawser, 'Salvage Song', about giving up her domestic items for aircraft construction; she imagines an aeroplane chased by her kettle (p. 145).

30. Sheila Gregg, undated letter to Victor Selwyn, p. 1. The letter containing the original submission is dated 15 November 1983.

31. SOTA Box 2 BA-BL, folder BEN-BEV.

32. Vernon Scannell, *Not without Glory: Poets of the Second World War* (London: Woburn Press, 1976), p. 22.

33. Jack Bevan's memoir *Through the Donkey's Ears* (Maidstone: George Mann, 1997) presents a different case of writing 'in action' to Scannell and Morris. Whilst training in Lincolnshire (summer 1940), Bevan 'jotted down on the inside of a cigarette packet some lines of a poem that suddenly came to me out of part of me not present' (p. 35); he later read 'my most recent poems' to other trainees (p. 45). As a sign of his lack of creativity on active service, Bevan notes that he kept—but never opened—a book of Keats's poems with him for the entire Italian campaign (p. 102). (Keith Douglas similarly stashed a book of Shakespeare's sonnets during the desert war, as recounted in *Alamein to Zem Zem*, ed. John Waller, G. S. Fraser and J. C. Hall (London: Faber, 1966), p. 22.) However, Bevan notes that even during action he was writing on cardboard and a signals pad (p. 54).

34. SOTA Box 16 G, folder GA.

35. *Poems of the Second World War*, p. 176.

36. Jack Bevan, *My Sad Pharaohs* (London: Routledge and Kegan Paul, 1968), p. 107. The less specific phrase 'decades later' is used in *Poems of the Second World War* (p. 177).

37. *Poems of the Second World War*, p.227.

38. SOTA Box 11 D and Box 16 G.

39. SOTA Box 2 BA-BL.

40. SOTA Box 15 F.
41. *Return to Oasis*, p. xx.
42. *Poems from the Desert: Verses by Members of the Eighth Army* (London: George G. Harrap, 1944), pp. 45–46; *Return to Oasis*, p. xx.
43. SOTA Box 18 H, folder HE (p. 1).
44. SOTA Box 43 W-separates.
45. The opening lines of the final stanza in the typescript have also been cut: 'Seeds which fall to the earth | may become death or birth.'
46. *More Poems of the Second World War*, p. 271. The difference, of course, is that the soldiers react to Semprun as a former inmate of Buchenwald: 'They stand amazed before me, and suddenly, in that terror-stricken gaze, I see myself—in their horror' (p. 3).
47. Roger Luckhurst, *The Trauma Question* (London: Routledge, 2008), p. 58.
48. In Colin Rushton's *Spectator in Hell: A British Soldier's Story of Imprisonment in Auschwitz* (Chichester: Summersdale Pubs, 2007), Arthur Dodd suffers 'nigh-on forty years of nightmares' (p. 145) as well as 'migraines and other stress-related sicknesses' (p. 148); Terry Gorman endures 'post-traumatic stress' (p. 174) and John Stevens is diagnosed with motor hysteria (p. 211). In her Ph.D. on Northfield Hospital and 'Treating and Preventing Trauma' (University of Salford, 2004), Thalassis discusses 'military psychiatry in the Second World War. Focusing almost exclusively on the British Army, it recounts how the military came to employ psychiatrists (and a few psychologists) to reform its recruitment and promotion procedures and to treat its psychiatric casualties. In addition, [the thesis] explores how psychiatrists responded to these challenges with new selection procedures and therapeutic regimes. The military purpose in employing psychiatrists and psychologists was to reduce manpower wastage and this was the principle that underscored psychiatry in the different military contexts in which it was practiced' (p. 1). Not all military personnel suffered after the war, of course: Selwyn's comment appertains to his own experience and others, such as R. J. Fayers, who wrote to Selwyn (22 February 1985) that '[a]fter a very long period after the war I turned off all interest in [the] RAF and war' (Box 15F (p. 1)).
49. Ralph H. Dargue, letter to Victor Selwyn (2 August 1987), p. 1.
50. Box 18 H, folder HARV-HAY. The letter is undated (p. 1).
51. Linda M. Shires, *British Poetry of the Second World War* (London: Macmillan, 1985), pp. 57–68.
52. See, for example, *Poems of the Second World War*, pp. xviii–xix.
53. World War I poetry does not entirely maintain these distinctions, of course, as in the uncovering in 'Strange Meeting' of the poet as the killer of the enemy friend. However, World War II poetry develops the unstable categories further, I argue, and highlights the figure of the poet as killer much more clearly in poems such as 'Vergissmeinicht' and 'Ubique'. Other reasons for the neglect of World War II poetry include the difficulties in critically addressing a body of work that arose from different continents: as Martin Gilbert writes in *Descent into Barbarism*, 'The range of combat zones is too large, the nature of the fighting too diffuse, the perils on land, sea and air too varied, the burdens of occupation and belligerency are too crippling, and the desperation of human suffering and loss are too intense, for easy summation' (p. 705). In contrast, the poetry of World War I consists of a more uniform iconography. Another problem is the sheer volume of published poems. As an example, the Eighth Army set up a poetry competition in February 1943 (which led to the submission of Kersh's false testimony): 403 poems were submitted by 280 authors (*Poems from the Desert*, p. 5). In *English Poetry*

of the Second World War (London: Mansell Publishing, 1986), Catherine W. Reilly identifies 2,679 World War II poets (p. vii).

54. Raul Hilberg, *Perpetrators Victims Bystanders: The Jewish Catastrophe 1933–1945* (London: Lime Tree, 1993), p. ix.
55. Levi, *The Drowned and the Saved*, p. 33. These categories are also unstable and problematic elsewhere; for example, in relation to the testimony in Alison Owing's *Frauen: German Women Recall the Third Reich* (New Brunswick, NJ: Rutgers University Press, 1993). 'Bystander testimony' might be the most appropriate term for the women's memoirs, but that would assume that perpetrator testimony is 'active' in the sense of initiating murder, rather than perpetuating Nazi ideology, as in the case of many of the women. In contrast, Hilberg includes German bankers in his list of perpetrators.
56. SOTA Box 2, folder BEN-BEV.
57. Primo Levi, *The Black Hole of Auschwitz*, ed. by Marco Belpoliti, trans. by Sharon Wood (Malden, MA: Polity Press, 1985), p. 86. In *Commandant of Auschwitz*, trans. by Constantine Fitzgibbon (London: Pan Books, 1982), Hoess's first attempt to evoke sympathy is through a description of his early childhood, where '[m]y sole confidant was a pony' (p. 29). The dangers of readerly identification can lull the reader into Hoess's desired, empathetic reaction. At the same time, the opposite effect of constantly taking Hoess's crimes into consideration can mean that his rare balanced evaluations of his actions are rejected by an outraged reader. Examples of what Levi terms mendacity are rife. He makes it clear early on in the testimony that he dislikes violence against his inmates ('My sympathies lay too much with the prisoners', p. 86) at the same time as he later dispassionately discusses the various ways in which to dispose of the transports in Auschwitz. Hoess attempts to explain his crimes in terms of his work ethic and need to obey orders; he argues that a soldier in democratic England would have done the same with the slogan 'My country, right or wrong' (p. 163). His virulent anti-Semitism ('the extermination of the Jews [...] brought the Jews far closer to their ultimate objective', p. 201), amongst other factors, make it rather difficult for the reader to agree with Hoess's conclusion that 'the commandant of Auschwitz [...] had a heart and [...] was not evil' (p. 205).
58. Victor Selwyn, 'Return to Oasis', *Times Literary Supplement*, 13 February 1981, p. 168e. There are clearly different delineations of perpetrators: Hilberg uses the term only once in his (first) chapter on Hitler (p. 16), and even then in the plural to refer to his inner circle, as if it would be embarrassing to lump together the enormity of Hitler's crimes with the list of perpetrators in 'The Establishment' (Chapter 2), such as the Dresdner Bank (p. 22).
59. See, for example, *From Oasis into Italy* (p. xxiv): 'they really did believe they were fighting for a better world, a more compassionate society, the possibility of an international organisation to defend the peace'. Philippa Lyon complies with Selwyn in *Twentieth-Century War Poetry*: 'In the Second World War, there is often a fundamental acceptance of the necessity for war' (p. 13). Adam Piette (in *Imagination at War* (London: Macmillan, 1995)) and Mark Rawlinson challenge this notion of the 'just war'. For Rawlinson, 'The justifications of this struggle were far from clear to those who wrote and those who fought' (*British Writing of the Second World War* (Oxford: Oxford University Press, 2000), p. 207).
60. R. W. Johnson, 'A Formidable Proposition (Review of Antony Beevor's *D-Day: The Battle for Normandy*)', *London Review of Books*, 10 September 2009, pp. 21–22 (p. 21).
61. Hitchcock, p. 80.

62. Johnson, p.21. The review recounts that 'A British army report acknowledged that its troops were in the habit of shooting SS men out of hand', adding: 'Many of them probably deserve to be shot in any case and know it' (p. 22). Prisoners were considered a burden which 'would only slow up the essential breakout from the beach-head. Orders might still be given not to kill prisoners, but once it happened there was no fuss and no further questions were asked' (p. 22).

63. Kendall, 'Gurney and Fritz', p. 152. 'Strange Meeting' has been read as the archetypal pacifist text of the World War One, but as Kendall notes (p. 152), it also comprises one of the few texts in which the 'business of killing' is represented, when the narrator is revealed to be the frowning killer of the strange friend.

64. Paul Fussell, *Wartime: Understanding and Behavior in the Second World War* (Oxford: Oxford University Press, 1989), p. ix. Fussell comments on a photograph of British and French generals in 1939: 'All look entirely inadequate to the cynicism, efficiency, brutality, and bloody-mindedness that will be required to win the war' (p. 7).

65. Box 21 H Separates (2).

66. SOTA Box 26 M. In one of the first Oasis poems—printed in the original 1943 anthology—Almendro (Denis Saunders) muses in a more complex way on the business of killing. 'Night Preceding Battle' contains the stanza:

> Today I killed a man. God forgive me!
> Tomorrow I shall sow another political corpse,
> Or be dead myself. And strangely
> I am satisfied to be applauded killer.
> Holy Mary plead my duties sin's legality.
> Is there no end, reason, answer? Damn the sea!
> (*Poems of the Second World War*, p. 55)

Auden's concept of the necessary murder does not quite assuage Almendro's guilt or suggest religious exculpation. Saunders understands the politically sanctioned kill, but still asks Holy Mary to plead to God for his 'duties sin'. As in Douglas's poetry—and unlike in World War I verse—the poet openly admits his pride 'to be applauded killer'. The reason for the necessary murder might be said to lie within Germany's expansionist and genocidal policies, yet—as with a striking number of Oasis poets in the archive—the narrator does not recognize this, and aligns his thinking with the predominant World War I sense—after the 1960s—that the war is avoidable and potentially absurd. John Buxton submitted his collection *Such Liberty* (London: Macmillan, 1944) to the archive, and, in 'On Reading Some War Poems', attacks civilians who 'scorn the enemy they never saw [. . .] It makes me sick, this smug self-righteousness | This certainty that we can kill with right | Denied our enemies' (p. 35).

67. For Hamilton, in *A Poetry Chronicle* (London: Faber, 1973), 'Vergissmeinicht' suffers from 'a reticence stiffening into the tight lipped insensitivity of the officers' mess' (p. 62). In *Wartime and Aftermath: English Literature and Its Background 1939–60* (Oxford: Oxford University Press, 1993), Bergonzi argues that 'Vergissmeinicht' has 'the starkness of a poster, and needs to be complemented by other and rather subtler poems' (p. 75). Douglas's best poems are a mixture of 'tough-mindedness and sensitivity': moral response masquerades here as an evaluation of aesthetic value. As Mark Rawlinson argues persuasively in *British Writing of the Second World War*, World War II literature in general 'disappoints the desire for a reprise of the literature' of World War I due to its implication in 'the reproduction and invention of alternative justifications of violence' (p. 3). The war poet 'as injurer is a factor

which the popular reception is largely silent about' (pp. 13–14). Douglas and Victor West use the same word—'exhilaration'—to describe their feelings after war action: such responses are difficult to reconcile with the politics of anti-war war anthologies (*From Alamein to Zem Zem*, p. 43; 'Second World War Memoirs of V. West', p. 193).

68. Felman and Laub, p. 5.
69. The introduction to the testimony section in *The Future of Memory*, ed. by Rick Crownshaw, Jane Kilby, and Antony Rowland (Oxford: Berghahn Books, 2010), pp. 113–21.
70. Roger Bowen, 'In the Interstices of War' (review of *Return to Oasis*), *Times Literary Supplement*, 7 November 1983, p. 11a.
71. *From Oasis into Italy*, p. i.
72. *Poems of the Second World War*, p. 177.
73. K. N. Batley, 'Chindit', *The Voice of War*, p. 244.
74. *Return to Oasis*, pp. 176–78.
75. *Keith Douglas*, p. 294. In *Service Slang* (London: Faber, 1943), J. L. Hunt and A. G. Pringle refer primly to 'Bullshit' as '***': 'A coarse expression of transatlantic origin [. . .] widely used between men in the services. By this they mean anything that they regard as eyewash, rubbish, and pure bluff—external show unsupported, as they see it, by necessity, achievement, or knowledge' (pp. 18–19).
76. SOTA Box 26 M. Morris regards a visit of reporters and photographers as 'an example of official bullshit; the published reports, when they filtered home from England were nauseating—whatever they did for morale at home' (p. 2).
77. 'The Second World War Papers of NT Morris' (N. T. Morris P116). The competition took place in December 1942, for the Fiftieth Battalion. Its timing was pertinent, since Operation Torch in November 1942—including the U.S. invasion force—'transformed the balance of power throughout the Mediterranean' (Gilbert, *Descent into Barbarism*, p. 473). The idea of writing about 'My Most Exciting Desert Adventure' might have seemed strange in the context of the fall of Tobruk and Sebastopol in the summer of 1942, where the ensuing conflict 'was to bring the Allies to the brink of disaster' (p. 450), but after El Alamein in October 1942 and the recapture of Tobruk in November, the initiative had been regained.
78. Letter to Hall (10 June 1943) in Graham, p. 287. In *Alamein to Zem Zem*, Douglas deploys the word in this sense to refer to Divisional Headquarters' inefficiency and inaction (p. 24).
79. Adorno, *Minima Moralia*, p. 52.
80. John Jarmain, *Poems* (London: Collins, 1945), pp. 38–40 (p. 38).
81. Bevan, *Through the Donkey's Ears*, pp. 283, 227.
82. Michael Hamburger, *The Truth of Poetry: Tensions in Modern Poetry from Baudelaire to the 1960s* (Manchester: Manchester University Press, 1982), p. 255.
83. SOTA Box 44 V. West.
84. SOTA Box 44 V. West (no page numbers).
85. Adorno, 'Cultural Criticism and Society', p. 34.
86. Jacqueline Simms, letter to Victor West (4 March 1992), p. 1. Simms writes, 'The writing is very uneven, despite a moving fidelity to your experiences [. . .] it leads you to accept the provisional and approximate [. . .] weaknesses [. . .] can't be subsumed under the "anti-poetry" heading.' Despite this evaluation, Simms encourages a resubmission, which West appears to have understood as a provisional acceptance of his work. He appears to have told the Imperial War Museum that Oxford University Press have accepted

his manuscript: an internal memorandum in Box 44 from 'Phil to Rod' (23 October 1992) states that 'I rang OUP. They have no plans to publish Victor West, who "keeps sending [them] stuff" and have made absolutely no commitments to him'.

87. Bernard Bergonzi, *War Poets and Other Subjects* (Aldershot: Ashgate, 1999), p. 32.

88. *From Oasis into Italy*, p. i.

89. Hugh Haughton, 'Anthologizing War', in *The Oxford Handbook of British and Irish War Poetry*, ed. by Tim Kendall (Oxford: Oxford University Press, 2007), pp. 433, 440. In a letter to Selwyn held in the archive (Box 2), Sir John Betjeman writes about the gift of *Return to Oasis* and comments that they are 'good poems' (8 October 1980 (p. 1)).

90. *Return to Oasis* (p. v): 'it takes a war [. . .] to move man to [. . .] write the finest verse'.

91. The selection of four poems out of twenty thousand SOTA items requires some explication. The emphasis of this book is, of course, on poetry, which immediately discounts thousands of the fascinating SOTA items, including prose memoirs, photographs, and letters. I have focussed on some of the most striking poems by different authors in the archives and anthologies, which is why I do not focus on a body of various poems by more famous World War II poets such as Alun Lewis, Hamish Henderson, Henry Reed, or Sidney Keyes. I have also tried to balance a rereading of a canonical poem ('Vergiss-meinicht') via Oasis testimony with the introduction of lesser-known authors such as Jack Bevan (whose erudite prose memoir, *Through the Donkey's Ears* bears comparison—with its classical references—to Levi's *If This Is a Man*). Through my choice of poems and poets, I have also tried to reflect the fact that testimony can come in many different forms from the same author. As well as the poems, I engage with Jarmain's, Bevan's, Morris's, Whitfield's, and West's letters; Bevan's memoir; Morris's pantomime; West's autobiography and literary criticism; and Douglas's prose and photographs. A criticism could be made that I 'privilege the perspective of the combatant soldier' with a 'quasi-sublime fascination with violence' in the poems (Rawlinson, pp. 11, 16), but given Selwyn's emphasis on collecting poetry 'in action', this inevitably comprises the emphasis of the Salamander/Oasis archive. Throughout the discussion (but most pertinently in relation to Jarmain and West) I compare World War II and Holocaust poetry, primarily to point out the (unnoted) similarities between different forms of poetry as testimony. There is little discussion of the context of 1940s poetry because the soldier poets were simply, in the majority of cases, unaware of contemporaneous poems. Many of the poems owe more to Georgian aesthetics rather than the Apocalyptics.

92. Levi, *If This Is A Man*, p. 17. Guy Sajer, a German soldier serving on the eastern front, similarly deploys the domestic image of the fire to convey his exasperation over readers of testimony: 'Too many people learn about war with no inconvenience to themselves. They read about Verdun or Stalingrad without comprehension, sitting in a comfortable armchair, with their feet beside the fire, preparing to go about their business the next day, as usual' (quoted in Hynes, *The Soldiers' Tale*, p. 285).

93. Delbo, *Auschwitz and After*, p. 84.

94. Margaret-Anne Hutton, *Testimony from the Nazi Camps: French Women's Voices* (London: Routledge, 2005), p. 51.

95. *Poems of the Second World War*, p. 70; Levi, *If This is a Man*, p. 17.

96. Anonymous, 'Forward', in John Jarmain, *Poems* (London: Collins, 1945), pp. 7–15 (p. 7).

97. Letter to Kate (30 June 1942), pp. 2, 3 (Major WJF Jarmain 07/20/1).

98. The ms poem is dated 23 January 1930 (07/20/1).
99. Letter to Michael [Barkway] (21 April 1943) (07/20/1), p. 5. Jarmain does
    not construct a rigid opposition between war and civilization in this letter:
    > Yes, we are on the foreshore. That *is* luxury, better than silver salt cel-
    > lars and glass tumblers. My house—the doova six foot by five foot by
    > four foot deep: I cannot stand upright in it—is only fifteen paces from
    > the water's edge: each morning at six-thirty I walk from my bed into
    > the sea and then dry in the sun before showing. What are your eleva-
    > tors and electric coffee-machines to that? (Coffee is unobtainable here
    > anyway, so why worry?) (p. 5)

    Battalion life is constrictive and liberating: at the same time as the exact
    measurements bemoan the hampered writing conditions, Jarmain celebrates
    the freedom of swimming, which contrasts with civilization's artefacts.
100. See Jarmain, p. 8, and the 'Salute to the Soldier Poets' article held in Jar-
    main's file (p. 54).
101. Jarmain's argument is similar to Sidney Keyes's in the more famous metat-
    estimony poem 'War Poet'. Both poets 'looked for peace', but found war as
    a compelling subject instead (*Poems of the Second World War*, p. 94); how-
    ever, the latter ends with the more radical, surrealist image of the war poet,
    whose face 'is a burnt book | And a wasted town'.
102. *Poems of the Second World War*, pp. 175–77 (p. 175). The second sentence
    appears to end after forty-nine lines, but the punctuation arguably becomes
    confused at this point: the question about the charge boxes reads as a paren-
    thetical clause, as the 'and' indicates before the recollections recommence (p.
    176). Throughout the poem, conventional punctuation proves inadequate to
    the 'verbal energy' of the fragmented memories.
103. *Rudyard Kipling's Verse: Inclusive Edition, 1885–1918* (London: Hodder
    and Stroughton, n.d.), pp. 550–51. In the last stanza of 'Ubique', Bevan
    quotes from Catallus's 'Home-Coming to Sirmia'. '[P]eregrino labore fessi'
    comes from the passage 'O quid solutis est beatius curis, cum mens onus
    reponit, ac peregrine labore fessi venimus larem ad nostrum' ('what is love-
    lier than to be free from cares, when the mind lays down its burden and we
    can return, weary from foreign toil, to our own home'). Catallus refers to
    Lake Como, having come back from visiting his brother's grave. The quota-
    tion supports Bevan's complex engagement with the concept of 'home' in
    'Ubique'. Catallus's lines come to him when Bevan fires his last rounds at
    Como as the war ends, and they appear to offer a redemptive vision of his
    future home in Britain. However, Como—and other Italian places familiar
    to Bevan through the classics—also offers the poet a kind of 'home': the
    prose testimony is full of instances where the Italian landscape appears *heim-
    lich*, and the poet unlocks its classical associations. In contrast, his British
    'home' appears unwelcoming when Bevan returns—as recounted in *Through
    the Donkey's Ears*—to a house of strangers. Despite such erudition, 'Ubique'
    is not without its aesthetic faults, such as clumsy line breaks. In contrast,
    Through the Donkey's Ears—with its references to Dante, Keats, etc.—bears
    comparison with Levi's classically informed prose, and constitutes a scandal-
    ously neglected piece of prose testimony about World War II.
104. The title of the memoir refers to the name for binoculars held on a tripod. My
    point about chronological linearity is true in general for *Through the Don-
    key's Ears*. For example, the first incident recorded in 'Ubique' which occurs
    in the prose testimony comprises the 'gun-barrel peeled | back like a steel
    banana skin' (p. 175). This accident occurs towards the end of *Through the
    Donkey's Ears*: 'I rush out to Number One and see it as a steel banana peeled
    back on itself'; one of the gunners is wounded ('a massive hole in his thigh')

by the 'jagged and cruel shafts of steel' which rain 'down from the sky' (p. 353). However, the prose is not always chronological: in the space of three pages (pp. 235–37), Bevan moves between his discovery of Doric temples at Poseidonia (p. 235) to discovering an Amalfi church 'Months after the war ended' (p. 236) and then previously visiting Naples (p. 237).

105. Felman and Laub, p. 12. The 'series of impressions' also allows Bevan to convey the distortions of time in heightened moments: the 'saws' from the destroyed gun come down 'thousands of minutes later' (p .175) and the final rounds at Como go on 'for ever and ever' (p. 177).

106. As opposed to the willed and relatively unproblematic process of recollection, deep memory registers fractures in the testimony's narrative. The witness can also be reduced to silence by the pressures of deep memory (Lawrence Langer, *Holocaust Testimonies* (New Haven, CT: Yale University Press, 1991), p. 21).

107. Anne Whitehead, *Memory* (New York: Routledge, 2009), p. 15. The importance of these final lines to Bevan is evident in their redeployment as metatestimony at the beginning of *Through the Donkey's Ears* (p. 10).

108. In *Through the Donkey's Ears*, the 'carapace' comprises the military training and chaos of the war, which forestalls reflection of his experiences (p. 369). Bevan recounts the suicide attempt as an unconscious act: 'I hear a click, and am suddenly aware that I have taken out my revolver, pointed it at my temple, and pulled the trigger. I replace it in the holster. There are three rounds in the six-round chamber. It is like a dream sequence. What in hell possessed me?' (pp. 319–20). He also recounts on several occasions how the 'grey shapes' pierce the 'carapace', using the traditional traumatic sign of the ghost. In the forward to the prose testimony (pp. 13–14), he states that he 'laid the ghosts to rest for more than half a lifetime' (p. 13) before quoting approvingly from *Propertius*: 'There *are* ghosts. Death does not end everything' (p. 14). By the end of the book, he insists that the 'ghosts [will still] rise up and insist upon their rights': this image of traumatic entrapment echoes Levi's description of spectral inmates demanding his guilty attention in the poem 'The Survivor'. Bevan also uses the traumatic sign to describe his own split identity: when he spots a former Cambridge friend near Calenzeno, he writes, 'We are both ghosts from another [pre-training] world' (p. 226). In a final twist to the ghost metaphor, Bevan recounts a recurrent war dream in which he confronts his own ghostly absence: he returns from leave and cannot find his kit (p. 384).

109. Piette, p. 214. Piette is quoting from R .N. Currey's *Poets of the 1939–1945 War* (London: Longmans, Green, 1960), pp. 40–41.

110. The description on page 315 of the dead German soldiers then moves to an incident uncannily similar to that of Douglas's 'Vergissmeinicht': 'At my feet is a sodden scrap, a faded photograph. I pick it up and see the image of a woman's face. On the back, in flowing Gothic script, is written *Gisela*'.

111. One such incident is recorded on page 281 when Bevan sees a funeral cortege with an old woman carrying a coffin: 'With all the arrogance of invaders who flout long-established local customs, we have the coffin transferred to the shoulders of the younger man'.

112. *Poems of the Second World War*, pp. 231–32 (p. 231).

113. Mark Mazower, *Inside Hitler's Greece: The Experience of Occupation 1941–44* (New Haven, CT: Yale University Press, 1993), p. 173.

114. SOTA Box 44 V. West.

115. 'The Second World War Memoirs of V West' (PP/MCR/239), p. 195.

116. Anne Whitehead discusses Proust's concepts of voluntary and involuntary memory in *Memory*, pp. 101–14.

117. I am referring here, of course, to Theodor Adorno's discussion of 'barbaric' poetics in 'Cultural Criticism and Society', p. 34.

118. *Schindler's List*, dir. Steven Spielberg (1993).

119. Letter to Selwyn (1 September 1989), p. 2 (SOTA Box 44 V. West).

120. West's poetry collection *The Horses of Falaise* (London: Salamander Imprint, 1975) records his success as an artist in the post-war period: the Royal Academy accepted his first two paintings in 1950 (pp. 27–28).

121. Sue Vice, 'False Testimony', in *The Future of Memory*, ed. by Crownshaw, Kilby, and Rowland, pp. 155–64. Vice refers in the example I give below to Martin Gray's embellished testimony about the Warsaw ghetto, *For Those I Love*, trans. Anthony White (London/Sydney: Pan Books, 1975).

122. West's letter to M. Suddaby (12 February 1974) requests these documents.

123. 'Elegy for an 88 Gunner' (rather than 'Vergissmeinicht') features in *Return to Oasis* (p. 84), *Poems of the Second World War* (p. 71), and *The Voice of War* (pp. 35–36).

124. Hamilton, p. 62; Piette, p. 206.

125. Hynes, *The Soldier's Tale*, p.144.

126. Kendall, 'Gurney and Fritz', p. 151; *Poems of the Second World War*, p. 71. All further references to 'Elegy for an 88 Gunner' appertain to the latter publication. The quotation is ambiguous: the corpse could also be 'almost [. . .] with content'. If the description belongs to the soldier, then 'almost' might register a slight uneasiness behind the ironic tone.

127. 117 BC MS 20c Douglas (c) Photographs.

128. Struk, pp. 12–13.

129. *From Alamein to Zem Zem*, pp. 67–68, 28.

130. *The Voice of War*, pp. 251–52; *Poems of the Second World War*, p. 287. Louis-Ferdinand Céline refers to the process of looting during World War I in *Journey to the End of the Night* and comments on its psychological impetus. French soldiers looted 'to take their minds off their troubles, to make it look as if they did have years before them. Everybody likes that feeling' (p. 38).

131. *Poems of Keats*, ed. by Edmund Blunden (London: Collins, 1955), p. 251. Aird refers to 'the swart and turbaned train'; Alford to the 'rudely gathered folds on her swart bosom'. In 'Solitary' (ii), Percy Shelley describes a 'swart Pariah in some Indian grove' (details taken from the English Poetry database). 'Swarthy' comes from the definition of 'swart' in the OED (2nd edn). The association of the Axis corpse with pagans is interesting in the context of the Allied forces' depiction of themselves as crusaders during the African campaign. V. A. Castleton's letter to the Trust (Box 9 C Separates) comments on an attached Christmas aerograph sent from the Middle East on 11 November 1943, which depicts the Allies as a Crusader on a horse, with the flag of 'Egypt/Tripolitania/Tunisia/Italy', facing a swastika flag before a castle (29 March 1981, p. 1). Due no doubt to the controversy caused, and confused iconography, 'the leaflet was hastily withdrawn as it was thought to offend the Egyptians'.

132. A. Banerjee, *Spirit above Wars: A Study of the English Poetry of the World Wars* (London: Macmillan, 1976), p. 129. 'Copybook' is ambiguous; it could also mean exemplary.

133. In the sketch 'Gun + Crew' reprinted in *Return to Oasis* (p. xxxiv), the gun, not the humans, comprises the centre of the picture.

134. Jahan Ramazani, *Poetry of Mourning: The Modern Elegy from Hardy to Heaney* (Chicago: University of Chicago Press, 1994), p. 7.

135. Hynes, p. xiii. Hynes uses 'myth' in the sense of a simplified narrative, rather than an imaginative fabrication.

136. Box 21 H Separates (2).
137. *Ruins of Memory: Rethinking the French Past*, ed. by Pierre Nora, trans. by Arthur Goldhammer (New York: Columbia University Press, 1996–98), I, p. 8.

NOTES TO CHAPTER 4

1. I am particularly grateful to Jane Kilby, Michael Rothberg, and Ursula Tidd for our discussions about Charlotte Delbo during the composition of this chapter.
2. Hynes, *The Soldier's Tale*, p. 25.
3. Felman and Laub, p. xviii.
4. Derek Attridge, *J. M. Coetzee and the Ethics of Reading: Literature in the Event* (Chicago: University of Chicago Press, 2004), p. xii.
5. In 'The Question of Community in Charlotte Delbo's *Auschwitz and After*', Thomas Trezise also notes that in the first two volumes of the trilogy 'many of the texts [. . .] remain undecidable in terms of the distinction between poetry and prose' (*MLN*, 117 (2002), 858–86 (p. 871)).
6. *Auschwitz and After* comprises the three volumes of the trilogy. There are no isolated poems between pages 147 and 209 of *Auschwitz and After*.
7. In *Convoy to Auschwitz: Women of the French Resistance*, trans. by Carol Cosman (Boston: Northeastern University Press, 1997), Delbo stresses, 'At Birkenau, time flowed differently' (p. 35). In the 'Daytime' section of *None of Us Will Return*, she asks, 'What is longer than a day?' (p. 47); the section concludes that whilst working in the marshes, 'It is day for a whole eternity' (p. 48).
8. This section includes the lines: 'Daylight on the marshland where tall, golden reeds shine. | Daylight on the marsh where insects with eyes full of terror labor to the point of exhaustion [. . .] It is day till the end of day'.
9. Claude Prévost, 'Entretien avec Charlotte Delbo', quoted in Nicole Thatcher, *A Literary Analysis of Charlotte Delbo's Concentration Camp Re-Presentation* (Lewiston: Edwin Mellen, 2000), p. 7.
10. Felman and Laub, p. 5.
11. Levi, *If This Is a Man*, pp. 398, 381.
12. *If This Is a Man*, in *Survival in Auschwitz* (New York: Touchstone, 1996): in the interview with Philip Roth, Levi says that the 'model (or, if you prefer, my style) was that of the "weekly report" commonly used in factories: it must be precise, concise, and written in a language comprehensible to everybody in the industrial hierarchy' (p. 181).
13. Dean, p. 153.
14. Gillian Rose, *Mourning Becomes the Law: Philosophy and Representation* (Cambridge: Cambridge University Press, 1996), p. 50. Rose contrasts Levi's work with that of Tadeusz Borowski, whose short stories make you 'witness brutality in the most disturbing way' (p. 50). It is not clear 'from what position' you are reading—from the perspective of a victim, perpetrator or complicit inmate, and the reader emerges 'shaking in horror [. . .] with yourself in question, not in admiration for the author's Olympian serenity (Levi)' (p. 50).
15. Levi, *If This Is a Man*, p. 111. Dominick LaCapra outlines his conception of 'empathic unsettlement' in *Writing History, Writing Trauma* (Baltimore, MD: Johns Hopkins University Press, 2001), pp. 40–41.
16. 'Introduction by Lawrence L. Langer', in *Auschwitz and After*, pp. ix–xviii, p. xvi.

17. Charlotte Delbo, *Auschwitz et Après I: Aucun de Nous ne Reviendra* (Paris: Les Éditions de Minuit, 1970), p. 69. The original French is as follows: 'Le vent souffle et siffle et gémit. C'est le gémissement qui monte des marais, un sanglot qui gonfle, gonfle et éclate et s'apaise dans un silence de frisson, un autre sanglot qui gonfle, gonfle et éclate et s'éteint'. Prose and poetry merge from the beginning of the testimony. The first paragraph ('People arrive [. . .]') is prosaic prose; the second switches to poetry when the emphasis is on the line rather than the sentence (as with the enjambment of 'those who are leaving | a station [. . .]') (p. 3). Anaphora ('Some came from Warsaw [. . .] some from Zagreb') also distinguishes the poetic prose: this is more prevalent in the original French, where '*Il y a*' starts the first five sentences (p. 9). Whereas Levi begins his chronology before the deportation in *If This Is a Man*, Delbo deploys a more playful, punning, and literary opening: irony persists when the narrator observes that 'dolls can be smothered too' (p. 7); perpetrator rhetoric occurs with the sentence, 'All those Jews have mouths full of gold, and since there are so many of them it adds up to tons and tons' (p. 9). Bitter irony is contained in the fragment about 'those who imagined they found a safe place for their children in a Catholic convent school where the sisters are so kind' (p. 8): such references to betrayal and collaboration occur throughout Delbo's work and reach their apogee in *The Measure of Our Days* when Alice 'hang[s] herself in her kitchen. Winters are sad in the country' (p. 300).
18. The original French contains half (end) rhymes, 'plaine [. . .] marais [. . .] wagonnets' (p. 69).
19. Rowland, *Holocaust Poetry*, passim.
20. Kofman, p. 36. In *Traumatic Realism: The Demands of Holocaust Representation* (London: University of Minnesota Press, 2000), Michael Rothberg reads the café incident as Delbo's resistance to the 'possibility of [the testimony] becoming a "master" narrative' (p. 159).
21. As Amira Bojadzija-Dan argues in 'Reading Sensation: Memory and Movement in Charlotte Delbo's *Auschwitz and After*', this unsettling chronology 'unhinges the reader from the safety of historical distance' (in *Memory and Migration: Multidisciplinary Approaches to Memory Studies*, ed. by Julia Creet and Andreas Kitzmann (Toronto: University of Toronto Press, 2011), pp. 194–209 (p. 199)).
22. In *The Age of Atrocity* (Boston: Beacon Press, 1978), Lawrence Langer refers to Pierre's response as a kind of 'intellectual tourism' (p. 236).
23. The character Françoise in Delbo's play *Who Will Carry the Word* similarly comments, 'We'll never be able to make them see what we have seen' ('Who Will Carry the Word', trans. by Cynthia Haft, in *The Theatre of the Holocaust*, ed. by Robert Skloot (London: University of Wisconsin Press, 1982), pp. 267–326 (p. 318)). The dialectical desire to make the reader 'see' can be partly attributed to the apathy greeting survivors in France: Madeleine Doiret 'suffers [in 1965] from the indifference, ignorance, and incomprehension of those who were not deported' (*Convoy to Auschwitz*, p. 66). Delbo also worries that even for those who are not ignorant, the Holocaust has become a closed unit of historical memory: 'Today people know [. . .] Auschwitz [. . .] they think they know' (p. 138). This inability to connect the ramifications of the Holocaust with the present leads to Delbo's links in her testimony between the Holocaust, the Algerian War, and Vietnam (as Michael Rothberg illustrates in *Multidirectional Memory*).
24. Seweryna Szmaglewska, *Smoke over Birkenau* (Warsaw: KiW, 2008). See, for example, 'But then you have horrible days, when all reason is dulled and the warnings are forgotten' (p. 46). As Trezise notes, '"Il faut donner à voir"

conveys the imperative of *making seen* or *showing*, an imperative of which Delbo knew only too well both that its fulfilment is impossible and that this impossibility does not in any way diminish the force of the imperative itself' (p. 865n). Delbo seems to want the reader to 'succeed in maintaining a tension between proximity and distance, between identification and estrangement, a tension that Dominick LaCapra has aptly characterized as "empathic unsettlement"' (p. 868).

25. 'Circumscribed' suggests that the 'horror' cannot be avoided, and that it forces Delbo to write about it. Similarly, Delbo's sacrilegious attack (akin to Levi's subversion of the morning prayer in 'Shemà') on the Christian iconography of suffering encompasses the need to make Christians compare the agony of Christ over 'three days and three nights' to 'those who agonized through so many agonies' in the camps (p. 10).

26. Langer draws on Delbo's distinctions between external, intellectual memory and deep memory in Charlotte Delbo, *Days and Memory* (Evanston, IL: Marlboro Press/Northwestern University Press, 2001), p. 3. These terms are themselves indebted to Proust's model of in/voluntary memory. Brett Ashley Kaplan discusses these links in *Unwanted Beauty: Aesthetic Pleasure in Holocaust Representation* (Urbana: University of Illinois Press, 2007), pp. 46–51. In the 'Thirst' section of *None of Us Will Return*, Delbo illustrates Proust's model succinctly when she states, 'I feel this taste in my mouth even today as soon as I think of this water, even when I do not think of it' (p. 72).

27. In *Inherit the Truth 1939–1945* (London: Giles de la Mare, 1996), Anita Lasker-Wallfisch notes that typhus sufferers in Auschwitz suffered from impaired eyesight and hearing (p. 78).

28. Thatcher quotes the interview with Prévost where Delbo states that 'It is truthful what conforms to reality. What is *true* contains a part of subjectivity' (p. 31). In contrast, Trezise warns that this version of *véridique* could be misleading in that 'such a normative objectification of experience leaves no room for an "uncertain sense of reality"' (p. 870).

29. Thanks are due here again to Jane Kilby for discussing such passages with me during sessions on the Representing the Holocaust module at the University of Salford.

30. In contrast to my argument here, Kaplan contends (less ambiguously) that for Delbo 'beauty in "the worst" functioned as a survival mechanism' (p. 15).

31. Delbo's critique of music chimes with Shirli Gilbert's criticism of the idea that music in the camps must always enact a 'spiritual resistance', 'a life-affirming survival mechanism through which [prisoners] asserted solidarity in the face of persecution, the will to live, and the power of the human spirit' (*Music in the Holocaust: Confronting Life in the Nazi Ghettos and Camps* (Oxford: Clarendon Press, 2005) p. 2).

32. My italics. Shirli Gilbert quotes from *Auschwitz and After* (p. 158), but not in the context of Delbo's engagement with Alma Rosé or music in general. Gilbert discusses the Viennese musician at length: when she arrived at the camp 'she was already something of a legend. She had established a reputation for herself as an accomplished violinist in pre-war Europe [. . .] Many former inmates emphasized the unprecedented relationship that she enjoyed with the SS, and the high esteem in which they held her' (p.181).

33. Borowski, *This Way for the Gas*, p. 99 (my italics).

34. In 'The Tulip' section of *None of Us Will Return*, the aesthetic is potentially redemptive: 'Down at the bottom of the ditch' the inmates 'were digging, the tulip's delicate corolla bloomed' (p. 61). The cherished memory of the tulip

then becomes contaminated when they realize it belongs to the SS, just as the poetry of the house as a 'ship', '[w]hipped by the squalls' (p. 60), is undermined by the knowledge that it is a house belonging 'to the SS in charge of the fishery' (p. 61).

35. This process of learning *Le Misanthrope* functions as the equivalent of Levi's Ulysses chapter in *If This Is a Man*. The inextricability of Ravensbrück and the memory process result in the reader appreciating the appropriateness of Delbo accidentally leaving *Le Misanthrope* in the camp (p. 218).

NOTES TO CHAPTER 5

1. Mole, pp. 18–19; Vice, p. 7.
2. Quoted in Agamben, p. 41.
3. Levi, *Collected Poems*, p. 5; *If This Is a Man*, pp. 48, 49.
4. *Collected Poems*, p. 5.
5. The reference here is to the American edition of *If This Is a Man*, *Survival in Auschwitz*: in the interview with Philip Roth, Levi says that the 'model (or, if you prefer, my style) was that of the "weekly report" commonly used in factories: it must be precise, concise, and written in a language comprehensible to everybody in the industrial hierarchy' (p. 181).
6. Ian Thomson, *Primo Levi* (London: Vintage, 2002), p. 223.
7. Levi, *The Drowned and the Saved*, p. 52.
8. Jay Losey, '"The Pain of Remembering"': Primo Levi's Poetry and the Function of Memory', in *The Legacy of Primo Levi*, ed. by Stanislao G. Pugliese (New York: Macmillan, 2005), p. 120.
9. T. S. Eliot, *Selected Poems* (London: Faber, 1961), p. 53.
10. Indeed, 'The Survivor' begins and ends with literary quotations, from Coleridge in the first instance and then Dante's *Inferno* (canto 33, l. 141). For an in-depth discussion of Levi's reading of Coleridge, and his reworking of the lines from Coleridge's poem, see Lina Insana's *Arduous Tasks: Primo Levi, Translation and the Transmission of the Holocaust* (Toronto: University of Buffalo Press, 2009).
11. Levi, *Ad Ora Incerta*, p. 11.
12. Agamben, p. 13.
13. Significantly, the phrase is not used in Delbo's *Auschwitz and After*: the female equivalents of the musulmann are described more compassionately than in Levi's texts. This difference illustrates that the musulmann is located within a continuum of masculinity between virility (both physically and intellectually) and emaciation.
14. Sofsky quoted in Agamben, p. 44; Joram Warmund, 'The Grey Zone Expanded', in *The Legacy of Primo Levi*, pp. 163–74 (p. 167).
15. Levi, *The Black Hole of Auschwitz*, p. 42.
16. Quoted in Mole, p. 103.
17. Quoted in Mole, p. 11.
18. Quoted in Agamben, pp. 166–67.
19. Tony Harrison, *V* (Newcastle: Bloodaxe Books, 1989 (1985)).
20. This poem appears at the beginning of *If This Is a Man* (p. 17): I refer to this version in the following quotations.
21. Thomas Gray, 'Elegy in a Country Churchyard', in *The Poems of Thomas Gray, William Collins, Oliver Goldsmith*, ed. by Roger Lonsdale (London: Longman, 1969), pp. 103–41 (p. 103).
22. Patricia Yaeger, 'Consuming Trauma; or, The Pleasures of Merely Circulating', in *Extremities: Trauma, Testimony and Community*, ed. by Nancy K.

Miller and Jason Tougaw (Urbana: University of Illinois Press, 2002), pp. 25–51 (p. 41).

23. I am paraphrasing Yaeger here (p. 46) in her description of distracted activities after someone reads an article about suffering in the *New York Times*.
24. Delbo, *Auschwitz and After*, p. 84.
25. *The Oxford Companion to the Bible*, ed. by Bruce M. Metzger (Oxford: Oxford University Press, 1993), p. 628.
26. 'There is Auschwitz, and so there cannot be God'. The quotation comes from Ferdinando Camon, *Conversations with Primo Levi*, trans. by John Shepley (Marlboro: Marlboro Press, 1989), p. 68. In his preface to Katzenelson's *The Song of the Murdered Jewish People*, Levi states, 'There is no longer a God in the "void and empty" skies' (*The Black Hole of Auschwitz*, p. 23).
27. *Shema: Collected Poems of Primo Levi*, ed. by Ruth Feldman and Brian Swann (London: Menard Press, 1976), p. 13.
28. Thomson, p. 226; Agamben, p. 58.
29. In *The Black Hole of Auschwitz*, Levi writes that the poem 'had been dancing around my head even while I was in Auschwitz, and which I had written down a few days after my return' (p. 25).
30. Rowland, *Tony Harrison*, pp. 25–26.
31. J. A. Cuddon, *A Dictionary of Literary Terms* (London: Penguin, 1982), p. 236.
32. Martin Gilbert, *The Holocaust: The Jewish Tragedy* (London: HarperCollins, 1987), p. 809.
33. Terry Eagleton, 'Material Girl No More . . . ', *THES*, 16 February 2007, pp. 16–17 (p. 17). To be fair, Eagleton is (rightly) criticizing celebrities' obsession with alternative spiritual sources.
34. Borowski, *This Way for the Gas*, p. 22.
35. Thomson, p. 506; Bruno Vasari, *Mauthausen Bivacco Della Morte* (Florence: Giuntina, 1991).
36. Quoted in Thomson, p. 506.
37. Emma Wilson, 'Material Remains: *Night and Fog*', in *OCTOBER*, 112 (spring 2005), 89–110 (pp. 95, 100).
38. Geoffrey Hill, *The Triumph of Love* (London: Penguin, 1999).
39. Carole Angier, *The Double Bond: Primo Levi, a Biography* (London: Viking, 2002), p. 445.
40. See note 1. Gubar, *Poetry after Auschwitz*; Gubar, 'The Long and Short of Holocaust Verse'.
41. *Witness and Memory*, p. 46.

NOTES TO CHAPTER 6

1. Felman and Laub, pp. xv–xvi.
2. The box in the Working Class Movement Library is labelled 'Ben Ainley, Voices, Autobiography'. These meetings took place in St James's Road (p. 1). An introduction to the autobiography notes, 'In recent years, Ben has given his energy and experience to developing the latent literary and artistic talent that lies dormant in the working class. This lead to the publication of "Voices"' (p. 2). The main text of the autobiography does not cover the later part of Ainley's life, when he began to edit the magazine.
3. These details are taken from a Mick Jenkin's memoir of Ainley, delivered as a funeral oration in 1977. Jenkins was a childhood friend of Ainley's. The memoir is held in the 'Intro Folder 1' of the *Voices* archive in the Working Class Movement Library. It reveals that Ainley also taught at Burnage High

School before Chorlton High School, and that he was elected to the District Committee of the Party in 1925. He was also a political speaker in Stevenson Square. The first time he turned up he lasted two minutes and was outshone by the established speaker Bill Gee. The next time Ainley lasted twenty minutes. There was clearly a tradition of political speaking in this Square near Piccadilly, since a photograph survives in the Manchester Local Image Collection from 1890 depicting a rapt crowd listening to a public speaker. (The Image Collection is owned by Manchester City Council.)

4. Extract from Tom Woodin, 'Building Culture from the Bottom Up: The Educational Origins of the Federation of Worker Writers and Community Publishers', *History of Education*, 34.4 (July 2005), 345–63 (reproduced by Ken Clay on www.mancvoices.co.uk). Woodin has the TUC Resolution 42 date as 1962, but the 1960 date is correct.

5. According to Woodin's article, the Resolution emphasized 'the importance of the arts in the life of the community and looked for greater participation by the trade union movement in all cultural activities' (www.mancvoices.co.uk). Arnold Wesker was artistic director of Centre 42 when it began in 1961 (see www.arnoldwesker.com for Wesker's comments on the Resolution and Centre 42). In *Class Act: The Cultural and Political Life of Ewan MacColl* (London: Pluto Press, 2007), Ben Harker notes that the organization ended in 'battered egos, bad blood and monstrous debts' (p. 165).

6. In private correspondence with Rick Gwilt, he commented that Unity of Arts was the loosely constituted group which originally published *Voices*. The idea was to create a 'progressive alliance of people working in different art forms': Ted Morrison, one of the editorial board members of the magazine who lived at 110 Edge Lane, where meetings used to be held, even renovated his cellar to accommodate the various art forms. Gwilt commented that the other art forms did not take off, and by the time Gwilt took over the editorship the Unity of Arts Association had been dropped as it had become meaningless.

7. Box 17 FWWCP Voices.

8. Ainley's aims for the Unity of Arts are printed as a 'President's Statement' (p. 2). The 'Unity of Art Society AIMS' (printed on the first page of the leaflet) are to gather together those 'who want to practise or take part in whatever form they wish in the Arts, namely, painting, sculpture, drama, music, poetry, etc. We aim not only to practise and improve our art, but to help others, learn from each other, and take art to the people, by way of exhibitions, performing plays, reading poetry, choir and folk singing, through Trade Union Branches, political meetings, peace organisations and other meetings of such character. We also hope to recruit from these meetings members who wish to participate in some form of the arts, but have not been able to do so hitherto'.

9. The first quotation is from Woodin's article in *History of Education* (www.mancvoices.co.uk). The second is from Ken Clay's introduction to the website.

10. The Labour Club reading took place on 15 July 1975 at 8 p.m. The *Voices* archive in the Working Class Movement Library contains a box of general information concerning the magazine, including letters, manuscripts, and photographs. A reference to New Cross Labour Club is contained in a letter by Ainley about the reading in Old Mill Street in Ancoats. (The letter is dated 1 July 1975.) A box labelled 'Ben Ainley Voices' in the Working Class Movement Library contains a 'Voices' poster which advertises a 'London Premier Event' at the Half Moon Theatre on 29 February 1976. The London 'Voices' group was set up as a reading group, according to Woodin,

but it then developed into a writing workshop. The group met at the Metropolitan Tavern on the corner of Farringdon Road and Clerkenwell Road in 1976. One of the leading lights of the Hackney Writers' Workshop was the educationalist Ken Worpole. According to *Voices* 18 (Autumn 1978), Worpole was at this time a full-time worker for Centreprise Bookshop in Hackney (p. 9).

11. These details are taken from Rick Gwilt's memoir of Ben Ainley held in the general *Voices* box in the Working Class Movement Library archive. The meetings in Edge Lane took place in the winter of 1973–74 (p. 3). Gwilt comments that they could have had a detrimental effect on Ainley's already poor health.

12. Details taken from Gwilt's memoir (p. 4). This meeting took place in December 1976. Gwilt comments that he 'was against the idea on principle—it seemed to me a betrayal of everything *Voices* stood for. In the event, it turned out to be a non-starter' (p. 4). The identity of this lecturer in question is Max Adereth, who taught French at the University of Lancaster. A picture at http://www.es.lancs.ac.uk/luss/Slugs/images/JohnSellers/ depicts Adereth at a demonstration with one of the left luminaries involved in *Voices*, the poet Adrian Mitchell. Adereth was an expert on committed French literature and the British Communist Party. A letter held in the 'Ben Ainley Voices' box reveals that Ainley was also in contact with Greg Wilkinson (Manchester Studies) from the Institute of Advanced Studies at Manchester Polytechnic about *Voices*. Wilkinson wrote to Ainley (30 April 1976) about Fed meetings.

13. Ken Clay refers to the Arts Council comment in his introduction to the website www.mancvoices.co.uk. McGovern's short story 'Whatever Happened to the Good Samaritan?' appeared in *Voices* 15 (9 new series) (Autumn 1977), pp. 5–7.

14. Felman and Laub, p. xv. By 'figure' I refer to my discussion in the Introduction about Paul de Man's reading of autobiography as a 'figure of reading' rather than a genre.

15. Friedrich Engels, *The Condition of the Working Class in England* (Oxford: Oxford University Press, 1999), p. 9.

16. Robert Tressell, *The Ragged Trousered Philanthropists* (London: Grafton Books, 1965). *Voices* began long before the post-millennial popularity of working-class memoirs and 'mis lit'. Tressell's novel is an example of posthumous testimony since, despite the literary embellishments, it remains a 'true' representation of everyday suffering in the lives of Hastings housepainters at the turn of the century. As an article in *Voices* 2 correctly surmises, Tressell, as he argues in his preface, invented nothing (p. 14).

17. Pierre Bourdieu and Alain Accardo, *The Weight of the World: Social Suffering in Contemporary Society* (Stanford, CA: Stanford University Press, 1999), pp. 4, 627. In relation to Jonquil Street, Bourdieu describes the inhabitants sensing an 'immense void': they are 'not unlike the survivors of an immense collective disaster, and they know it' (p. 6). I am not suggesting that working-class experience is coterminous with suffering: as the early, hedonistic exploits of Arthur Seaton indicate in Alan Sillitoe's *Saturday Night, Sunday Morning*, this can be far from the case. *Voices* is also full of celebrations of labour: in issue 27, Ron Oliver reminisces about of '[t]he hiss of rams and the rumble of the tubs' in the poem 'The Pit's Closed' (p. 4).

18. Wilkinson writes in *Suffering: A Sociological Introduction* (Cambridge: Polity, 2005) that 'The actual quality of the *lived experience* of suffering rarely appears as the direct focus of sociological study' (p. 2).

19. Crispin Aubrey and Charles Landry, '"Breaking Cover"—In Other Words: The Alternative Press', *International Journal of Lifelong Education*, 26.1

(2007), 89–104 (reproduced by Ken Clay on www.mancvoices.co. uk). Aubrey and Landry are discussing the Federation in general.
20. Fanny Morgan, 'Onomatopoeia', *Voices* 3 (n.d.), p. 23.
21. Lauren Berlant, 'The Subject of True Feeling: Pain, Privacy, and Politics', in *Transformations: Thinking through Feminism*, ed. by Sara Ahmed, Jane Kilby, Celia Lury, Maureen McNeil, and Beverley Skeggs (London: Routledge, 2000), pp. 33–47 (p. 33).
22. Žižek, *Violence*, pp. 8, 11.
23. Žižek, *Violence*, p. 11.
24. Dean, p. 111.
25. Laura S. Brown, 'Not Outside the Range: One Feminist Perspective on Psychic Trauma', in *Trauma: Explorations in Memory*, ed. by Cathy Caruth (London: Johns Hopkins University Press, 1995), pp. 100–12 (p. 102). I must thank Stef Craps for reminding me in Aarhus about this chapter.
26. John Kirk, *Twentieth-Century Writing and the British Working Class* (Cardiff: University of Wales Press, 2003), pp. 1–2.
27. Carolyn Steedman, *Landscape for a Good Woman* (London: Virago Press, 1995), p. 8.
28. Steedman quotes approvingly from Ronald Fraser's *In Search of a Past* (1984): '"What actually happened is less important than what is felt to have happened. Is that right?" says Ronald Fraser to his analyst, and his analyst agrees' (p. 145). The Laub reference is to the chapter 'Bearing Witness, or the Vicissitudes of Listening' from Felman and Laub, pp. 57–74, p. 59.
29. The Adlam poem appears in *Voices* 19 (Spring 1979), p. 34. Poetry has always been an important form for working-class testimony. Ken Clay recalls the radical journal *Northern Star* from the 1840s, which invited poetry submissions and then found itself inundated. The editors then stated that 'the Poets must really give us a little breathing time. We have heaps upon heaps accumulating which we cannot find room for' (www.mancvoices.co.uk).
30. Quoted in P. M. Ashrat, *Introduction to Working Class Literature in Great Britain, Part 1: Poetry* (no publication details, 1978), p. 199. The book was presented as a gift to the founders of the Working Class Movement Library, Edward and Ruth Frow.
31. *Voices* 17 (Spring/Summer 1978), p. 10.
32. The origins of 'get' are obscure. It could refer to illegitimate offspring (as in James Joyce's 'the bloody thicklugged sons of whores' gets' from *Ulysses*), or to the 'gate' (a funnel-shaped object used in letting molten iron into a sand mould), or to 'Geat', Scandinavian people, of whom Beowulf is a famous literary example.
33. Jane Kilby, *Violence and the Cultural Politics of Trauma* (Edinburgh: Edinburgh University Press, 2007), p. xiv.
34. Adorno, *Minima Moralia*, p. 25.
35. Karl Marx, *Capital, Vol 1: A Critical Analysis of Capitalist Production* (London: Lawrence and Wishart, 2003), p. 233.
36. Attridge, *The Singularity of Literature*, p. 9.
37. Morrison conceded that the literary quality of the magazine had improved from issue 1 to issue 20 (*Voices* 22 (Autumn 1980), p. 1). Ken Clay concurs with Morrison when he admits that '[s]nooty critics, and I was one of them, complained in its early days that, as literature, *Voices* wasn't much cop. Maybe it was sociology or even politics but literature?—no' (www.mancvoices.co.uk). Clay reproduces a letter from the Arts Council from 1978: the Literature Finance Committee in this instance was not convinced that the Federation's productions were of 'solid literary value'; they were 'successful in a social, therapeutic sense, but not by literary standards'.

38. The review is held in the general *Voices* box.
39. *Voices* 9, pp. 7–8.
40. Margaret-Anne Hutton, *Testimony from the Nazi Camps: French Women's Voices* (London: Routledge, 2005).
41. According to Crispin Aubrey and Charles Landry in 'Breaking Cover', the Arts Council subsequently funded the post of a literature development officer for the Federation of Worker Writers and Community Publishers, which cost £5500. The Federation had bid for £20,000 funding.
42. *Voices* 17 (Spring/Summer 1978), pp. 1–2.
43. Theodor Adorno, 'Commitment', in *Aesthetics and Politics*, trans. by F. MacDonagh, and ed. by R. Livingstone, P. Anderson, and F. Mulhern (London: New Left Books, 1977), pp. 177–95 (p. 177).
44. See, for example, the introduction to *Holocaust Poetry* (Edinburgh: Edinburgh University Press, 2005), pp. 1–27.
45. Derek Attridge, 'Can We Do Justice to Literature?', *PN Review*, 182 (July–August 2008), 16–22 (p. 16).
46. Brown, p. 107.

NOTES TO CHAPTER 7

1. See, for example, my discussion in Chapter 2 of Delbo's attempt to make the reader 'see' violence at the same as she often refers to the impossibility of non-survivors 'seeing' the camps.
2. Judith Butler, *Precarious Life: The Powers of Mourning and Violence* (London: Verso, 2004), p. 7; Richard Gray, *After the Fall: American Literature since 9/11* (Oxford: Wiley-Blackwell, 2011), p. 1. By the 'events of 9/11' I refer primarily in this chapter to the destruction of the Twin Towers, rather than the attack on the Pentagon and the airplane crash in Shanksville, Philadelphia. The reason for this lies in poems' focus on the events in Lower Manhattan, particularly in the anthology I examine here (*Poetry after 9/11: An Anthology of New York Poets*, ed. by Dennis Loy Johnson and Valerie Merians (Hoboken, NJ: Melville House, 2002)), as well as in 9/11 literature more widely, rather than any denial of the importance of the Pentagon attack and crash to the events unfolding on 11 September 2001.
3. Kristiaan Versluys, *Out of the Blue: September 11 and the Novel* (New York: Columbia University Press, 2009), p. 1.
4. Laura Frost, 'Still Life: 9/11's Falling Bodies', in *Literature after 9/11*, ed. by Ann Keniston and Jeanne Follansbee Quinn (Abingdon: Routledge, 2008), pp. 180–206.
5. After quoting from Paul Celan's 'Todesfugue'—which emphasizes Frost's point about 9/11 being a 'Holocaust subject'—Kinnell writes, 'This is not a comparison but a corollary' (the poem is available at www.princetonindependent.com/issue11.02/item3.html). Even a 'corollary' suggests a connection, however, in a similar way to comparative singularity.
6. John Updike, *Terrorist* (Oxford: Isis, 2007); Mohsin Hamid, *The Reluctant Fundamentalist* (London: Hamish Hamilton, 2007). Fictional engagements with victims of 9/11 have, following the arguments above, been more cautious. Many examples do exist, of course, such as Frédéric Beigbeder's *Windows on the World* (London: HarperCollins, 2004), Jonathan Safran Foer's *Extremely Loud & Incredibly Close* (London: New York, 2006 (2005)), and Don DeLillo's *Falling Man* (London: Picador, 2007). Foer's novel forms a postmodern rewriting of Marguerite Duras's *La Douleur*, trans. Barbara Bray (London: Collins, 1986) in its location of mourning not in fragmented,

and agonized, modernist prose but in the return to life of the child narrator through arbitrariness—primarily symbolized in the search through the Blacks in the telephone directory—humour and play.

7. This focus on 9/11 poets inevitably brings up the issue of the hyper-visibility of the event in Western culture. In '"There Is No Poetry in This": Writing, Trauma, and Home', Michael Rothberg argues, 'It ought not to be understood as minimizing the suffering of survivors and families of victims of the September 11 attacks to point out that, however "unique" those attacks were, the hyper-visibility of "American" suffering reflects disproportionate U.S. political, economic, and media power at least as much as it reflects the specific terrors of the events' (*Trauma at Home: After 9/11*, ed. by Judith Greenberg (Lincoln: University of Nebraska Press, 2003), pp.147–57 (p. 150)). In *Violence*, Slavoj Žižek turns the discussion to the moveable feast of the term 'perpetrator' when he asks, 'Why should [Henry] Kissinger, when he ordered the carpet bombing at Cambodia that led to the deaths of tens of thousands, be less of a criminal than those responsible for the Twin Towers collapse? Is it not because we are victims of an "ethical illusion"?' (p. 38). Žižek's thought unusually dovetails with Butler's at this point, since her discussion of grievable lives in *Precarious Life* includes the deconstruction of this 'ethical illusion': 'We reserve "acts of terror" for events such as the September 11th attacks on the United States, distinguishing these acts of violence from those that might be justified through foreign policy decisions or public declarations of war [. . .] In the United States, we have been surrounded with violence, having perpetrated it and perpetrating it still, having suffered it, living in fear of it, planning more of it, if not an open future of infinite war in the name of "war on terrorism"' (pp. 2, 28).

8. Levi, *The Drowned and the Saved*, p. 63.

9. I must thank Michael Rothberg for directing me towards this oral history project. The 11 September 2001 Oral History Narrative and Memory Project has recorded nine hundred hours of interviews with over six hundred people, 'to allow individuals to speak about their experiences outside the frameworks quickly developed by official media and government accounts' (www.library.columbia.edu/indiv/ecoh/new-projects/9–11html) (accessed 29 September 2012)). There may be an idealistic sense here that subjectivity is never interpolated, but the vast archive is important in the voice it gives to 'those who were discriminated against in the aftermath and those who lost work or who were unable to work', as well as 'large clusters of people directly affected or near the site of the towers'. Excerpts were then published in *After the Fall: New Yorkers Remember September 2001 and the Years that Followed*, ed. by Mary Marshall Clark, Peter Bearman, Catherine Ellis, and Stephen Drury Smith (New York: New Press, 2011). Other examples of testimony in this localized sense include the Naudet brothers' film of the firefighters of New York experiencing the events of 9/11, and other collections of written testimony, such as *Tower Stories: An Oral History of 9/11*, ed. by Damon DiMarco (Santa Monica, CA: Santa Monica Press, 2007). This focus on the particularity of the events might be said to problematically reinscribe the notion of Americans (or, more specifically, New Yorkers) as a priori victims, but is, I would argue, necessary in order to distinguish between different kinds of witnessing and confront the fact that we know very little about the events of 9/11. There are also, it must be stressed, occasions when the testimony of the survivors was sought, but rejected, as in the case of some firefighters who argued that giving an account of the events appeared too close, for them, to a judicial indictment of their labour (Ann Cvetkovich, 'Trauma Ongoing', in *Trauma at Home*, ed. by Greenberg, p. 63).

10. Since I interpret this poem primarily as a performance piece, I would direct the reader to the various commanding performances of 'first writing since' on YouTube. The poem is also available as a written text at http://fas.camden. rutgers.edu/events/Perspectives1poem.html (accessed 3 September 2012). The poem is fast becoming *the* canonical poem on 9/11. Rothberg, for example, praises it throughout '"There Is No Poetry in This": Writing, Trauma, and Home' as an example of multicultural sensitivity and linguistic complexity. Although I agree with much of his excellent (and groundbreaking) analysis of the poem, I am more critical of the ending in my discussion of the poem later in this chapter.

11. Theodor Adorno, *Prisms*, trans. by S. and S. Weber (London: Neville Spearman, 1967), pp. 177–95 (p. 64).

12. Liedeke Plate, 'Bearing Witness: Gender and the Poetry of 9/11', *Women's Studies*, 37.1–16 (2008), 1–16 (p. 2). In 'The Comic Supplement' section of *In the Shadow of No Towers* (New York: Pantheon, 2004), Art Spiegelman recalls that '[p]oetry readings seemed to be as frequent as the sound of police sirens in the wake of September 11—New Yorkers needed poetry to give voice to their pain, culture to reaffirm faith in a wounded civilisation. I must have heard W. H. Auden's 'September 1, 1939' a dozen times in those weeks'.

13. Karen Alkalay-Gut, 'The Poetry of September 11: The Testimonial Imperative', *Poetics Today*, 26.2 (Summer 2005), 257–79 (p. 1). Versluys evaluates the outpouring of Internet poetry as 'large quantities of amateur versifying', which amount 'to nothing more than eerily comic doggerel' (p. 9).

14. In her preface, Butler refers to a post-9/11 'apprehension of the precariousness of life' (p. xvii).

15. Sigmund Freud, 'Mourning and Melancholia', in *A General Selection from the Works of Sigmund Freud*, ed. by J. Rickman (London: Hogarth Press, 1937), pp. 142–61. For a critical engagement with the differences, and similarities, between mourning and melancholia, see the 'Theories of Mourning: From Psychoanalysis to Deconstruction' section in Rowland, *Tony Harrison*, pp. 150–60. In his talk 'Poetics of Anxiety and Security: The Problem of Speech and Action in Our Time' (available at www.backdoorbroadcasting. net), Homi Bhabha attempts to account for the iteration of 'September 1, 1939': 'Amidst the burnt offerings that poetry brought to the city of ashes'. Bhabha interprets the poem as a form of symbolic capital and recounts that Paul Muldoon and Adrienne Rich recited 'September 1, 1939' at several memorial services and that radio stations broadcasted the text. He also announces an anecdote whereby bookstalls in New York were running out of poetry. Read (inappropriately) by bloggers as prophesy, Bhabha accounts for the poem's popularity in terms of its engagement with smell (recalling the 'dioxins, asbestos, shattered glass, mercury and metal dust'), and a 'threshold moment' in history, as well as its reference to arrogant skyscrapers and cycles of violence. 'September 1, 1939', for Bhabha, hence takes up the position of 'displaced third discourse' in relation to a private–public binary, which brings 'poetry into the politics of the everyday'.

16. Johnson and Merian, p.ix. Plate reads the chief's comment as an implicit gender reading of poetics, in which 'the call for "no more poetry" is a call for the regain of self-control that is also a re-inscription of masculine mastery of public space' (p. 12). A more mundane explanation is possible; that, unlike with the food and flowers, the firemen could not find anywhere to place the loose paper securely, or satisfactorily.

17. Nancy K. Miller, 'Reporting the Disaster', in *Trauma at Home*, ed. by Greenberg, pp. 39–47 (p. 46).

18. By 'problematically' I mean that there are a variety of different conceptions of the witness within the city itself, as I argue later in this chapter in relation to the Greenberg volume, and differing accounts of the importance of geographical specificities. The experiences of rescue workers and firefighters at Ground Zero were clearly different from those of witnesses in Chinatown; which, again, differ from those of the inhabitants of Brooklyn (such as Hammad) and the Upper West Side (as Greenberg discusses in *Trauma at Home*, pp. 21–35). In *After the Fall*, paramedic James E. Dobson bemoans a rigid hierarchy of heroes and suffering, in which the firefighters are followed by the police, so that '[y]ou had policemen working that day at Ninety-sixth Street and First Avenue [near the top of Central Park] who are considered heroes. Okay? You have people [like me] at Ground Zero when the buildings came down, and people don't even know them from Adam' (pp. 1–14). (The editors also write about the 'acts of survival', such as Dobson's, which are 'complicated by their reality of needing to abandon someone in order to survive as the towers began to collapse. These were the stories that the unreal histories of heroism performed in the media excised' (p .xxii).) In contrast, for 'witnesses' outside New York City dangers include the fantasy of proximity and over-identification: in her preface to *Names of the Dead: An Elegy for the Victims of September 11* (New York: Penguin, 2004), Diane Schoemperlen writes, 'I did not know anyone who died on September 11. But for weeks at a time I felt closer to these three thousand dead people that I had never met than I did to anyone in my own life' (p. xiii; quoted in Plate, p. 1).

19. Kristeva, pp. 316–17. Other icons of 9/11 include the famous photograph of the falling man, described as the 'true' story of 9/11 in *The Falling Man* documentary (available on YouTube). Such icons still occlude the variety of stories to be told in the Oral History Narrative and Memory Project.

20. Versluys, pp. 1, 5.

21. In 2011 the mayor of New York, Michael Bloomberg, announced that the term 'Ground Zero', with its connotations of the atom bombings in 1945, should no longer be used, and that the area should be referred to as the site of the World Trade Center or the National September 11th Memorial and Museum. As well as attempting (artificially) to mark a completed period of 'true' mourning, the renaming marks absence and remembrance, instead of the contingency of 'Ground Zero' after the attacks. In this chapter, I use the term to denote the contemporaneous site of destruction—in relation, for example, to the labour of the rescue workers.

22. Versluys, pp. 4, 7 (my italics).

23. Suleiman, p. 546.

24. Anne Whitehead, 'Trauma and Resistance in Art Spiegelman's *In the Shadow of No Towers*', in *The Future of Memory*, ed. by Richard Crownshaw, Jane Kilby, and Antony Rowland (New York: Berghahn Books, 2010), pp. 233–44 (p. 237).

25. *In the Shadow of No Towers* (my italics). For Brian Conley, interviewed as part of the Oral History Narrative and Memory Project, that 'something' referred specifically to the cordon below Fourteenth Street: 'It's almost as if New York has this incredible rift in it. People below Fourteenth Street—many are still walking around like zombies—and above Fourteenth Street, they're still shopping and carrying on their lives as if nothing had happened. I think there's something wrong with that' (*After the Fall*, p. 111).

26. Working with the Red Cross with victims of trauma in the days following 9/11, Boulanger was appalled that volunteers only had to show their university ID card. She thought, 'My God! You shouldn't be doing this. You'll

be getting people from the English department coming in here. This is outrageous' (*After the Fall*, pp. 257–58).

27. *In the Shadow of No Towers*, p. 1.
28. *Trauma at Home*, p. 46.
29. As Cristina Archetti outlines in her excellent article on 'News Coverage of 9/11 and the Demise of the Media Flows, Globalization and Localization Hypotheses', *International Communication Gazette*, 70.6 (2008), 463–86, we have to be careful of asserting that the media coverage of 9/11 was the same in all countries. After studying the elite press framing of 9/11 in the United States, Italy, France, and Pakistan from the two months after the event, Archetti concludes that her findings 'neither support the existence of international news flows, nor the idea that news is becoming homogenised on a global scale' (p. 463). The extent to which 'news in different parts of the world mirrors American news' varies (p. 467), and there is 'no evidence that the American news framing of 9/11 is being imposed on news in foreign countries' (p. 463).
30. Jill Bennett, 'The Limits of Empathy and the Global Politics of Belonging', *Trauma at Home*, pp. 132–38 (p. 132).
31. Ian McEwan's early response to 9/11, published the next day in the *Guardian*, argues that it was precisely the distance from the events which was so traumatic for viewers: 'it was our safe distance from it all that made it so terrifying [. . .] This was an obscenity. We were watching death on an unbelievable scale, but we saw no one die. The nightmare was in this gulf of imagining. The horror was in the distance. Only television could bring this' ('11.09.2001: The Day the Earth Stood Still', p. 2). McEwan is attuned to effects of mediation, with the editing of certain images, which contrasts with the 'horror' of proximity in, for example, the visceral reports of the Oral History Narrative and Memory Project, such as the priest's recollection of blessing a nose crushed onto a piece of rubble and a rescue worker coming across a dead woman impaled on a steel girder.
32. See www.911_digitalarchive.org/chinatown/ (accessed 17 September 2012).
33. *After the Fall*, p. xvi.
34. In an interview, the local politician Margaret Chin recalls that the zone resulted in unemployment, because '[y]ou couldn't get supplies in and out' (*Guardian (G2)*, 6 September 2011, p. 21). The interviewer Ed Pilkington then notes, 'Tourism to Chinatown also vanished overnight. Everyday life became a toil, because the streets were blockaded and tightened security made movement almost impossible'. Chin worked for Asian Americans for Equality, 'trying to rebuild the community and ensure that people did not get forced out of their homes as the developers moved in'. She is still preoccupied with the health of local inhabitants after 9/11: she suffers from breathing difficulties and skin allergies, has helped others to get federal funds for proper health care, and 'is still fighting to have cancer recognised among the list of illnesses induced by 9/11'.
35. Conley, an artist, lived in Tribeca: his landlord illegally demanded rent for September and October 2001, since his home and studio 'were in a cordoned-off police zone' (*After the Fall*, p. 114). He eventually had to hand over his Red Cross aid money to the landlord to sever the lease and settle his arrears.
36. Frost notes that 'Art Spiegelman invokes the Holocaust comparison at several points of *In the Shadow of No Towers*, suggesting that the feelings of victimhood he experienced on 9/11 are comparable to those experienced by Jews in Europe on the eve of the Holocaust' (*Trauma at Home*, p. 204).
37. Butler, p. xvii.

38. The metrical break occurs at the end of the Alexandrine: 'Hysteria of morning. A clearing, the half-gnawed'. This reading is dependent upon not reading the full stop as the equivalent of a syllable in the middle of the line. If the opening is read in this way, the line becomes regular iambic heptameter.

39. Jean Baudrillard, *The Spirit of Terrorism*, trans. by Chris Turner (London: Verso, 2002), p. 27.

40. Robert Sheppard, 'Full of Unlikely Treasure', in *Warrant Error* (Bristol: Shearsman, 2009)(written September–October 2001), p. 1. On September 11, Sheppard refers to the footage presciently as 'a hi tech hot spot hijacking the lifeworld'.

41. See www.news.nationalgeographic.com/news/2001/09/pictures/110908 (accessed 18 September 2012). Baudrillard writes of, and O'Brien deliberately avoids, the 'unforgettable incandescence of the images' (p. 4): the former confronts the undeniably gripping nature of the iconic footage and photographs, and the taboo of confronting the aesthetics of these visual responses. Jensen and Conley in the Oral History Narrative and Memory Project refer to the fascination and excitement displayed by some witnesses as the 'incandescent' scene unfolded itself (pp. 51, 103–04), but both are careful to distinguish their reactions from these impious responses; such reactions do not, of course, feature in the iconic footage of disorientated bystanders. Controversial reactions to the images—such as Karl Heinz Stockhausen and Damian Hirst's contention that the event committed a work of art—might be written off as the insensitive responses of secondary witnesses at a remove, unlike the witnesses in the Oral History Narrative and Memory Project or New York poetry anthology. Yet Spiegelman himself freely admits to this attractive 'incandescence' as a primary witness. He refers to the 'AWESOME' spectacle of the glowing tower before it collapses (p. 1), and crosses his fingers that it will not be repeated soon: 'I'd feel like such a jerk if a new disaster strikes while I'm still chipping away at the last one' (p. 1). In contrast, the poems I discuss in this chapter avoid engaging with the event's potential aesthetics and prefer the poetics of indirection ('Aubade 2'), and paradoxes of in/articulacy ('How to Write a Poem after September 11th'; 'first writing since'). Writers' avoidance of 'AWESOME' aesthetics demonstrates an understandable reluctance to admit to the terrorists' success in creating an 'unforgettable incandescence'. Iconic *National Geographic* pictures of the burning towers and aftermath (such as Florio's) can be read, in one sense, as perpetrator photographs. Hence James Young worries about the construction of the 9/11 memorial: it 'could even become the terrorists' victory monument to the deadly success of their attacks' ('Remember Life with Life: The New World Trade Center', in *Trauma at Home*, ed. by Greenberg, p. 217).

42. Simon Armitage, *Out of the Blue* (London: Enitharmon, 2008), p. 28. The TV version was first shown on the anniversary of 9/11 in 2006 (*Out of the Blue*, dir. by Ned Williams (Silver River/Channel 5, 2006)).

43. Frédéric Beigbeder, *Windows on the World* (London: HarperCollins, 2005), p. 110.

44. Laurence Golstein, 'The Response of American Poets to 9/11: A Provisional Report', *Michigan Quarterly Review*, 48.1 (Winter 2009) <www.quod.lib. umich.edu> (accessed 3 September 2012).

45. 'Poetics of Anxiety and Security: The Problem of Speech and Action in Our Time' (available at www.backdoorbroadcasting.net).

46. Henry Reed, 'Lessons of the War (I. Naming of Parts)', in *Collected Poems*, ed. by Jon Stallworthy (Manchester: Carcanet, 2007), pp. 47–60 (p. 49). Reed describes (up to a point) the machinations of rifle firing, of course, rather than using imperatives. The surreal juxtaposition of the bees, branches, and

gardens with the military discourse echoes Moustaki's switch from imperatives about 9/11 to the seemingly unconnected depiction of the mayor cutting
a ribbon and the invocations to 'Say: the bakery was out of cake | The dogs
in the pound howled' (*Poetry after 9/11*, p. 96).

47. In *After the Fall: American Literature since 9/11*, Richard Gray argues that,
'like Beigbeder, Armitage risks accusations of tastelessness and exploitation
by using a fictionalised character and placing him within the reality of the
attacks' (p. 79). Clichés 'could reflect very accurately what many on-the-spot
witnesses thought as they watched the attacks' but Gray ultimately thinks
that 'they merely reiterate trite observations' (pp. 82, 84). Gray critiques
the *banality* of vicarious testimony in relation to 9/11: '"Jesus!" says the
blonde in Ralph Lauren. "Let's get the hell out of this sauna"' (Beigbeder,
p. 65). In *Out of the Blue*, Armitage self-consciously represents vicarious-
ness through the mixture of witnessing modes and prosopopoeia: 'A shoe'
is 'freeze-framed against the open sky' (p. 16), and the narrator sees 'it now,
over and over | frame by frame by frame', when the second plane hits (p. 23).
The main difference between Beigbeder and Armitage is that, even though
both emphasize the artifice of their texts, Armitage takes the verisimilitude
more seriously: the prose-poem section (7) representing the chaos following
the attack is certainly effective (pp. 19–20); more so on the page, without
the distracting melodrama of Rufus Sewell. Even if Beigbeder's banality of
testimony is read through his self-conscious critique of the impossibility of
re-creating the events of 9/11, the results and clichés are nevertheless sometimes irritating and insensitive, as when the narrator—stuck in Windows on
the World restaurant—comments, 'Restaurants cook up all kinds of stuff,
just usually not the customers' (p. 185).

48. Wendy Cope, 'Spared', *Observer*, 14 October 2001, p. 5. Cope draws on her
epigraph from Emily Dickinson's work, 'That Love is all there is | Is all we
know of Love'. The poem actually draws on a range of amorous discourse,
from Vera Lynn's popular World War II song 'We'll Meet Again' (which
Cope inverts with 'Knowing we'll never meet again') and Philip Larkin's
famous ending to 'An Arundel Tomb' ('What will survive of us is love') to
The Beatles' 'All You Need Is Love'.

49. Martin Randall, *9/11 and the Literature of Terror* (Edinburgh: Edinburgh
University Press, 2011), p. 152n.

50. The poem works best as a powerful performance piece: one version can be
accessed at www.youtube.com/watch?v=0fhWX2F6G7Y (accessed 4 October
2012). I primarily refer to this performed version in the ensuing quotations.
An earlier written version is available at http://fas.camden.rutgers.edu/events/
Perspectives1poem.html. In 'Precocious Testimony: Poetry and the Uncom-
memorable', Jeffrey Gray argues that the beginning of the twenty-first century
might see the end of a 'bland, desacralized, conversational poetry, whether
"engaged" or "not"' (*Literature after 9/11*, ed. by Keniston and Quinn , pp.
261–84 (p. 279)). Hammad's Ginsberg-like, prosaic poetry could be said to be
'conversational' and 'engaged', but her performances are certainly not 'bland'.

51. *After the Fall*, p. xxiii.

52. See Edition.cnn.com/2001/US/09/11/bush.speech.text/.

53. Quoted in Butler, p. 2.

54. I refer here to the YouTube version of the poem cited above.

NOTES TO THE CONCLUSION

1. De Man, p. 920.

2. Guyer, pp. 31–42.
3. Semprun, *Literature or Life*, p. 13.
4. Semprun, pp. 240, 201. This does not mean that non-professional testimony is not worthy of further study, however: there are different gradations of such 'rough' testimonies. Semprun's detection of an 'avalanche of facts' and 'confused scraps of meaning' appertains, for example, to Murray Kessler's description of the destruction of the Jewish community in the Polish region at Cracau (http://www.shtetlinks.jewishgen.org/Frysztak/FrysztakHOLO.htm). In contrast, Jan Demczur's account of his escape from the 9/11 attacks with the aid of a squeegee is utterly compelling, despite the welter of details in the forty-five other narratives in the book (*Tower Stories*, pp. 76–92). Narrative pleasure may have something to do here with the intervention of the editor, Damon DiMarco, in shaping the testimonies. In this sense, the 'hybrid' testimony in *Tower Stories* differs from the 'rough' testimony about Cracau, which was published, without editorial assistance, on the internet. Felman and Laub's groundbreaking book is concerned only with professional testimony, but in the forthcoming volume *The Future of Testimony*, the editors discuss the recent academic interest in 'rough' and popular testimony that Semprun dismisses too blithely.
5. Delbo, *Auschwitz and After*, p. 153.
6. Tressell, p. 566.
7. Alkalay-Gut, p. 258.
8. Adorno, 'On Lyric Poetry', p. 37
9. Borowski, *Selected Poems*, p. 89.
10. Raymond Federman, *La Voix dans le Cabinet de Débarras (The Voice in the Closet)* (Buffalo, NY: Starcherone Books, 2001).
11. *From Oasis into Italy*, p. xvii.
12. Antelme, p. 34.

Bibliography

I do not refer to any of the archival material in this bibliography: items in the Salamander Oasis archive, for example, are listed in the individual chapters.

PRIMARY SOURCES

Armitage, Simon, *Out of the Blue* (London: Enitharmon, 2008)

Beigbeder, Frédéric, *Windows on the World* (London: HarperCollins, 2005)

Bevan, Jack, *My Sad Pharaohs* (London: Routledge and Kegan Paul, 1968)

——, *Through the Donkey's Ears* (Maidstone: George Mann, 1997)

Blunden, Edmund, ed., *Poems of Keats* (London: Collins, 1955)

Borowski, Tadeusz, *Selected Poems*, trans. by Tadeusz Pióro with Larry Rafferty and Meryl Natchez (Walnut Creek, CA: Hit & Run Press, 1990)

——, *This Way for the Gas, Ladies and Gentlemen*, trans. by Barbara Vedder (New York: Penguin, 1967)

Burk, David, Denis Saunders, and Victor Selwyn, eds, *Oasis: The Middle East Anthology of Poetry from the Forces* (Cairo: Salamander Society, 1943)

Butts, Dennis, and Victor Selwyn, eds, *Schools Oasis: Poems of the Second World War* (Cheltenham: Nelson Thornes, 1992)

Céline, Louis-Ferdinand, *Journey to the End of the Night*, trans. by Ralph Manheim (London: John Calder, 1988)

Clark, Mary Marshall, Peter Bearman, Catherine Ellis, and Stephen Drury Smith, eds, *After the Fall: New Yorkers Remember September 2001 and the Years That Followed* (New York: New Press, 2011)

Cope, Wendy, 'Spared', *Observer*, 14 October 2001, p. 5

Delbo, Charlotte, *Auschwitz and After*, trans. by Rosette C. Lamont (New Haven, CT: Yale University Press, 1995)

——, *Auschwitz et Après I: Aucun de Nous ne Reviendra* (Paris: Les Éditions de Minuit, 1970)

——, *Convoy to Auschwitz: Women of the French Resistance*, trans. by Carol Cosman (Boston: Northeastern University Press, 1997)

——, *Days and Memory* (Evanston, IL: Marlboro Press/Northwestern University Press, 2001)

——, 'Who Will Carry the Word', trans. by Cynthia Haft, in *The Theatre of the Holocaust*, ed. by Robert Skloot (London: University of Wisconsin Press, 1982), pp. 267–326

DiMarco, Damon, ed., *Tower Stories: An Oral History of 9/11* (Santa Monica, CA: Santa Monica Press, 2007)

Drewnowski, Tadeusz, ed., *The Correspondence of Tadeusz Borowski*, trans. by Alicia Nitecki (Evanston, Illinois: Northwestern University Press, 2007)

Duffy, Carol Ann, *Rapture* (London: Picador, 2005)

Eliot, T. S., *Selected Poems* (London: Faber, 1961)

Federman, Raymond, *La Voix dans le Cabinet de Débarras (The Voice in the Closet)* (Buffalo, NY: Starcherone Books, 2001)

Feldman, Ruth, and Brian Swann, eds, *Shema: Collected Poems of Primo Levi* (London: Menard Press, 1976)

Forché, Carolyn, ed., *Against Forgetting: Twentieth-Century Poetry of Witness* (New York: W. W. Norton, 1993)

Freud, Sigmund, 'Mourning and Melancholia', in *A General Selection from the Works of Sigmund Freud*, ed. by J. Rickman (London: Hogarth Press, 1937), pp. 142–61

Graham, Desmond, ed., *Keith Douglas: The Letters* (Manchester: Carcanet Press, 2000)

Hart-Davis, Rupert, ed., *Sassoon: The War Poems* (London: Faber and Faber, 1983)

Hoess, Rudolf, *Commandant of Auschwitz*, trans. by Constantine Fitzgibbon (London: Pan Books, 1982)

Jarmain, John, *Poems* (London: Collins, 1945)

Johnson, Dennis Loy, and Valerie Merians, eds, *Poetry after 9/11: An Anthology of New York Poets* (Hoboken, NJ: Melville House, 2002)

Levi, Primo, *Ad Ora Incerta* (Garzanti, 1984)

——, *The Black Hole of Auschwitz*, trans. and ed. by Marco Belpoliti, and trans. by Sharon Wood (Malden, MA: Polity Press, 1985)

——, *Collected Poems*, trans. by Ruth Feldman and Brian Swann (London: Faber, 1988)

——, *The Drowned and the Saved*, trans. by Raymond Rosenthal (London: Abacus, 1989)

——, *If This Is a Man/The Truce*, trans. by S. Woolf (London: Abacus, 1987)

——, *Moments of Reprieve*, trans. by Ruth Feldman (London: Abacus, 1987)

——, *Survival in Auschwitz* (New York: Touchstone, 1996)

Lonsdale, Roger, ed., *The Poems of Thomas Gray, William Collins, Oliver Goldsmith* (London: Longman, 1969)

Miłosz, Czesław, *The Captive Mind* (London: Penguin, 2001)

——, ed., *Post-War Polish Poetry* (Harmondsworth: Penguin, 1970)

Owen, Wilfred, *Collected Letters*, ed. by Harold Owen and James Bell (Oxford: Oxford University Press, 1967)

Owing, Alison, *Frauen: German Women Recall the Third Reich* (New Brunswick, NJ: Rutgers University Press, 1993)

Poems from the Desert: Verses by Members of the Eighth Army (London: George G. Harrap, 1944)

Reed, Henry, *Collected Poems*, ed. by Jon Stallworthy (Manchester: Carcanet, 2007)

Reid, Christopher, ed., *Letters of Ted Hughes* (London: Faber, 2007)

Ross, Alan, *Poems* (London: Harvill Press, 2005)

Rudyard Kipling's Verse: Inclusive Edition, 1885–1918 (London: Hodder and Stroughton, n.d.)

Rushton, Colin, *Spectator in Hell: A British Soldier's Story of Imprisonment in Auschwitz* (Chichester: Summersdale Pubs, 2007)

Schiff, Hilda, ed., *Holocaust Poetry* (London: HarperCollins, 1995)

Schoemperlen, Diane, *Names of the Dead: An Elegy for the Victims of September 11* (New York: Penguin, 2004)

Selwyn, Victor, ed., *The Voice of War: Poems of the Second World War* (London: Penguin, 1996)

Selwyn, Victor, Erik de Mauny, Ian Fletcher, G.S. Fraser, and John Waller, eds, *Return to Oasis: War Poems and Recollections from the Middle East 1940–1946* (London: Shepheard-Walwyn, 1980)

Selwyn, Victor, Erik de Mauny, Ian Fletcher, and Robin Ivy, eds, *More Poems of the Second World War: The Oasis Selection* (London: J. M. Dent & Sons, 1989)

Selwyn, Victor, Erik de Mauny, Ian Fletcher, and Norman Morris, eds, *Poems of the Second World War: The Oasis Selection* (London: J. M. Dent & Sons, 1985)

Selwyn, Victor, Dan Devin, Erik de Mauny, and Ian Fletcher, eds, *From Oasis into Italy: War Poems and Diaries from Africa and Italy 1940–1946* (London: Shepheard-Walwyn, 1983)

Semprun, Jorge, *Literature or Life*, trans. by Linda Coverdale (New York: Penguin, 1997)

Siedlecki, Janusz Nel, Krystyn Olszewski, and Tadeusz Borowski, *We Were in Auschwitz*, trans. by Alicia Nitecki (New York: Welcome Rain Publishers, 2000)

Siedlecki, J. N., *Beyond Lost Dreams* (Edinburgh: Pentland Press, 1994)

Silkin, Jon, ed., *The Penguin Book of First World War Poetry* (Harmondsworth: Penguin, 1981)

Sir Gawain and the Green Knight, Pearl and Sir Orfeo, trans. by J. R. R. Tolkien (London: Unwin Hyman, 1979)

Spiegelman, Art, *In the Shadow of No Towers* (New York: Pantheon, 2004)

Stallworthy, John, ed., *Owen: the War Poems* (London: Chatto and Windus, 1994)

———, ed., *Wilfred Owen: The Complete Poems and Fragments* (London: Oxford University Press, 1983)

Steedman, Carolyn, *Landscape for a Good Woman* (London: Virago Press, 1995)

Szmaglewska, Seweryna, *Smoke over Birkenau* (Warsaw: KiW, 2008)

Thwaite, Anthony, ed., *Philip Larkin: Letters to Monica* (London: Faber, 2010)

Tressell, Robert, *The Ragged Trousered Philanthropists* (London: Grafton Books, 1965)

West, Victor, *The Horses of Falaise* (London: Salamander Imprint, 1975)

Zych, Adam A., ed. and trans., *The Auschwitz Poems* (Oświęcim: Auschwitz-Birkenau State Museum, 1999)

SECONDARY SOURCES

Aaron, Frieda W., *Bearing the Unbearable: Yiddish and Polish Poetry in the Ghettos and Concentration Camps* (New York: State University of New York Press, 1990)

Adorno, Theodor, 'Commitment', in *Aesthetics and Politics*, trans. by F. MacDonagh and ed. by R. Livingstone, P. Anderson, and F. Mulhern (London: New Left Books, 1977), pp. 177–95

———, 'Cultural Criticism and Society', in *Prisms*, trans. by S. and S. Weber (London: Neville Spearman, 1967), pp. 17–35

———, *Minima Moralia: Reflections from Damaged Life*, trans. by E. F. N. Jephcott (London: Verso, 1978)

———, 'On Lyric Poetry and Society', in *Notes to Literature*, trans. by Shierry Weber Nicholsen (New York: Columbia University Press, 1991), pp. 37–54

———, 'Rede über Lyrik und Gesellschaft', in *Gesammelte Schriften II: Noten Zur Literatur* (Frankfurt: Suhrkamp, 1974), pp. 49–68

Agamben, Giorgio, *Remnants of Auschwitz*, trans. by Daniel Heller-Roazen (New York: Zone Books, 2002)

Alkalay-Gut, Karen, 'The Poetry of September 11: The Testimonial Imperative', *Poetics Today*, 26.2 (Summer 2005), 257–79

Angier, Carole, *The Double Bond: Primo Levi, a Biography* (London: Viking, 2002)

Antelme, Robert, 'Poetry and the Testimony of the Camps', in *On Robert Antelme's 'The Human Race': Essays and Commentary*, ed. by Daniel Dobbels (Evanston, IL: Northwestern University Press, 2003), pp. 31–37

Archetti, Cristina, 'News Coverage of 9/11 and the Demise of the Media Flows, Globalization and Localization Hypotheses', *International Communication Gazette*, 70.6 (2008), 463–86

Attridge, Derek, 'Can We Do Justice to Literature?', *PN Review*, 182 (July–August 2008), 16–22

——, *J. M. Coetzee and the Ethics of Reading: Literature in the Event* (Chicago: University of Chicago Press, 2004)

——, *The Singularity of Literature* (London: Routledge, 2004)

Banerjee, A., *Spirit above Wars: A Study of the English Poetry of the World Wars* (London: Macmillan, 1976)

Barthes, Roland, *The Rustle of Language*, trans. by Richard Howard (Oxford: Basil Blackwell, 1986)

Baudrillard, Jean, *The Spirit of Terrorism*, trans. by Chris Turner (London: Verso, 2002)

Bergonzi, Bernard, *War Poets and Other Subjects* (Aldershot: Ashgate, 1999)

——, *Wartime and Aftermath: English Literature and Its Background 1939–60* (Oxford: Oxford University Press, 1993)

Berlant, Lauren, 'The Subject of True Feeling: Pain, Privacy, and Politics', in *Transformations: Thinking through Feminism*, ed. by Sara Ahmed, Jane Kilby, Celia Lury, Maureen McNeil, and Beverley Skeggs (London: Routledge, 2000), pp. 33–47

Bhabha, Homi, 'Poetics of Anxiety and Security: The Problem of Speech and Action in Our Time' <www.backdoorbroadcasting.net>

Bloxham, Donald, and Tony Kushner, *The Holocaust: Critical Historical Approaches* (Manchester: Manchester University Press, 2005)

Bojadzija-Dan, Amira, 'Reading Sensation: Memory and Movement in Charlotte Delbo's *Auschwitz and After*', in *Memory and Migration: Multidisciplinary Approaches to Memory Studies*, ed. by Julia Creet and Andreas Kitzmann (Toronto: University of Toronto Press, 2011), pp. 194–209

Bosley, Keith, 'The Khaki Muse', *Times Literary Supplement*, 6 July 1984, p. 760b

Boswell, Matthew, *Holocaust Impiety* (Basingstoke: Palgrave Macmillan, 2011)

Bourdieu, Pierre, et al., *The Weight of the World: Social Suffering in Contemporary Society* (Stanford, CA: Stanford University Press, 1999)

Brown, Laura S., 'Not outside the Range: One Feminist Perspective on Psychic Trauma', in *Trauma: Explorations in Memory*, ed. by Cathy Caruth (London: Johns Hopkins University Press, 1995), pp. 100–12

Butler, Judith, *Precarious Life: The Powers of Mourning and Violence* (London: Verso, 2004)

Caesar, Adrian, *Taking It Like a Man: Suffering, Sexuality and the War Poets* (Manchester: Manchester University Press, 1993)

Camon, Ferdinando, *Conversations with Primo Levi*, trans. by John Shepley (Marlboro: Marlboro Press, 1989)

Campbell, James, 'Combat Gnosticism: The Ideology of First World War Poetry Criticism', *New Literary History: A Journal of Theory and Interpretation*, 30.1 (1999), 203–15

Caruth, Cathy, ed., *Trauma: Explorations in Memory* (London: Johns Hopkins University Press, 1995)

Crownshaw, Rick, *Afterlife of Holocaust Memory in Contemporary Literature and Culture* (Basingstoke: Palgrave Macmillan, 2010)

Crownshaw, Rick, Jane Kilby, and Antony Rowland, eds, *The Future of Memory* (Oxford: Berghahn Books, 2010)

Currey, R. N., *Poets of the 1939–1945 War* (London: Longmans, Green, 1960)

de Man, Paul, 'Autobiography as De-Facement', *MLN*, 94.5 (December 1979), 919–30

Dean, Carolyn J., *Aversion and Erasure: The Fate of the Victim after the Holocaust* (Ithaca, NY: Cornell University Press, 2010)

Derrida, Jacques, *Sovereignties in Question* (New York: Fordham University Press, 2005)

Douglas, Ana, and Thomas A. Vogler, eds, *Witness and Memory: The Discourse of Trauma* (London: Routledge, 2003)

Eaglestone, Robert, *The Holocaust and the Postmodern* (Oxford: Oxford University Press, 2004)

Eagleton, Terry, 'Material Girl No More . . . ', *THES*, 16 February 2007, 16–17

Engels, Friedrich, *The Condition of the Working Class in England* (Oxford: Oxford University Press, 1999)

Felman, Shoshana, and Dori Laub, *Testimony: Crises of Witnessing in Literature, Psychoanalysis, and History* (New York: Routledge, 1992)

Fussell, Paul, *The Great War and Modern Memory* (Oxford: Oxford University Press, 1977)

——, *Wartime: Understanding and Behavior in the Second World War* (Oxford: Oxford University Press, 1989)

Gilbert, Martin, *Descent into Barbarism: A History of the 20th Century 1933–1951* (London: HarperCollins, 1999)

——, *First World War* (London: HarperCollins, 1995)

——, *The Holocaust* (London: HarperCollins, 1986)

Gilbert, Shirli, *Music in the Holocaust: Confronting Life in the Nazi Ghettos and Camps* (Oxford: Clarendon Press, 2005)

Golstein, Laurence, 'The Response of American Poets to 9/11: A Provisional Report', *Michigan Quarterly Review*, 48.1 (Winter 2009) <www.quod.lib.umich.edu>

Graham, Desmond, *The Truth of War: Owen, Blunden, Rosenberg* (Manchester: Carcanet, 1984)

Gray, Richard, *After the Fall: American Literature since 9/11* (Oxford: Wiley-Blackwell, 2011)

Greenberg, Judith, ed., *Trauma at Home: After 9/11* (Lincoln: University of Nebraska Press, 2003)

Grossman, Morris, 'The Holocaust, or, Once More with Feeling', *Centennial Review*, 35.3 (Fall 1991), 625–60

Gubar, Susan, 'The Long and Short of Holocaust Verse', *New Literary History*, 35.3 (Summer 2004), 443–69

——, *Poetry after Auschwitz: Remembering What One Never Knew* (Bloomington: Indiana University Press, 2003)

Guyer, Sara, 'Before *The Human Race*: Robert Antelme's Anthropomorphic Poetry', in *Critical Survey*, 20.2 (2008), 31–42

Hamburger, Michael, *The Truth of Poetry: Tensions in Modern Poetry from Baudelaire to the 1960s* (Manchester: Manchester University Press, 1982)

Hamilton, Ian, *A Poetry Chronicle* (London: Faber, 1973)

Harker, Ben, *Class Act: The Cultural and Political Life of Ewan MacColl* (London: Pluto Press, 2007)

Hartman, Geoffrey, 'The Humanities of Testimony: An Introduction', *Poetics Today*, 27.2 (2006), 249–60

Hatley, James, *Suffering Witness: The Quandary of Responsibility after the Irreparable* (Albany: State University of New York Press, 2000)

Haugh, Rachel, 'Versed in War: The Preservation and Publication of Second World War Poetry by the Salamander Oasis Trust' (unpublished doctoral dissertation, 2009)

Haughton, Hugh, 'Anthologizing War', in *The Oxford Handbook of British and Irish War Poetry*, ed. by Tim Kendall (Oxford: Oxford University Press, 2007)

Hibberd, Dominic, *Wilfred Owen: A New Biography* (London: Weidenfeld and Nicolson, 2002)

Hilberg, Raul, *Perpetrators Victims Bystanders: The Jewish Catastrophe 1933–1945* (London: Lime Tree, 1993)

Hitchcock, William I., *Liberation: The Bitter Road to Freedom, Europe 1944–1945* (London: Faber, 2008)

Hunt, J. L., and A. G. Pringle, *Service Slang* (London: Faber, 1943)

Hutton, Margaret-Anne, *Testimony from the Nazi Camps: French Women's Voices* (London: Routledge, 2005)

Hynes, Samuel, *The Auden Generation: Literature and Politics in England in the 1930s* (London: Faber, 1979)

——, *The Soldier's Tale: Bearing Witness to Modern War* (London: Pimlico, 1998)

Insana, Lina, *Arduous Tasks: Primo Levi, Translation and the Transmission of the Holocaust* (Toronto: University of Buffalo Press, 2009)

Johnson, R. W., 'A Formidable Proposition (Review of Antony Beevor's *D-Day: The Battle for Normandy*)', *London Review of Books*, 10 September 2009, 21–22

Kaplan, Brett Ashley, *Unwanted Beauty: Aesthetic Pleasure in Holocaust Representation* (Urbana: University of Illinois Press, 2007)

Kendall, Tim, 'Gurney and Fritz', *Essays in Criticism*, 59.2 (2009), 142–56

——, 'Wilfred Owen's Concern', in *Modern English War Poetry* (Oxford: Oxford University Press, 2006), pp. 46–64

Keniston, Ann, and Jeanne Follansbee Quinn, eds, *Literature after 9/11* (Abingdon: Routledge, 2008)

Kilby, Jane, *Violence and the Cultural Politics of Trauma* (Edinburgh: Edinburgh University Press, 2007)

Kirk, John, *Twentieth-Century Writing and the British Working Class* (Cardiff: University of Wales Press, 2003)

Kistner, Ulrike, 'Writing "After Auschwitz": On the Impossibility of a Postscript', *Acta Germanica*, 21 (1992), 171–83

Kofman, Sarah, *Smothered Words*, trans. by Madaleine Dobie (Evanston, IL: Northwestern University Press, 1998)

Kristeva, Julia, 'For Shoshana Felman: Truth and Art', in *The Claims of Literature: A Shoshana Felman Reader*, ed. by Emily Sun, Eyal Peretz, and Ulrich Baer (New York: Fordham University Press, 2007), pp. 315–21

LaCapra, Dominick, *Writing History, Writing Trauma* (Baltimore, MD: Johns Hopkins University Press, 2001)

Lane, Arthur E., *An Adequate Response: The War Poetry of Wilfred Owen and Siegfried Sassoon* (Detroit, MI: Wayne State University Press, 1972)

Langer, Lawrence, *The Age of Atrocity* (Boston: Beacon Press, 1978)

——, *Holocaust Testimonies* (New Haven, CT: Yale University Press, 1991)

Losey, Jay, '"The Pain of Remembering": Primo Levi's Poetry and the Function of Memory', in *The Legacy of Primo Levi*, ed. by Stanislao G. Pugliese (New York: Macmillan, 2005), pp. 119–24

Luckhurst, Roger, *The Trauma Question* (London: Routledge, 2008)

Lyon, Philippa, ed., *Twentieth-Century War Poetry* (Basingstoke: Palgrave Macmillan, 2005)

Mazower, Mark, *Inside Hitler's Greece: The Experience of Occupation 1941–44* (New Haven, CT: Yale University Press, 1993)

McEwan, Ian, '11.09.2001: The Day the Earth Stood Still', *Guardian*, 12 September 2001, p. 2

Miller, J. Hillis, *The Conflagration of Community: Fiction before and after Auschwitz* (Chicago: University of Chicago Press, 2011)

Mole, Gary D., *Beyond the Limit-Experience: French Poetry of the Deportation, 1940–45* (New York: Peter Lang, 2002)

Nader, Andrés, *Traumatic Verses: On Poetry in German from the Concentration Camps, 1933–45* (Rochester, NY: Camden House, 2007)

Nora, Pierre, ed., *Ruins of Memory: Rethinking the French Past*, trans. by Arthur Goldhammer (New York: Columbia University Press, 1996–98)

Piette, Adam, *Imagination at War* (London: Macmillan, 1995)

Plate, Liedeke, 'Bearing Witness: Gender and the Poetry of 9/11', *Women's Studies*, 37 (2008), 1–16

Purkis, John, *A Preface to Wilfred Owen* (London: Longman, 1999)

Ramazani, Jahan, *Poetry of Mourning: The Modern Elegy from Hardy to Heaney* (Chicago: University of Chicago Press, 1994)

Randall, Martin, *9/11 and the Literature of Terror* (Edinburgh: Edinburgh University Press, 2011)

Rawlinson, Mark, *British Writing of the Second World War* (Oxford: Oxford University Press, 2000)

Reilly, Catherine W., *English Poetry of the Second World War* (London: Mansell Publishing, 1986)

Rose, Gillian, *Mourning Becomes the Law: Philosophy and Representation* (Cambridge: Cambridge University Press, 1996)

Rothberg, Michael, *Multidirectional Memory: Remembering the Holocaust in an Age of Decolonisation* (Stanford, CA: Stanford University Press, 2009)

——, *Traumatic Realism: The Demands of Holocaust Representation* (London: University of Minnesota Press, 2000)

Rowland, Antony, 'The Future of Testimony', in *The Future of Memory*, ed. by Rick Crownshaw, Jane Kilby and Antony Rowland (New York: Berghahn Books, 2010), pp. 113–22

——, *Holocaust Poetry* (Edinburgh: Edinburgh University Press, 2005)

——, 'Interview with Tadeusz Pióro (re Tadeusz Borowski's *Selected Poems*)', in *Holocaust Poetry*, ed. by Robert Eaglestone and Antony Rowland (*Critical Survey*, 20.2 (2008)), pp. 43–52

——, *Tony Harrison and the Holocaust* (Liverpool: Liverpool University Press, 2001)

Rudolf, Anthony, 'Rescue Work: Memory and Text', *Stand*, 5.3 (2004), 80–112

Scannell, Vernon, *Not without Glory: Poets of the Second World War* (London: Woburn Press, 1976)

Selwyn, Victor, 'Return to Oasis', *Times Literary Supplement*, 13 February 1981, p. 168e

Shires, Linda M., *British Poetry of the Second World War* (London: Macmillan, 1985)

Sokołowska-Paryż, Marzena, *The Myth of War in British and Polish Poetry 1939–1945* (New York: Peter Lang, 2002)

Struk, Janina, 'The Death Pit', *Guardian*, 27 January 2004, pp. 12–13

Suleiman, Susan Rubin, 'Problems of Memory and Factuality in Recent Holocaust Memoirs: Wilkomirski/Wiesel', *Poetics Today*, 21.3 (Fall 2000), 543–59

Swift, Daniel, *Bomber County: The Lost Airmen of World War Two* (London: Penguin, 2010)

Tesio, Giovanni, 'At *an Uncertain Hour*: Preliminary Observations on the Poetry of Primo Levi', in *Primo Levi: The Austere Humanist*, ed. by Joseph Farrell (New York: Peter Lang, 2005), pp. 160–70

Thatcher, Nicole, *A Literary Analysis of Charlotte Delbo's Concentration Camp Re-Presentation* (Lewiston: Edwin Mellen Press, 2000)

Thomson, Ian, *Primo Levi* (London: Vintage, 2002)

Todman, Dan, *The Great War: Myth and Memory* (London: Continuum, 2005)

Trezise, Thomas, 'The Question of Community in Charlotte Delbo's *Auschwitz and After*', *MLN*, 117 (2002), 858–86

Versluys, Kristiaan, *Out of the Blue: September 11 and the Novel* (New York: Columbia University Press, 2009)

Vice, Sue, 'Holocaust Poetry and Testimony', *Critical Survey*, 20.2 (2008), 7–17

Wachtell, Cynthia, *War No More: The Anti-War Impulse in American Literature 1861–1914* (Baton Rouge: Louisiana State University Press, 2010)

Warmund, Joram, 'The Grey Zone Expanded', in *The Legacy of Primo Levi*, pp. 163–74

White, Hayden, *Tropics of Discourse: Essays in Cultural Criticism* (Baltimore, MD: Johns Hopkins University Press, 1978)

Whitehead, Anne, *Memory* (New York: Routledge, 2009)

——, 'Trauma and Resistance in Art Spiegelman's *In the Shadow of No Towers*', in *The Future of Memory*, ed. by Richard Crownshaw, Jane Kilby, and Antony Rowland (New York: Berghahn Books, 2010), pp. 233–44

Wiesel, Elie, 'The Holocaust as Literary Inspiration', in *Dimensions of the Holocaust* (Evanston, IL: Northwestern University Press, 1990)

Wilkinson, Ian, *Suffering: A Sociological Introduction* (Cambridge: Polity, 2005)

Wilson, Emma, 'Material Remains: *Night and Fog*', *OCTOBER*, 112 (Spring 2005), 89–110

Yaeger, Patricia, 'Consuming Trauma; or, The Pleasures of Merely Circulating', in *Extremities: Trauma, Testimony and Community*, ed. by Nancy K. Miller and Jason Tougaw (Urbana: University of Illinois Press, 2002), pp. 25–51

Young, James, 'Interpreting Literary Testimony. A Preface to Rereading Holocaust Diaries and Memoirs', *New Literary History*, 18.2 (Winter 1987), 403–23

——, *Writing and Rewriting the Holocaust* (Bloomington: Indiana University Press, 1988)

Žižek, Slavoj, *Violence* (London: Profile Books, 2008)

Index

Made in the USA
Columbia, SC
28 November 2023

27329907R00107